ENGLISH INSTITUTIONS

General Editor
LORD STAMP

*CAMBRIDGE
UNIVERSITY PRESS*
*LONDON: BENTLEY HOUSE
NEW YORK, TORONTO, BOMBAY
CALCUTTA, MADRAS: MACMILLAN
TOKYO: MARUZEN COMPANY LTD*

Canterbury Cathedral, from the north-west

HERBERT HENSLEY HENSON
Sometime Bishop of Durham
Hon. Fellow of All Souls College, Oxford

THE
CHURCH
OF
ENGLAND

CAMBRIDGE
AT THE UNIVERSITY PRESS
1939

PRINTED IN GREAT BRITAIN

GENERAL EDITOR'S PREFACE

A British traveller in the United States just after the Coronation was likely to be hard put to it to explain the Church of England even to himself. There is often no more difficult task than to justify what one takes for granted. The Jubilee, the Royal Wedding, the Archbishop of Canterbury at the time of the Abdication, and above all the Coronation Ceremony in the Abbey—brought direct to the American by cinema or radio—had just served to make the entire American nation conscious of the "Established" Church of England. There were questions that I hesitated to answer through too *much* knowledge. But there were many more I parried through too *little*, concerning that institution which most of us unconsciously assume we know all about. But never did I so realize its anomalous and its paradoxical position, its superficial and yet its fundamental significance, until I had to put into understandable words my replies to that disarmingly direct and uncompromising cross-examination.

No description of England would convey much sense of reality without an account of its formative and sustaining institutions, and of those institutions the Established Church would come into the "short list" of any exponent. And yet the average man has but the sketchiest notions of the true position and characteristics of the Church. The respectable and prosperous intellectual classes, doing little or nothing to sustain her or revere her in everyday life, use her socially, and—through respectable scorn for the bare civil alternatives—in weddings and memorial services, with an occasional function of national or institutional significance. Yet in times of attack they are to be relied on to put her first and resent any belittlement of her claims.

The Coronation Service woke up not America alone to the problem of "Church and State". One prominent public man in London exclaimed to me: "This has been a field day for the Church—well, I must say they've delivered the goods."

To the layman the character of the State nexus is not often in the forefront of his mind. An occasional flash of perception brings it all back. To me, one such was when we received the final news from the House of Commons about the Debate on the New Prayer Book, and my neighbour, the venerable Bishop Knox, stood on my doorstep, after his long leadership in the fight for his passionately held convictions, with the mien and the voice of an Old Testament Prophet, thanking God for this "deliverance". Another such flash was on a recent Easter Sunday when the fortuitous shuttle of holiday-making took a very high judicial dignatory indeed and myself to the same little Anglican Church in Cornwall, where, after a service outrageous by any ordinary standards, we met on the churchyard path, and he exclaimed —incensed in every sense of the word—"And what is this we have been at? Is it the Church of England by law established? *This ought to be stopped!*"; and I thought of the worthy Bishop—one time of a famous Nonconformist public school—to whom the responsibility might fall, and I did not envy him his job of "stopping it".

Of all our Institutions, this has the most need to be studied in its historic development if it is to be understood—a fact which this volume definitely recognizes.

This venerable Institution has two sides, the political and the religious. It has survived the deepest political vicissitudes and has been modified by them far less than by the internal change in its religious content, and all this notwithstanding the fact that it has kept its creed, liturgy and internal form of government almost unchanged for centuries. In one of its darkest hours, one

William Stampe, D.D., "the imprisoned, plundered, exil'd Minister of God's word at Stepney", delivered his soul in sermons at the Hague, and sent them forth to his old flock after eight years' absence (*A Treatise of Spiritual Infatuation*, 1650) and spoke of the Church of England as the establishment of religion in its purity and lustre, "that which should be most dear unto a nation"—it could "never have receaved so deepe a wound, from any Infernal Stratagem, as from the plausible pretensions of refining and securing it unto us. How well it is refined, and secured, yourselves may judge by the present Complexion of our Deare mother, strip'd and mangled and wounded unto death by the sonns of her owne bowells. Her Government dissolved; Her Feastes (the Religious Commemorations of the great mysteries of Salvation) abolished; Her Sacred formes of prayer (the sweet harmony, and agreement of harts, and voyces) vilified and scorned....Her Champions (that should maintaine her Doctrine against the frauds and fallacies of her subtile and malicious adversaries) expelled, and banished the *Schooles of the Prophets*; Her doctrine...invaded and tramped into a muddie puddle; Her Discipline discharged and threatned....Her Temples either defaced and demolished; or else locked up by the *Militarian Power*. In so much that in one of her Cities...namely Lincoln, the Sacramental Bread and Wine hath not been communicated for three years together. And the true Protestant Religion (which by solemn Protestation we were obliged to maintaine) is now squeezed into such a narrow roome, that few or none dare own the profession of it, unlesse it be upon the scaffold...."

It is almost inconceivable that a Church could survive the subsequent disputations on government, discipline and relation to authority such as one may find through the myriad pages of Richard Baxter. (He indeed anticipated the modern idea of an alternative liturgy as a suitable means of accommodating a wide range of thought in a single communion.) But that strides the centuries.

No one could do justice to the Church of England as an institution unless he were in it and of it, deeply dyed. And yet not too much so. He would still not do justice, unless he had the objective faculty to stand outside and judge it, changing in history and political standing, as a social force—judge it dispassionately, fearlessly, without apology, but with pride. Few men could attempt this appraisal. The impressive performance of Bishop Henson —which it would be presumptuous of me to praise—is evidence that he is one of those few. Maybe his book will get him into trouble in some quarters. He has never minded trouble. But it will get him appreciation and gratitude in many others—and that too will never move him overmuch.

STAMP

CONTENTS

ILLUSTRATIONS

1, 3, 4 and 8 supplied by Rischgitz, London
2 and 7 supplied by Mallinson, Cambridge
6 supplied by The Times
5 reproduced by permission of The Clerk of the Parliaments

AUTHOR'S PREFACE

When I received from Lord (then Sir Josiah) Stamp a proposal that I should "consider writing the volume on the Church of England" in the series on "English Institutions", which he had undertaken to edit for the Cambridge University Press, I felt it requisite to point out that, in view of my publicly stated conviction that recent events had rendered the Establishment morally indefensible, I might well be thought unfitted for the task to which he was good enough to invite me. However, after consulting the Syndics, he assured me that I might have an absolutely free hand. Accordingly I proceeded to prepare what I called a *Speculum Ecclesiae Anglicanae*, describing the actual working of the Church, and setting out my impressions and conclusions with respect to it. This book, then, is neither a history of the Church of England, nor a treatise on ecclesiastical law, but a "speculum" or mirror in which the working institution is displayed. Only so much history has been introduced, and so much law, as appeared in my judgment indispensable for a just estimate of the existing situation. It is obvious that the question of Disestablishment could not be wholly omitted, but it forms no part of the general scheme, and for the most part I have contented myself with indicating my own position, stating as fairly as I can the relevant facts, and leaving the reader to draw his own inferences.

Disestablishment has for the time being fallen out of practical politics. Partly, the public has ceased to concern itself with merely ecclesiastical questions; and, partly, the old reasons for objecting to the Establishment have ceased to be relevant. The victory of Democracy has removed the civil disabilities of non-Anglicans; such

privileges as linger are neither greatly valued by their
possessors, nor greatly resented by others. The severest
critics of Establishment are now found within the
membership of the Established Church. Moreover, the
strange revolt against Christianity, which has swept over
a great part of the continent, has created a natural
reluctance in English minds to take any action which
might have the appearance of hostility to Christianity.
This sentiment is both intelligible and respect-worthy,
and even though it be misdirected, is not likely to grow
weaker. Its immediate effect is to provide a popular
apology for the Establishment.

At the same time, it is apparent that the monstrous
development of Erastianism in Totalitarian Germany
has made a profound and painful impression in England.
It has opened the eyes of many English Churchmen to
the dangerous possibilities latent in Establishment, and
inclined them to resent and resist claims on the part of
the English State which, albeit in principle unwarranted,
have in the past been readily conceded. Few considering
English Churchmen to-day would endorse without large
reserve Archbishop Tait's address on the constitution of
the Church of England at the Lambeth Conference of
1878.[1]

The Church of England is a national institution, but
it is also a spiritual society, an organized branch of the
Catholic or universal Christian Church. Its functioning
as a national institution may, or may not, assist fulfilment of the higher obligations implicit in its spiritual
character. Among these must be reckoned the maintenance of right relations with the other branches of the
Christian society, and the faithful wardship of the
Christian religion. Moreover, a living Church must take
its due part in the evangelization of the non-Christian
world. The efficiency of the national institution is finally

[1] *V. Life*, ii, 369–370.

conditioned by the healthy activity of the spiritual society. Some consideration of the Ánglican "Via Media", and of the relations of the Church of England with other Christian Churches, could not be excluded from my plan, and I have allowed myself to discuss with some freedom the situation created by, or, perhaps, disclosed by, the recently published *Report* of the Archbishops' Committee on Doctrine in the Church of England. This *Report* has been generally recognized as a document of outstanding importance, and cannot be overlooked by any serious student of English religion. The authoritative character of the *Report*, the great ability and various outlook of its authors, and above all the high quality of the *Report* itself, combine to clothe it with exceptional interest and value. It will take rank with the Clerical Subscription Act (1865), the Appeal on Church Unity issued by the Lambeth Conference (1920), and the Revised Prayer Book (1928) as marking a stage in the advance of the Church of England out of an insular self-centredness into a genuinely Catholic mind.

It is apparent that a complete view of the Church of England would include much that has been perforce omitted, since inclusion would have enlarged the book excessively. Thus nothing has been said about the amazing multiplicity of organizations within the Church, designed to meet the needs of various sections of the community, a multiplicity which arouses anxiety in many minds which are neither ill-informed nor unsympathetic. Waste of resources, both financial and personal, dissipation of interest and energy, a certain lop-sidedness of religious emphasis, and an imperilling of ecclesiastical discipline are mischiefs which shadow all well-intentioned attempts to substitute private essays for corporate effort. The conditions under which "Societies", maintained by "voluntary contributions", can wisely be permitted within the Church, constitute a problem which is equally urgent, complicated, and important. It must soon engage the anxious attention of the Bishops.

One considerable omission, perhaps, needs explanation. I have left unconsidered the large and perplexing subject of the Ecclesiastical Courts. I did so deliberately, because the Ecclesiastical Courts have largely fallen out of use since the House of Commons, by rejecting the Prayer Book Measure (1928), threw the Church back into the anarchic confusion, which the Royal Commission (1906) described, and which the Revision of the Prayer Book was designed in some measure to remedy. The present situation is confessedly undignified, unreasonable, and unstable. The Bishops are attempting to govern the Church, apart from the law, by such authority as their episcopal office can command. Their hold on the clergy is measured by the extent of deference which the clergy may feel conscientiously bound to accord to their oath of canonical obedience. It is understood that, apart from moral offences which affront the general conscience, and which are happily very infrequent, the parochial incumbents need fear no coercive discipline, however freely they may break the law which controls the conduct of public worship. The clerical conscience, assisted by the fatherly advice of the Bishops, is to serve as an alternative to the Act of Uniformity, enforced by the Courts. Such a situation cannot be either satisfactory or secure.

When the English nation is again free to interest itself in its domestic concerns, and again gives attention to the working of the Established Church, it is certain that the issue of Disestablishment will once more present itself. It is not likely that its settlement will again be postponed.

H. HENSLEY HENSON
Bishop

July, 1939

CHAPTER 1

HISTORICAL INTRODUCTION

The Church of England as it now exists is the most enigmatic and baffling of the national institutions. It is the very embodiment of paradox. Theoretically it is the Church of the English nation; actually its effective membership is claimed by no more than a petty fraction of the citizens. It is a reformed Church, but it refuses fellowship with all other reformed churches, with the partial exception of the Church of Sweden. It is at once the most authoritative, and the least disciplined of all Protestant churches, the proudest in corporate pretension, the feeblest in corporate power. With all this, the Church of England has been illustrated by a great succession of scholars, statesmen, thinkers, pastors, and saints; and, though it can no longer pretend to embrace within its membership the entire community of English Christians, it does still include a larger variety of social and intellectual types than any other denomination in the country. Indeed, it is not excessive to say that it is accepted, for widely differing reasons, by "all sorts and conditions of men", and draws to itself a measure of general respect which is curiously contrasted with the self-belittlement which is not rarely audible within its membership. Alike in its paradoxical aspect, and in its spiritual vitality, the Church of England presents a fascinating problem to the student of Christianity. As the oldest and most interesting of the national institutions, it appeals irresistibly to the considering English citizen.

The enigmatic character of the modern Church of England is, perhaps, explicable by the conditions under which it has come to be what it is. Race and geography have counted for much; the character of the original conversion and the course of the national history have counted for much more. The influence of individuals and the effect of continental movements have had their place, an important place, in the process. Some consideration of these shaping forces must precede any serviceable study of the existing institution.

The conquerors of Britain in the sixth and seventh centuries of the Christian era were of Teuton stock, and in their new surroundings they preserved with remarkable tenacity many of the social and political features of their homelands. It seems to be probable that the conquered Britons survived far more generally than once was thought, and no doubt they told potently on their conquerors. The modern Englishman has a mixed ancestry. He is a Teuton with a difference.

Whatever effect the racial type of the English may have had on the Christianity which they accepted was emphasized by the fact that the ecclesiastical development proceeded in the comparative freedom from external influences which is implicit in the fact of insularity. It is difficult to overstate the magnitude of this factor in the life of the English people, and in the shaping of their religion. Local peculiarities were able to survive behind the protecting barrier of the seas, which, without that protection, had certainly perished. The very aspect of the country attests the preserving power of insularity. Why does England possess such amazing wealth of parish churches scattered throughout the country in unwalled towns and open villages? It is mainly because the island kingdom escaped the ravages of continental warfare, and could in unparalleled degree find security apart from fortifications. Racial individualism, which in Germany hindered the growth of nationality, became, in England, the very principle of national independence. In later times, when the strong repressive domination of the medieval Church had been shattered, this racial individualism took the morbid form of fissiparous sectarianism. This circumstance also left its mark on the Church of England.

The effects of race and habitat on English religion must needs be matters of speculation rather than of assured knowledge, but when we consider the circumstances in which the English people received Christianity, and seek to trace the consequences which followed from them, we enter the well-mapped territory of historical record.

In two respects the Conversion of the English was exceptional. It was the result of missionary efforts directed from abroad: and its process and character have been better recorded than in any comparable instance. The names and achievements of the founders of Christianity in the provinces of the Roman Empire are for the most part unknown. They were not professed evangelists, but men and women who spread their religion incidentally and unconsciously as they "went about their lawful occasions". From time to time they stand out to view in the lurid glare of persecution, but for the most part they only survive in their work. It is not possible to assign precise dates and occasions to the achievements by which the great transition from paganism to Christianity was effected. When the barbarians from beyond the Rhine poured into the Roman provinces, they found themselves everywhere confronted by a strongly organized Christian Church. It was far otherwise with the Conversion of the English. British

Christianity appears to have had little influence over the pagan invaders. Whether the surviving British population amidst which the victorious English settled was numerous, and whether it was generally Christian, cannot be certainly ascertained. What appears indisputable is, that contact with it left English paganism intact. The dark period which links the age of Gildas with the age of Bede, during which the English established themselves in Britain, cannot have witnessed any effective missionary efforts on the part of the British Church, for, when the curtain rises on the Heptarchy in the pages of Bede's *History*, the English are apparently ignorant of Christianity, and firmly attached to their ancestral paganism. The Christian religion is brought to them by the accredited representatives of foreign churches.

Christianity had a less impeded course in Britain than elsewhere, for it brought the spiritual message to the English with a relatively small admixture of irrelevant attractions. There were in the partially Romanized island comparatively few cities which might in Britain, as in Gaul, have become citadels of Christian civilization in the social confusion of barbarian conquest. The earliest English Church was a rural church. This fact is indicated by the choice of the sees of the bishops. "They were in many cases selected in full agreement with the German instinct of avoiding cities; and planted in villages which served as a nucleus for the later towns."[1]

It has been the singular good fortune of the Church of England to have had the record of its foundation preserved by a native writer of outstanding merit. "Alone among the historians of his age", is the judgment of the late Professor E. W. Watson on the Venerable Bede, "he had the statesmanship to know what was of permanent importance, and the skill to record it clearly and fully."[2]

---

[1] *V.* Stubbs, *Constitutional History*, vol. I, ch. vii.
[2] *V. Bede*, edited by A. H. Thompson, p. 59, Oxford, 1935.

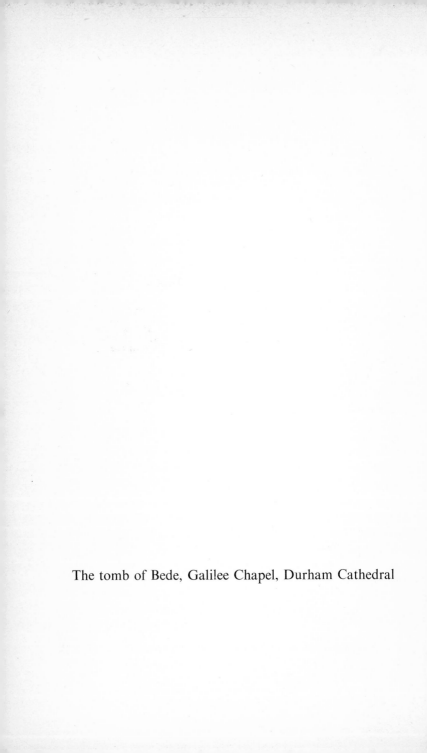

The tomb of Bede, Galilee Chapel, Durham Cathedral

No other Church possesses so vivid, trustworthy, and copious a record of its origins. Bede's *Ecclesiastical History of the English Race* is enriched by narratives which have taken rank among the choicest treasures of the Christian Church.

Two features of the Conversion must be noted as having affected lastingly the later development of English Christianity—the predominance of Monasticism, and the close connexion with the Roman Papacy.

"The conversion of England", writes Stubbs, "was accomplished principally, if not wholly, by monks either of the Roman or of the Irish school; and thus the monastic institution was not, as among the earlier converted nations, an innovation which rooted its claims for reverence on the sanctity or asceticism of its professors; it was coeval with Christianity itself; it was the herald of the Gospel to kings and people, and added the right of gratitude to that of religious respect and superstitious awe. Hence the system occupied in England and in the countries converted by English missionaries a position more really honourable and better maintained than elsewhere."[1]

The monkish missionaries came from two churches, widely disparate in discipline and temper. Very early in the history of the newly founded English Church the issue of its religious allegiance had to be determined. Would Ireland or Rome "call the tune" for England? Most happily for the Church of England that issue was decided at the Synod of Whitby (A.D. 664) in favour of Rome. English Christianity was rescued from the spiritual incoherence and ecclesiastical confusion which finally befell the Church of Ireland, and was brought into the main stream of European religious and cultural development as part of the Papal Dominion.

[1] *V. Historical Introductions to the Rolls Series*, by William Stubbs, collected and edited by Arthur Hassall, p. 366.

The predominance of Monasticism held the Church of England very closely to the continent and to the Papacy since it was on the continent that the great Monastic Orders had their governing centres, and since these Orders depended on the Papacy both for their independence of diocesan control and for the maintenance of their domestic discipline. Inevitably they became the mainstays of Papal Power within the nation. When, therefore, the direct political association with the continent was severed by the loss of the overseas dominions of the English monarch; and when, at a later period, the island kingdom entered on the Hundred Years' War with France, the monasteries, by virtue of their close relations with the continent and with the Papacy, were brought into a position of grave practical difficulty. Their interests were no longer identical with those of the nation, and might (as actually happened during the French War) even be apparently antagonistic. During the "Babylonian Captivity" (A.D. 1305–1376) the Popes, living at Avignon, had become almost confessedly the obedient tools of French policy. It followed inevitably that the close connexion of the monasteries with the Papacy seemed to stamp on them an anti-patriotic character. They were in spite of themselves immersed in the odium which attached to the Papacy in English eyes. At the Dissolution in the sixteenth century the English monasteries were unable to offer any considerable or effective resistance to the king because they had long before fallen out of accord with the national feeling which the king embodied. The monks were notoriously subjects of a power with which the nation was in conflict.

Apart from its direct effect on the monasteries, which it exploited and helped to ruin, the influence of the Papacy on the Church in England, throughout the Middle Ages, can hardly be overstated. Rome touched England at many points. It was closely interwoven with foreign politics: it affected potently the conflict with the monarchy out of which the parliamentary system was developed: it enhanced, while it resisted, the power of the monarchy; and, finally, it provided the occasion for revolt, and in some sense determined its character. Nor did the revolt make an end of Papal influence, though it revolutionized its method. Among the major forces which have determined the development of the Church of England since the Reformation none can take a greater place than that of the controversy which still continues between the apologists of the Church of England and the protagonists of the ever-waxing pretensions of the Roman Popes. Domestic dissidence and ecclesiastical isolation have been by-products of the controversy with the Papacy.

The key to a right understanding of the modern Church of England lies in a just appreciation of the unique character of the English Reformation. The general movement in Western Christendom which in the sixteenth century transformed the Renaissance into the Reformation throughout a great part of Christendom was coloured by the history of the various communities which together constituted the spiritual dominion of the Roman Popes. No two countries were quite alike. In every one the great experience was locally determined.

In England the monarchy played a decisive part. The royal supremacy is the distinctive feature of the English Establishment. Historically it has a twofold character. On the one hand, it involved the repudiation of external authority, the breach with the Papacy: on the other hand, it secured the subjection of the Church to the State within the nation. Both in its external aspect, as the triumph of national independence, and in its internal aspect, as the effective subordination of the Church to the State, the royal supremacy was deeply rooted in the past.

The pre-Norman English Church was disfigured by many abuses, the consequences of pagan habit, of insularity, and of invasion, but its loyalty to Rome never wavered. The Norman Conquest brought in its train a religious reformation. William the Conqueror had the moral support of the Pope's blessing when he invaded England, and he brought with him, not merely the articulated feudalism of Normandy, but also the ascetic ecclesiasticism of Cluny. Alongside the masterful monarch stood his friend and mentor, the hardly less masterful archbishop. By the combined action of these two remarkable men, William and Lanfranc, the English Church was transformed, its lack of discipline was corrected, its standards of ecclesiastical duty were raised, and it was carried out of its perilous insular individualism into the main stream of European religion. One feature, however, distinguished England from the continent—the strength of the monarchy. Under the strong hand of its kings, England enjoyed a measure of internal order greater than could elsewhere be found. The power of the English monarch made possible an attitude of independence towards the Papacy which was unparalleled, and became part of the national tradition.

The medieval English king was closely held to the Pope, for not only was he, as a member of the Catholic Church, subject to the Vicar of Christ, but also, as a sovereign, he could not wisely ignore the supreme head of the spiritualty within his realm, nor leave out of count in his foreign policy so potent an international force as the Papacy. The king's attitude towards the Pope varied with his situation. When his interest coincided with that of the nation, he was defiant: when it conflicted, he was yielding. The financial requirements of both authorities were increasing, for the king's government, as it became better organized and more efficient, was ever more costly; and his wars at frequent intervals compelled him to embark on vast extraordinary expenditures, and the Popes, alike as Heads of the Church organizing crusades against infidels and heretics, and despatching missionaries to the pagans, and as local rulers governing, waging war, and pursuing secular policies, required immense revenues. A *modus vivendi* was discovered in this community of financial need. The English hierarchy found itself between the hammer of royal taxation and the anvil of Papal extortion. At the close of the Middle Ages the king's authority over the Church of England was in the temporal sphere effectively supreme, although the claims of the Papacy were formally uncontested, and its financial exactions condoned. The subjection of the national hierarchy was complete. Thus the ground had been prepared in England for the formulation of the royal supremacy and its effective expression by Henry VIII. The English hierarchy was already habituated to subjection before it was called upon officially to accept it. Erastianism had long been the atmosphere of England, when the storm of the Reformation broke on the Church.

Moreover, the Papacy at the end of the fifteenth century had so largely lost authority in Christendom that, when urgent need for the exercise of authority had suddenly emerged, it found itself practically powerless. The Popes had alienated the general conscience of Christendom, and broken up that unity of religious opinion which for so many generations had sustained their authority. The Papacy was at the lowest point of its fortunes when its authority was most directly challenged. In Germany, and throughout Christendom, its prestige had been irreparably damaged by the scandals of the Renaissance Pontiffs. Luther had publicly burned the Pope's bull amid popular enthusiasm in 1520, and the mercenaries of Charles V had horrified Christendom by the sack of Rome in 1527 before Henry VIII wrested from the reluctant and panic-stricken Convocations the recognition of his supreme headship in 1531. The rapid and easy course of the religious revolution in England is only intelligible when it is seen in the context of European history.

The enfeebled Papacy was confronted in England by a monarchy which had become beyond all precedent powerful. The wealth and influence of the sovereign had been greatly increased by the union of the Houses of York and Lancaster, and by the numerous forfeitures which the Wars of the Roses had occasioned. "In fact treason was more profitable to Henry VII than any other branch of his revenue." The feudal nobility, which had mostly perished, on the stricken fields of civil war or by the headsman's axe, was replaced by a new nobility which possessed neither its social influence nor its hereditary independence. The hierarchy of officials, as well secular as ecclesiastical, was largely composed of the king's personal attendants. The Tudor Court was the centre of the national system in a sense and measure which had never been the case in earlier times. The effect was favourable to the process of religious change.

The ecclesiastics who surrounded the throne of Henry VII and Henry VIII, and sanctioned with their presence and authority the acts of both those monarchs, invested royalty with a spiritual influence in the minds of the people which could not be disintegrated from it, or resumed when the Kings changed their religious principles, and dismissed their spiritual ministers.[1]

Thus the royal supremacy was no strange interruption of the normal movement of national history, but the natural outcome of the history itself.

It was, indeed, the distinctive method of the English Reformation to avoid the appearance of innovation, and

[1] *V*. Brewer, *The Reign of Henry VIII*, I, 69.

to ground its most revolutionary procedures on alleged precedents. These were often little more than formal, but they served to mitigate the shock of change, and they maintained the appearance of ecclesiastical continuity. Thus in the cardinal case of the royal supremacy, the king professed to have no other design than to maintain the ancient prerogatives of the Crown. When early in the reign of Henry VIII Dr Standish appealed to the king on the question of jurisdiction, Henry disclosed his point of view very clearly. This was in 1514, when Henry was far from designing a breach with the Pope. Seven years later, in 1521, he wrote his book against Luther, and was rewarded by Leo X with the famous title, which still retains its place in the style of the British sovereign, "Defender of the Faith". But the set of the king's mind had been sufficiently disclosed. Wolsey's ruin was effected by recourse to a statute of Richard II, which, by a cynical perversion of justice, was made to extend to the clergy since they, although they were but following the example of the king himself, had recognized Wolsey's legatine authority.

If one day more than another may be fairly fixed upon as that on which the English Reformation was in principle effected, and the Church *in* England became the Church *of* England, that day can hardly be other than 11 February, 1531, when the Convocation of Canterbury acknowledged the royal headship of the Church. This acknowledgment, it must never be forgotten, was neither willing nor unconditioned. It was wrung from the reluctant clergy as the price of the royal pardon.

In the Supremacy Act (1534) the conditioning clause to which the Convocations attached so much importance was dropped, and the obnoxious title was enacted in its original crudity:

albeit the king's majesty is and ought to be the supreme head of the Church of England, and so is recognized by the clergy of this realm in their Convocation, yet nevertheless for corroboration confirmation thereof...be it enacted by authority of this present Parliament that the king our sovereign lord, his heirs and successors kings of this realm, shall be taken, accepted, and reputed the only supreme head in earth of the Church of England, called Anglicana Ecclesia.

This Act was repealed by Mary, and revived by Elizabeth with a not insignificant change of title, governor being substituted for head. The use of the word "head" to express the royal supremacy was strongly objected against both by Papists and by Puritans. When the sovereign was a female the title appeared to be particularly inapt. Accordingly, Elizabeth, with her wonted caution, replaced it by the less obnoxious word "governor".

The point has been debated whether the title "Supreme Head" still belongs to the British sovereign. It was, as we have said, deliberately omitted from Elizabeth's Supremacy Act, but that Act by reviving the statute of Henry VIII concerning doctors of civil law may be said to have revived also the title of Supreme Head which is in that statute given to the king. "Thus", says Lindsay, "the very title Supreme Head of the Church of England was revived and bestowed on Elizabeth by this Parliament of 1559."[1]

Selden, a thorough-going Erastian, is reported to have said that there is "a great deal of difference between head of the Church and supreme governor", and, perhaps, if the titles be exactly understood, he was right. But it is certain that the adoption of the humbler title was not intended to indicate any diminution of authority.

The supremacy of Elizabeth expressly included all that was included in that of Henry VIII and Edward VI. Indeed it was even more extensive, for it was made to

[1] *V. History of the Reformation*, II, 394.

cover the case of "schisms", and the queen was empowered to delegate it to commissioners. The "admonition to simple men deceived by malicious" appended to the Royal Injunctions of 1559, and substantially included in the XXXVIIth Article of Religion, gives a moderate interpretation to the language of the Statute. It is explained that the queen does not "challenge authority and power of ministry of divine offices in the church", but only that authority "which is and was of ancient time due to the imperial crown of this realm":

that is, under God to have the sovereignty and rule over all manner persons born within these her realms, dominions, and countries, of what estate, either ecclesiastical or temporal, soever they be, so as no other foreign power shall or ought to have any authority over them.[1]

It is probable that Henry VIII did not perceive the full consequence of his action. To the end of his reign he seems to have clung to the notion that he could abolish the Pope and yet retain the Pope's religion. He left to his successors the problems, theological and disciplinary, which were implicit in the national independence within the ecclesiastical sphere which he had so crudely affirmed. The abolition of the Pope's authority compelled the improvisation of an effective substitute, and this was not easy to discover. It was not difficult to assert the national independence in the *political* sphere, and so far as the Papal supremacy had been in character and purpose *political*, it was easily cast aside. But to affirm independence in the *ecclesiastical* sphere was a far more formidable task. Christianity is not a national religion, and a Church which is genuinely Christian can never be unreservedly national. A parliamentary definition of heresy such as was contemplated by the Supremacy Act of 1559, could be no more than a temporary expedient,

---

[1] *V.* Gee and Hardy, *Documents*, pp. 438, 439.

for the doctrinal definitions of antiquity could hardly be adequate for the settlement of modern controversies. A national Establishment, stereotyped in statutes, and enforced in law-courts, would not only be difficult to reconcile with a Catholic religion, but would certainly fall out of accord, sooner or later, with the freely-developing life of the nation. The Papacy, in spite of many and gross scandals, had given coherence and authority to the ecclesiastical system of the Middle Ages. Local liberties had co-existed with submission to the central authority. But without the Papacy, without any central power, what should preserve the Christian society from complete disintegration? A famous attempt had been made in the fifteenth century to provide an alternative to the Papacy in a General Council, but after a brief fallacious triumph at Constance, it had petered out ignominiously at Basel. The Papacy, weakened and warned by its humiliation, had resumed its supremacy with the old problems unsolved, the old tendencies unweakened, and new questions clamouring for answer. In England men turned naturally to the monarch, who had brought order to the war-racked kingdom, and who alone could guarantee that political tranquillity which the waxing prosperity of the trading class imperatively required. If indeed reformation in the Church was to be effected, it would not be the Pope but the king who would be its instrument. But the king lacked one indispensable qualification, viz. a spiritual character. If but the monarchy could be equipped with a clear title to ecclesiastical control, it would be as irresistible in the spiritual sphere as in the temporal. It was precisely this qualification which the Reformers, armed with the Bible, were able to provide. Henry's appeal to political precedents might satisfy lawyers and antiquaries, and serve the convenience of diplomatists, but to religious men, bred in the tradition of medieval Christianity, it would carry little weight. It was otherwise with the appeal to the Scriptures, which the Church itself declared to be the infallible Word of God. It must be remembered that the Bible came to the laity with the charm of freshness, as well as with the authority of inspiration. Making all reasonable allowance for the vernacular versions which had circulated with ecclesiastical authority before the Reformation, it can hardly be reasonably disputed that the masses of the people were profoundly ignorant of the Scriptures. The translations of Luther in Germany, and of Tyndale in England, were immediately perceived to be powerful agents on the side of the religious revolution. On this point Reformed and Unreformed were agreed. The one exerted themselves to circulate the Scriptures in vernacular versions, the other to prohibit the circulation. The influence of the Bible on the English Reformation was nowhere more apparent than in its strengthening of the sovereign's ecclesiastical authority. For in the Bible men found, or thought they found, a clear title for the Royal Supremacy, and an august precedent for such a national church as the royal supremacy was shaping in England. In 1528 Tyndale, the illustrious translator of the Bible, published a volume which indicated a new attitude of mind towards the much agitated question of ecclesiastical reform. It was entitled, significantly, *The Obedience of a Christen man, and how Christen rulers ought to govern*. This book stated clearly "the governing principles of the English reformation—the final authority of scripture, and the supreme authority of the king in the state". The discussion was carried beyond the limited spheres of scholars and divines and brought into the market-place. With the English Bible in their hands, who could remain in doubt? Did not a national church exist by Divine appointment in ancient Israel? Could the English sovereign, reigning over a Christian nation, be possessed

of anything less than "that only prerogative which we
see to have been given to all godly princes in holy
Scripture by God Himself"? Hooker adopts the tone
of one who is laying down unchallengeable propositions.
"If, therefore," he asks, "with approbation from heaven,
the kings of God's own chosen people had in the affairs
of Jewish religion supreme power, why not Christian
kings the like power in Christian religion?"[1]

The lawyers co-operated with the Protestant divines.
Justinian went arm in arm with St Paul. Maitland has
pointed out the effect of the Civil Law which was now
ousting the Canon Law in the Universities wherever the
Renaissance was working change.[2]

The official doctrine of the Church of England, as set
out in the IInd Canon of 1604, credits the king's majesty
with

> The same authority in causes Ecclesiastical that the godly
> kings had amongst the Jews, and Christian Emperors in the
> Primitive Church.

Henry VIII was not slow to avail himself of the theory
which the preachers and lawyers asserted. In his colossal
egotism he imagined himself fully equal to the task of
ordering the belief and worship of his subjects. But it
was beyond his powers. Before he passed from the scene,
he too had failed. His death opened the floodgates of
innovation. The excesses of Edward's reign provoked
the savage reaction of Mary's, and then Elizabeth succeeded to the problem unsolved by her masterful father,
and made more difficult of solution by the decade of
revolution and counter-revolution which had followed
his death. It presented itself in changed circumstances.
The Reformation had passed into a new phase. Loyola
(*ob*. 1556) and Calvin (*ob*. 1564) had left their mark.

---

[1] *V. Ecclesiastical Polity*, Bk VIII, ch. III.
[2] *V. Canon Law in England*, p. 94.

The simple fervours of iconoclasm, and the drastic edicts of sovereigns, had given place to learned controversy and half-cynical state-craft. Statesmen were wearying of religious fanaticism, and casting about for some rational compromise which should make life tolerable to reasonable citizens of varying beliefs. Christendom, in short, was (to use a builder's phrase) "finding rest" within religious frontiers which would be permanent. The survival of a national church in England was not consistent with the victory of the rival extremes, Jesuit and Puritan. Against the Jesuit the victory of the National Church was complete because the Counter-Reformation, which the Jesuits inspired and embodied, was as hostile to the political as to the spiritual independence of the nation. Patriotism and religion blended in Elizabethan churchmanship. The half-century which followed the defeat of the Spanish Armada (1588) was the Golden Age of the Church of England, for then Church and State were effectively united by national sentiment. Against the Puritan the Church's victory was Pyrrhic. The Church only overcame the Puritans at the cost of its religious monopoly, that is, of its national character. So close was the interlacement of the religious and the secular forces within the nation, that a final settlement was only reached after the violences of the Civil War, and the great disillusionment of the Restoration. The murder of one sovereign and the abdication of another were requisite before men could acquiesce in the indispensable policy of mutual toleration. It has been said that "with toleration had come comprehension", but this implies a misunderstanding of the history. It was precisely the demonstrated failure of comprehension that forced the unreconciled but exhausted politicians to acquiesce in toleration. For toleration involved the definite failure of the older Anglicanism. Nonconformity in the original sense disappeared, for Puritanism would henceforward express itself as Dissent. The fact is that men's minds cleared slowly as experience disclosed and interpreted the issues raised by the repudiation of the Papacy. There was no promise of finality about the Elizabethan Settlement. The queen and her statesmen established only "a temporary equilibrium in Church and State, a government which was essentially a compromise between the old and the new spirit". But the religious compromise was more stable than the ecclesiastical, being grounded less on requirements of contemporary politics than on religious principles of abiding validity. The practical system was at best but a temporary makeshift, which was destined to break down in violent disaster within less than a half century of the great queen's death, but the theological scheme survived, because, under the stress of experience, it was found to disclose a reasonable and satisfying version of the Christian religion. Of all the Protestant Confessions that of the Church of England has sustained best the stern, continuing criticism of life.

The importance of the royal supremacy in the evolution of Anglicanism can hardly be overstated. It provided the framework within which it was possible to formulate such a delicately balanced version of Christianity. Only the power of the Tudor monarch could have enabled the achievement of the remarkable man who, through the critical years which witnessed the definite triumph of the Reformation in England, presided as Primate over the English Church. Of all the leading figures of the great transition from medievalism to Protestant Christianity that of Thomas Cranmer has been most belittled, and yet grows steadily in impressiveness as history reveals the quality of his work. By temperament, training, ability, and experience, the Archbishop was fitted for his task. A virtuous man in an evil age, without personal ambition amid a multitude of

self-seekers, merciful among persecutors, mild and for-
giving towards his opponents, a widely learned scholar
with a genuine scholar's candour and open-mindedness,
and, together with these graces, natural and acquired,
endowed with a genius for balanced and dignified English
speech which made him uniquely qualified to provide
the Church with its forms of public worship, Thomas
Cranmer stamped on the Reformed Church the characteristics which would finally be recognized as honourably
distinctive of the version of Christianity which it maintains—theological moderation, a deep and balanced
devotion, and a temper of comprehensive charity. The
English Prayer Book and the Thirty-nine Articles were
Cranmer's bequest to the Church of England, and they
remain after nearly four centuries its most treasured
possessions. While thus by his life's work Cranmer gave
order and meaning to the English Reformation, by his
martyrdom he made that work permanent. If ever the
famous saying of Tertullian may be justified, and the
blood of martyrs is the seed of the Church, it is when
applied to the martyrdoms of the two primates, Cranmer
and Laud. The one saved the English Reformation: the
other saved Anglicanism. Cranmer was in every respect,
except perhaps in physical courage, the superior of Laud,
but the considering student of English Christianity must
unite their names in his grateful recollection. Yet
Cranmer's superiority is unchallengeable. No name in
the long succession of Anglican worthies has such
apparent and supreme title to the homage and affection
of English churchmen.

The royal supremacy as understood by the Tudor
sovereigns was rather the logical expression of plenary
national autonomy than the assertion of extreme monarchical theory, or, to speak more exactly, the king and the
nation were so conjoined that the supremacy of the first
was implicit in the independence of the last. In the next

century there was a change of emphasis. The monarch was credited with an independent authority. According to the fantastic notion of hereditary right that then established itself, the royal supremacy was a personal prerogative. While, in the view of the Tudor sovereign, the exclusion of every foreign jurisdiction, whether Papal or imperial, was implicit in the "absolute" or "imperial" character of the English monarchy, in the view of the Stuart sovereign, the plenitude of ecclesiastical authority was vested in him by Divine hereditary right. In some sense it was true to say of the Tudor conception of the headship of the Church that it was constitutional. Of the headship as conceived by the Stuarts the constitutional aspect had been obscured by the mystical doctrine of inherent hereditary right. However extravagant might be the royalism of the preambles to their statutes, the Tudor sovereigns possessed the royal supremacy by a parliamentary title. The Stuarts succeeded to this title, but they preferred to emphasize another title older and higher than any which Parliament could confer or restrain—the title of Divine hereditary right. Whether constitutional or inherent, the royal supremacy could not but share the fortune of the other prerogatives of the Crown. Personal monarchy expired when James II abdicated the throne. The Revolution Settlement, which made an end of arbitrary government in England, implied for the Church of England the substitution of Parliament for the monarch. The change in the supremacy and the effect of the change could not but be considerable. The monarch's dictatorship was personal, and therefore temporary: the dictatorship in becoming parliamentary would be permanent.

In the course of the eighteenth century the development of the party system transformed the ecclesiastical authority of the sovereign into an asset of the party in office. This was clearly an incongruous and repellent development, yet however difficult it might be to harmonize the party system with the healthy working of a national church, it was not beyond the power of apologists to offer some plea for its acceptance. It could be argued that the royal supremacy had but returned to its originally constitutional character. It still reflected the completeness of national autonomy. The Christian nation which, in the sixteenth century, had uttered its mind in matters of religion through the monarch, now uttered its mind through Parliament. The House of Commons was composed of communicants who were the chosen representatives of the Christian nation. A Christian Church includes laity as well as clergy, and both have a clear right to take part in its government. Why should not the Christian laity utter its mind in Parliament, as the clergy in Convocation? But as the century advanced the situation steadily worsened. In 1717 the Convocation met for the last time for the transaction of business. The Union with Scotland brought a number of Presbyterians into the House of Commons, and thereby destroyed its definitely Anglican character. This anomaly, however, was easily condoned, for the number of non-Anglicans was petty, their Protestantism was undoubted, and their votes were convenient. The innovation did not essentially affect the situation. Purists might complain, but practical men were complaisant. It was far otherwise with the legislative changes which, in the course of the nineteenth century, destroyed all the legal securities for the Anglican, and even for the Christian, character of the electorate. The history discloses a progressive disqualification of Parliament for its original function as the House of Laity in a national church. Successively the gate of the constitution has been opened, first, to Protestant Nonconformists, then to Roman Catholics, then to Jews, finally to Atheists. The Christian character has been abandoned both in the constituencies and in Parliament. The crude fact is, that not a Christian monarch but a non-Christian Parliament controls the Church of England. Only the consideration and good sense which commonly mark the political action of English citizens have made possible the continuance of so gross and humiliating an anomaly.

The abolition of the Pope's authority involved the abandonment of the medieval theory of the Church, and necessitated the provision of a tolerable alternative. Absorbed by their immediate objects, the divorce on the king's part, the subjection of the clergy to lay control on the Parliament's, the agents of the momentous innovation were probably unaware of the inevitable consequences of their action. They had been following a well-trodden road when they challenged Papal interference in national politics. Conflict with the Papacy, it must be remembered, was a familiar feature of medieval Christianity. In the fourteenth century the embittered and protracted controversy between Lewis of Bavaria and the Avignonese Popes had brought under hostile criticism both the origin and the measure of Papal authority. Marsilius of Padua anticipated the arguments of Henry VIII. The Conciliar Movement of the following century had been with difficulty defeated, and in its course had raised questions which would not be easily answered, but had wonderfully damaged the current arguments for the Papal autocracy. England, in its insular isolation, had lagged behind the rest of Christendom, so that when, in the wake of the breach with Rome, Englishmen came into close contact with the religious revolution on the continent, they found themselves introduced at once into controversies far more searching than those which had engaged their minds at home. In Germany and in Switzerland the revolt against medieval religion had sprung from the distress of good men's consciences, and the disgust of thoughtful men's intelligence. England produced no masterful thinker like Luther, or Calvin, or Zuinglius, or Erasmus, to name the original leaders of the doctrinal and rationalistic movements on the continent. Political considerations, not moral repugnance to ecclesiastical abuses nor rational contempt for medieval superstition, induced the breach between England and Rome, but, that breach once effected, England could not but be drawn into the wider and more fundamental religious revolution which was developing in Europe. Wycliffe (*ob.* 1384) had, indeed, left a tradition of destructive criticism and pointed the way to drastic disendowment; but, as a thinker, he never really moved outside medieval scholasticism, and there is little reason for ascribing to Lollardism any considerable contribution to the English Reformation. Wycliffe's influence was greatest, not in England but in Bohemia, where he may fairly be regarded as the author of the Hussite movement, itself in turn a potent factor in the religious revolution in Europe.

It is, of course, true that political, moral, and intellectual motives and influences were co-operative in every movement of Reformation, but it is also true that these factors operated in varying measure, and that in the case of England the paramount factor was not moral or intellectual but political.

From this circumstance consequences of far-reaching importance have followed. In the first place, the polity of the Reformed Church did not grow out of the doctrinal and disciplinary changes, but preceded them. Henry himself remained to the day of his death an orthodox medievalist in every respect except that which affected the Pope's position in the Church. The Tudor statesmen were opportunists to whom change was unwelcome. They made the alterations in the ecclesiastical system as slight as possible. Even where meaning and reference had become different, the old names and forms were carefully maintained. The diocesan and parochial boundaries remained the same, and the endowments of the hierarchy were not confiscated. Bishops and incumbents were appointed to office in the accustomed way. The Spiritual Estate still had its representatives in the Upper House of Parliament. The Convocations still met, the Ecclesiastical Courts still functioned. Even the canon law retained a limited range and validity. In outward aspect the Church was little changed.

"This formal adherence to antiquity," observes Dixon, "this continued maintenance of the old constitution in all parts and branches, is the most characteristic and admirable feature of the English Reformation. But at the same time it must be carefully noticed that much of all this was no more than formal: that there was a real transference of power from one part of the old constitution to another; and that many things survived henceforth as shadows which had hitherto been of the force and activity of substance."[1]

This cautious retention of the medieval polity did undoubtedly preserve the Reformed Church from much of the violence and sacrilege which disgraced the Reformation outside England. The traveller in Scotland and Protestant Europe must needs reflect with thankfulness on the happy fortune which in his own country rescued from the ruthless fanaticism of popular zeal so many glorious monuments of medieval piety. But, if he be acquainted with the religious history of England, he will acknowledge that this good fortune has been dearly purchased by the religious division of the English people, and the internal confusions of the English Church. For the conservatism of the earlier phase of the English Reformation drew in its train the religious conflicts which marked the later. For when, in due course, the full force of doctrinal innovation reached England, the

[1] *V.* Dixon, *History of the Church of England*, I, 6.

new beliefs of the people had to find expression in an ecclesiastical system which had taken shape in an older world. The attempt to contain the "new wine" of Calvinistic doctrine and Presbyterian polity within the "old wine-skin" of the Tudor establishment was doomed to failure. It led through controversy, persecution, and civil strife to the final abandonment of the very ideal of national Christianity which had inspired the Elizabethan Settlement. The Toleration Act registered the triumph of political wisdom, and the disappearance of an ecclesiastical ideal.

It is interesting to observe how closely the changes of ecclesiastical theory reflected the circumstances of the national history. In the sixteenth century, when English nationality found full political expression, the Church *in* England became transformed into a national institution, the Church *of* England. Citizenship and churchmanship were identical. Religious dissent was potential treason, for it ever carried the implication of a foreign allegiance inconsistent with whole-hearted patriotism. Whether the foreign allegiance were Popish or Protestant made small difference. Its vice lay in its extra-national character. Under Henry VIII and Elizabeth the penal laws fell with impartial severity on the followers of Calvin and on those of Loyola. Neither Geneva nor Rome could be tolerated in England.

When all the efforts to restore the broken unity of Christendom by negotiation had definitely failed, the great controversy of the Reformation took a sterner and darker character. The epoch of the religious wars opened. Those wars were neither national nor dynastic, though both national and dynastic interests played a part in them, but essentially conscientious. Conflicting conceptions of truth, differing religious allegiances, incompatible versions of duty, were the springs of the most savage and destructive wars which have ever, until our own time, when again there is a strife of rival "ideologies", cursed the world. In this epoch the Tudor nationalism was necessarily transformed. England could not stand outside the wars of religion. It could not but be united to the rest of Protestant Christendom in a conflict which was in truth a desperate fight for very life against the superior forces of the Counter-Reformation. Elizabeth became, almost in spite of herself, the head of the Protestant interest in Europe, supporting against her own principles the Protestant rebels in Scotland, France, and Holland, and, by an irony of fate, strengthening by her foreign policy the very forces within her own kingdom which would finally destroy the balanced equilibrium of her ecclesiastical settlement. It was the misfortune and final undoing of the Stuarts that they never succeeded in realizing the transition from an English patriotism which naturally expressed itself in an "absolute" sovereign, to an English patriotism which could not but express itself in a passionate Protestantism.

The Reformation had raised ultimate issues—the right of the private conscience, the franchise of the intellect, the worth and authority of knowledge, the limits of spiritual authority, the conditions of civil liberty. These could not be pinched within local frontiers, or treated as merely national interests. They were more than counters in the game of dynastic policy. England, albeit almost fanatically insular, could not stand outside the conflict in which the very suppositions of her treasured independence were at stake. National interest compelled continental entanglement. The strength of the Elizabethan Church had been its sincere self-identification with the national interest: the fatal weakness of the Church under the Stuarts was its failure to accord with the national interest. It exchanged dependence on the nation for dependence on the monarch, and inevitably it shared the monarch's fortunes. The Puritans, who had been handicapped under the Tudors by their foreign con-

nexions, succeeded to the inheritance of national confidence which the established Church had forfeited. As
thoroughgoing advocates of the Protestant cause, they
commanded the support of that multitude of patriotic
Englishmen who, while tepid in their religious preferences, regarded with horror the prospect of a restoration
of Popery in the wake of Spanish victory. The Papacy
had become completely identified in English minds with
anti-national policies, and, therefore, it drew upon itself
the long-lasting suspicion and resentment of English
patriotism.

Protestantism, even in Anglican minds, outweighed
Monarchism. The Anglican clergy, who had since the
Restoration professed and proclaimed the slavish doctrine of non-resistance, joined hands with the Nonconformists, whom they had so hotly denounced and so
willingly persecuted, against a sovereign who was a
zealous Papist. The nation, divided religiously, was
politically united. Protestantism had become in the eyes
of considering English citizens the synonym of national
independence. Not his violations of law, but the dread
of his Romanizing zeal had deprived James II of his
firmest supporters. It was apparent to the least discern-
ing English churchman that the mighty instrument of
the royal supremacy could not safely be left in the hands
of a Roman Catholic monarch. This was the argument
that carried William of Orange, the acknowledged leader
of European Protestantism, to the throne of England.
When the Seven Bishops refused acceptance of James II's
illegal Declaration, the Church of England leaped into a
popularity which had had no parallel since the Spanish
Armada and the Gunpowder Plot. For once more the
nation divined that the Church of England was frankly
accordant with the national mind and could be trusted to
guard the national interest. The convictions created by
the crisis were stereotyped by legislation. Papists were expressly excluded from the provisions of the Toleration Act

(1689); and the Act of Settlement (1700) specifically shut out from succession to the Crown all members of the Royal House "that then were, or afterwards should be reconciled to, or shall hold communion with the see or Church of Rome, or should profess the popish religion, or marry a papist". The coronation oath was altered in order still further to secure the Protestantism of the sovereign, and it was enacted

that whosoever shall hereafter come to the possession of this crown shall join in communion with the Church of England, as by law established.

William himself was a Dutch Calvinist, and the princes to whom the title to the British Crown was transferred were German Lutherans: but all were unquestionably Protestants, and that was the main thing. Intercommunion with the Protestant churches of the continent was then an established practice among Anglicans. It has been maintained, probably with truth, that the Act of Settlement would not bar the accession of a qualified Nonconformist who was a Protestant Christian. The Supreme Head of the Established Church must be a Protestant. Nobody imagined that there was anything odd or undesirable about such a provision, for the Church of England in the seventeenth century was proud to describe itself as a Protestant Church. The determined Protestantism of the English people is more political than religious. Unquestionably the barbarities which earned for the most unfortunate and, perhaps, the most innocent of the Tudor sovereigns the hideous description, "Bloody Mary", created in English minds a traditional belief about Roman Catholicism which was not wholly just or fair, but the main root of the continuing prejudice was political. The "No Popery" dogma was burned into the national memory by the long association of Roman Catholicism with political disaffection. It has outlived the circumstances of its origin, and now survives as an intractable sentiment latent in the public mind which can be released into activity at the call of religious fanaticism, and may easily serve the interest of politicians who themselves regard it with merited contempt.

It is important to emphasize the political character of the Protestantism which achieved the English Revolution, for the religious development of the nation had tended in another direction. The conservative character of the English Reformation had given to the Reformed Church of England a stronger hold on the past than other Reformed Churches possessed. Much that had perished elsewhere in the storms of religious revolution had survived in England, and these older elements of the ecclesiastical system became more significant, and were valued more highly, as time passed. The intimate association with the monarchy which, in the sixteenth century, had saved the Church in England from the iconoclasm and Presbyterianism, elsewhere prevailing in the Protestant sphere, carried the Church in the seventeenth century into a fellowship with the monarchy which proved disastrous. Church and monarchy fell together. Both king and primate lost their heads in the Great Rebellion. The personal qualities of the sovereigns had told effectively on the development of opinion within the Church, for Tudors and Stuarts were alike in this respect, that both took their ecclesiastical supremacy very seriously. Henry VIII and James I were no mean theologians. Elizabeth and Charles I were keenly interested in church affairs. Among the Reformed Churches the National Church in England enjoyed an apparent and uncontested primacy. It alone had the prestige of a powerful state behind it, and it alone preserved the dignified aspect of a hierarchy in close association with a court. Moreover, it was relatively wealthy. Mark Pattison, in his illuminating biography of the Huguenot scholar, Isaac Casaubon (1559–1614), has drawn the picture of the Church of England under

James I, during that brief interval between the definite triumph of the Reformation and the catastrophe of the Civil War. Then, if ever, Burke's famous phrase was true to fact, and religion in England "reared its mitred front in Courts and Parliaments". Anglicanism was purging itself of its fanaticism, and leaving that element to the puritans.

"You must not suppose", Casaubon writes to Saumaise, "that this people is a barbarous people; nothing of the sort; it loves letters and cultivates them, sacred learning especially. Indeed, if I am not mistaken, the soundest part of the whole reformation is to be found here in England, where the study of antiquity flourishes together with zeal for the truth."[1]

While its national establishment separated the Church of England from the poverty and social insignificance of the Protestant communions, its continuing controversy with the Roman Church developed its self-consciousness, and created its apologetic. It is true to say, that Anglicanism took definite shape in controversy, and that it was stereotyped in the bitter crisis of political ruin. As the first fervours of the Reformation died down, a notable change in controversial method became apparent. Sir Edwyn Sandys, in his remarkable *Europae Speculum*, published at the very close of the sixteenth century, pointed out the character and effect of the difference. Under the influence of the Jesuits, the Papacy had organized its warfare against the Protestant rebels. The Jesuits had studied the methods of the enemy, and adopted them. In the earlier phases of the Reformation the Protestants had prevailed by their incessant preaching, by their popular publications, by their zeal for knowledge, by their activity in education. Now they found themselves encountered, and often surpassed, in all these respects.

As with preaching, so with devotional books, and

[1] *V. Isaac Casaubon*, pp. 327, 328.

learned treatises, and above all with educational activity. The Protestants were in danger of being driven out of the field. The Counter-Reformation swept victoriously over Hungary, Poland, France, Belgium, and the Rhineland, and seemed to be marching to complete triumph. To meet this new offensive a better equipped type of controversialist was required. The Church of England did not fail to provide a succession of apologists who met the Papist champions on equal terms, and were not defeated. The goodly array of Anglican apologists came on the scene, and if the controversy still continues, it has no longer the formidable aspect which it once possessed. The battle ceased to be limited to the field of Scripture. It extended to the patristic literature, and to the whole range of Christian history. Nothing is so quickly obsolete as controversial writing. Immediate effectiveness is always purchased by an early oblivion, for knowledge is ever growing: every question presents itself in unprecedented forms; and the force of every argument is determined by its relevance to actual conditions. There is no finality in apologetics. None but the curious or the student of opinion now turns the pages of the famous controversial writers of the past. Among the Anglican champions, Hooker and Chillingworth alone retain importance, for they carried the controversy of their time into the calmer region of ultimate principle, and summoned to the arbitrament of current disputes the final authority of the human reason itself. In their hands the issue was not merely concerned with a successful apology for Anglicanism, but with an investigation of the primary postulates of faith and morality.

Experience seemed to disallow the original Anglican assumption, for when the nation had decisively repudiated the National Church, and the Supreme Head had been deposed and murdered by his subjects, what could any longer be reasonably said about the spiritual autonomy of the nation vested in "the Lord's anointed"?

The years of exile abroad were sifting years for devout and considering Anglicans. The moral of their calamity was relentlessly pushed home by the agents of the Papacy. They were hard pressed by the Jesuit proselytizers, backed up by the personal insistence of Henrietta Maria and the colder political reasoning of the French king. It is certain that many of the exiled Royalists yielded to the arguments thus powerfully supported, and renounced membership in a national church which had vanished from the map of Christendom. For the most part, however, the exiled Royalists adhered to their religious allegiance, and followed the leading of Anglican scholars like Cosin, Bramhall, Jeremy Taylor, Thorndike, and Hammond, who in the teeth of immense difficulties separated from their books, and often hard pressed for the bare necessaries of life, made a valorous defence for their religious convictions. In these troubled years there was worked out a reasoned case for a version of Anglicanism which was properly independent of the Tudor theory of a national church, and rested on the deeper foundations of reason, Scripture, and antiquity. The Restoration, drawing in its train a fantastic royalism, gave a fresh lease of life to the old ecclesiastical nationalism, though, as we have already pointed out, the emphasis was now placed rather on the monarch's hereditary right than on the nation's spiritual autonomy. But the bigotry of James II completed the disillusioning process which the Royal Martyr's fate had begun. It became apparent that neither the nation nor the monarch could provide a secure foundation for Anglican theory. As the Church of England, dismayed and divided, became frankly subject to the State, it acquiesced involuntarily, and not without the vehement protest of the Nonjurors' secession, in the Erastian principle on which alone such subjection could be defended.

CHAPTER 2

CHURCH AND STATE

The Divine right of the individual human spirit was but dimly perceived by the ancients, and in its practical expression variously conditioned. The later Hebrew prophets proclaimed it as the essential distinction of human nature itself. It was tersely uttered in that verse of the Proverbs, which was a favourite text of the Cambridge Platonists, "*The spirit of man is the candle of the Lord*". It is this doctrine which is the fontal spring from which the age-long conflict of Church and State has flowed. It is a doctrine clearly capable of disastrous misconception and misapplication. The miserable record of fanaticism shows how often and how ruinously it has been distorted. There is no explosive force known to human experience more powerful than that of a large idea introduced into minds too small to comprehend it. This doctrine of the Divine right of the individual human spirit has shown itself to be precisely such an explosive force. The Cambridge Platonists themselves, who emphasized it, were in some measure protected by their own circumstances from forgetting the danger of its misapplication by ignorance, interest and ambition. Their lot was cast in an age of disordered individualism. They had witnessed with their own eyes the havoc wrought in Church and State by the frenzied fanatics of the Commonwealth. It is no mean evidence of their

own sanity and wisdom that, in the teeth of this experience, they yet did not refrain from championing the
truth of individual freedom. Conscience and reason (or
judgment), they affirmed, were the Divinely ordained
guides of human action, and these might not be thought
of as conceivably conflicting. "Conscience without
judgment", runs one of Whichcote's celebrated aphor-
isms, "is superstition, judgment without conscience is
self-condemnation." "To go against reason", runs
another, "is to go against God: it is the self-same thing,
to do that which the reason of the case doth require, and
that which God himself doth appoint. Reason is the
Divine governor of man's life. It is the very Voice of
God." It is ultimately this prophetic doctrine of the
Divine right of the individual human spirit which carries
the promise, nay which involves the necessity, of im-
mitigable conflict between man and every demand of
external authority, however strongly entrenched in
tradition, and heavily armed with coercive power, which
insults his reason or wounds his conscience. It is the
Magna Carta of the human spirit, the affirmation of
man's personal autonomy.

Religion then, as presented by the Hebrew Prophets,
albeit in their belief bound to national privilege, and
inspired by the vision of a time when the final victory
of the perfected nation should be welcomed by a subject
universe, carried ever at its core this truth about Man.
In himself, they taught, the individual has access to a
higher guidance than any that external authority can
provide, and can appeal from all mundane verdicts to a
more august tribunal than any which mundane power
can establish. This prophetic doctrine lays the axe at the
root of all totalitarian versions of external authority.
Ultimately, the persistent and many-sided problem of
the relations of Church and State grows from this creed.
Christianity has added to the requirement of the inspired

individual that of the inspired society. In the view of the Christian, religion is not merely a private philosophy guiding the life of the individual, but a social gospel interpreting and delimiting his civic obligation. From the first the Christian profession has implied membership of the Christian Church. The oldest Christian documents are Apostolic epistles to churches, and, when the religion of Christ emerges in history, it is in an ecclesiastical form. The Church confronts the State.

In theory, the Church's claim to obedience has the same authority as that of the individual conscience. When the Council of Jerusalem introduced its decision with the bold assumption, "*it seemed good to the Holy Ghost and to us*", claiming Divine inspiration for its own verdict, it struck a note which has been sustained throughout the history of Christendom. But that note has been as audible in the worst ecclesiastical pronouncements as in the best. The spiritual society, yielding with strange facility to the pressures of its mundane environment, has fallen into the same condemnation as the State, and has raised against itself the same revolt of the private conscience. For no external authority, however designated, spiritual or secular, Church or State, can rightfully require from the individual Christian an unlimited or unconditioned obedience. Its demands must be endorsed by the citizen's own conscience and reason before he can without loss of self-respect acknowledge their title to his acceptance. Indeed, from the Christian point of view, the convenient and conventional distinction between the secular and the spiritual spheres has no inherent validity. Both spheres lie within the empire of the Moral Law. From the Jews the Christian Church received the sublime conception of the Moral Law as the Will of the Creator, immutable and eternal as its Author. The intensely ethical character of Jewish religion grew from that conception, and not less the universal range of duty. The Messianic faith in Israel's final triumph in a righteously ordered universe sprang from the conviction that, since righteousness was the Will of God, it must finally prevail throughout the whole extent of His dominion. Christianity inherited, interpreted, and reaffirmed both the morality and the indestructible hope of Israel. "What has mattered in history", writes a learned modern Jew, "is not so much the Jewish revelation of the unity of God as the Jewish intuition of that God's moral nature."

Men need a vision which gives meaning to moral striving. This can take the form of one of two ideals in which present inequalities are redressed; the one that of a perfected social order, the other that of a perfected life-cycle. Both these ideals took shape in the Hebraic tradition, the former receiving more stress in Judaism, the latter in Christianity.[1]

Now the one vision, and now the other, has directed the course of Christian thought and life. Yet the correlation of both in a single service is essential if the true balance of Christian obligation is to be maintained. Ecclesiastical history is filled with the blunders and crimes of moral lopsidedness. Here, the ascetic, pursuing the ideal of personal salvation, has repudiated his secular duty; and there, the Erastian, seeking to win the world for Christ by the tempting method of complaisance, has betrayed his spiritual trust.

It is only in the context of these large considerations respecting religion in general, and Christianity in particular, that the practical problem, of which Establishment is presumed to provide a solution, can itself usefully be discussed. Perhaps it would not be untrue to say that the Old Testament has been more influential than the New in shaping the political thought and practice of Christendom. Medieval Christianity was, in its distinc-

[1] V. Cecil Roth, *The Jewish Contribution to Civilization*, p. 159.

tive features, a Christianized Judaism; and, when it gave place, after the great disruption of the sixteenth century, to local establishments of religion, these long continued to use its language, and to reflect its spirit. "*Cujus regio, ejus religio*" was no invention of the Protestant innovators, but a survival of medieval doctrine, which, though with lessened excuse and more apparent unreason, they accepted and maintained. Thus medieval intolerance persisted long in the sphere of the Reformation, and gravely compromised its character. But religious persecution, entirely consistent with medieval principles, was too plainly incompatible with the fundamental assumption, on which the Reformers were acting, to continue when once political opportunism ceased to demand it. The principle of private judgment could not be permanently combined with the practice of persecution. The deeper teaching of the Hebrew prophets, endorsed and emphasized by Christ, was seen to override and disallow the nationalistic suggestions of the Old Testament. The prophetic vision of Israel persisted, but it was ever more sharply distinguished from the ecclesiastical caricature which had seemed satisfying enough in the half-light of the Middle Ages. The practical problem which had divided Christendom for centuries presented itself in new forms within modern communities which were national and free. In England alone, the medieval framework of national religion was in unique measure preserved, so that the new wine of Protestant doctrine had perforce to be contained in wine-skins which by long-continued use had been stretched and strained.

The practical problem, of which Establishment offers a solution, is properly peculiar to Christendom, for, in Christendom, Church and State cover the same ground, and are (Christianly viewed) Divinely commissioned as allies in pursuit of the same ideal, which neither in isolation is able to reach, viz. the ideal of a perfect society. Their procedure is different for, while the Church is primarily concerned with the individual citizen, the State addresses itself to the society of citizens. But plainly these objectives cannot be rightly thought of as finally opposed. The perfect citizen is unthinkable apart from the rightly ordered society: a rightly ordered society presupposes perfect citizens. The interests of Church and State are ultimately identical. Conflict between them implies failure on the one side or on the other, or indeed on both. Since both are moving towards the same goal, which neither in isolation can attain, neither can rightly consent to be excluded from its own sphere. Both State and Church claim Divine Right. The State grounds its title to obedience on no less a foundation than the purpose of the Creator, disclosed in the gradual development of civilization. The Church, emerging later in history, adduces its Divine Founder's institution. Civil government reveals the action of the Divine Wisdom in human society:

> By me kings reign,
> And princes decree justice.
> By me princes rule,
> And nobles, even all the judges of the earth.[1]

Christianity, though often obscured and compromised by the "earthen vessels" of ecclesiastical system which preserve and express it, brings "the mind of Spirit" to the guidance of mankind.

Both State and Church are Divinely appointed instruments through which the Kingdom of God shall be set up on earth. Through their right and harmonious functioning in human society the prophetic dream of a world wherein dwelleth righteousness shall be finally realized: "*The earth shall be full of the knowledge of the*

---

[1] *V.* Proverbs viii. 15, 16.

Lord as the waters cover the sea." It was a happy thought which led Dean Stanley to inscribe above the high altar of Westminster Abbey the great legend of Christian hope: "*The kingdoms of the world are become the kingdoms of our Lord and His Christ.*" Did not Christ in His famous answer to the Pharisees accept both State and Church, and charter the great rivals for distinctive contributions to the single end? Caesar and God were united in His doctrine of human obligation and, if that doctrine did not solve the practical problem implicit in a recognition of both, it did at least disclose its range and character. The long experience of Christendom has left the problem unsolved. In the pagan state of antiquity there was no strife between Church and State because there was no rival to the State. In medieval Christendom there was, at least in theory, no strife, because there was no rival to the Church: but in the modern world the competing totalitarianisms of State and Church are rending society. Moreover, these historic totalitarianisms of Church and State must always finally confess their derivative character, and make their count with the older and more august totalitarianism of the individual self, which with Divine authority both authenticates and limits their demands.

In a famous and often quoted passage Hooker repudiates as "a gross error" the low estimate of "regal power" which would limit its concern to merely "men's temporal peace":

A gross error it is, to think that regal power ought to serve for the good of the body, and not of the soul: for men's temporal peace, and not for their eternal safety: as if God had ordained kings for no other end and purpose but only to fat up men like hogs, and to see that they have their mast. Indeed, to lead men unto salvation by the hand of secret, invisible, and ghostly regiment, or by the external administration of things belonging unto priestly order, (such as the word and sacraments are,) this is denied unto Christian kings: no cause in the world to think them uncapable of supreme authority in the outward government which disposeth the affairs of religion so far forth as the same are disposable by human authority, and to think them uncapable thereof, only for that the said religion is everlastingly beneficial to them that faithfully continue in it. And even as little cause there is, that being admitted thereunto amongst the Jews, they should amongst the Christians of necessity be delivered from ever exercising any such power, for the dignity and perfection which is in our religion more than in theirs.[1]

In this passage Hooker discloses an inadequate perception of the implications of his own argument, and he assumes much that was challenged even in the sixteenth century, and in the twentieth has long been abandoned. If the State were confessedly Christian, and if the Church were apparently united, it might not be wholly unreasonable to base a working unity of both on an agreed allocation of functions. But when neither of these conditions can be shown to exist, when the State is frankly non-Christian, and the Church is notoriously divided into sections, it is obvious that such a scheme of harmonious co-operation is altogether impracticable. Hooker in fact was the apologist of an Establishment which rested on assumptions, political, ecclesiastical, historical, and scriptural, which have lost validity. It was less the *arguments* of the Nonconformists than their *existence* that finally destroyed Hooker's case for a national church. The Church of England still retains the imposing façade of the Elizabethan Establishment which Hooker defended, but that façade is as delusive as it is picturesque. It belongs to a Past which can never return: it has little hold on the Present, and less hope for the Future. Its passing away, which cannot be long postponed, may conceivably release spiritual energies

[1] *V. Ecclesiastical Polity*, Bk VIII, ch. III, sec. 2.

which it can now only hamper and conceal. The English Establishment is only one more example of mutability. It may illustrate Wordsworth's famous lines:

> Truth fails not; but her outward forms that bear
> The longest date do melt like frosty rime,
> That in the morning whiten'd hill and plain
> And is no more; drop like the tower sublime
> Of yesterday, which royally did wear
> His crown of weeds, but could not even sustain
> Some casual shout that broke the silent air,
> Or the unimaginable touch of Time.

That eminent medievalist, Bishop Stubbs, delivers the conclusion to which his life-long studies had led him, when he warns us against facile solutions of the vexed problem implicit in Establishment:

The careful study of history suggests many problems for which it supplies no solution. None of these is more easy to state, or more difficult to handle, than the great question of the proper relation between Church and State. It may be taken for granted that, between the extreme claims made by the advocates of the two, there can never be even an approximate reconciliation. The claims of both are very deeply rooted, and the roots of both lie in the best parts of human nature; neither can do violence to, or claim complete supremacy over, the other, without crushing something which is precious. Nor will any universal formula be possible so long as different nations and churches are in different stages of development, even if for the highest forms of Church and State such a formal concordat be practicable.... For the historian, who is content to view men as they are and appear to be, not as they ought to be or are capable of becoming, it is no dereliction of duty if he declines to lay down any definition of the ideal relations between Church and State....

Even if it were possible that in a single state of homogeneous population and a fair level of property and education, the relations of religion, morality and law could be adjusted, so that a perfectly national church could be organized and a system of co-operation work smoothly and harmoniously, the fact remains that religion and morality are not matters of nationality. The Christian religion is a historical and Catholic religion; and a perfect adjustment of relations with foreign churches would seem to be a necessary adjunct to the perfect constitution of a single communion at home. In the middle ages of European history, the influence of the Roman church was directed to some such end. The claim of supremacy made for the see of Rome, a claim which its modern advocates urge as vehemently as if it were part of the Christian Creed, was a practical assertion that such an adjustment was possible. But whether it be possible or no in a changed state of society, the sober judgment of history determines that, as the world is at present moved and governed, perfect ecclesiastical unity is, like a perfect adjustment between Church and State, an ideal to be aimed at rather than to be hoped for.[1]

But, it must be asked, even conceding the necessity of some lack of logical completeness in the relations of Church and State, are there no essential conditions which any rightly acceptable compromise must satisfy? Has the Church no fundamental principles which it can only abandon at the fatal cost of spiritual suicide? What are the limits of a morally legitimate compromise which, in the interest of its spiritual task, the Church may accept? What is the true meaning of Establishment?

These unavoidable questions can only be usefully debated when there is agreement as to the content of the crucial terms, State and Church.

The Oxford Dictionary defines the State thus:

The body politic as organized for supreme civil rule and government: the political organization which is the basis of

[1] *V. Constitutional History*, 3rd edition (Oxford, 1884), vol. III, ch. XIX, p. 296..

Coronation processions of George IV and Edward VII

civil government (either generally and abstractly or in a particular country) hence the supreme civil power and government vested in a country or state.

The State may be organized on a despotic, or on a democratic, basis: it may be national or imperial: sovereign or subordinate; absolute or constitutional; religious or secular. The Church of Christ in its long history has had experience of every kind of State, and in the Middle Ages it became itself a State.

In modern England the State is democratic, supreme, and secular. Government reflects the will of an electorate which now includes practically the entire adult population of both sexes. Civic rights are unconditioned by any form of religious profession. The Roman Catholic, the Dissenter, the Pagan, and the Atheist have equal right with the Anglican to a share in the State's control of the Established Church. The sovereign is, indeed, still excluded from the right, which the humblest of his subjects possesses, to determine his own religious profession, but, though this exclusion could only be justified, if justified at all, by his ecclesiastical prerogative, and was in fact originally imposed because that prerogative had been grossly misused by James II, it is still maintained though the ecclesiastical prerogative of the Crown has, for all practical purposes, been transferred from the sovereign to his constitutional advisers. He must as Head of the National Church act on the advice of the prime minister, who is responsible to the House of Commons. Prayers are still read in both Houses of Parliament. The sovereign is still crowned with the archaic pomp of religious ceremony, but these traditional observances carry no real security that government shall proceed on Christian principles. Peers and Members of Parliament are free to be of any religion or of none, and the crowned and anointed monarch, in spite of his

Coronation Oath, has no direct authority in ecclesiastical affairs. Nevertheless to the State, thus in its constitution effectively secular, the Establishment secures complete legislative and judicial control of the Church. The Enabling Act (1919) did indeed confer on the Church Assembly the power of drafting measures to which Parliament might, if it so pleased, give statutory force, but the unlimited legislative power of Parliament was expressly preserved. This complete subordination of the Church to the State has often provoked misgivings, protests, and even secessions; but so long as the State limited its action to such matters as did not raise issues of Christian principle, the Establishment did not lack apologists, and there seemed no urgent reason for challenging it. But the situation has been drastically altered. The extension of the area of State action since the complete democratization of government has steadily ousted the Church from ground which from time immemorial it had regarded as its own. There is no civic concern which now lies outside the State's control. The laws of marriage, the education of the people, the regulation of the nation's reading, recreation, health, and social habits—all are now regarded as lying within the legitimate action of the State. Public opinion is increasingly insistent on State interference in the sphere of economics.

In these circumstances, the character of the Establishment has completely changed. The State no longer looks to the Church for many public services which formerly the Church was expected to render, but which now the State feels able to render more effectively from its own resources.

Inadequacy of material means on the part of the Church has co-operated with failure of religious interest on the part of the State in the process of emptying Establishment of effective meaning. In fact, Establishment has now become a very one-sided arrangement. The Church, though still in name and legal theory NATIONAL, and as such bound to national service, is left unhelped to satisfy the waxing religious obligations created by the nation's rapid development. The State no longer accepts any responsibility for so extending the parochial system that it shall match the new situation created by the re-housing and redistribution of the urban population which has marked the post-War period. More than a century has passed since Parliament voted money for the building of new churches. The State's material assistance has been limited to legislative manipulations of the Church's ancient endowments, not always to the Church's advantage, and it has thrown on the unhelped Church the heavy and continuing cost of maintaining the fabrics of the cathedrals and parish churches. Seventy years ago Church rates even for this purpose were abolished.

The question cannot but suggest itself, and press for answer—What advantage accrues to the Church of England as a result of the subjection to the secular State implicit in the Establishment?

It may indeed fairly be argued, that Establishment in some sense is a necessary condition of the Church's existence, and tenure of property. The spiritual society cannot function without the State's permission or acquiescence, nor can it hold property save under legal control, and for purposes which the State allows. The State may be Pagan, as in the Roman Empire; or Mohammedan, as in Persia; or Protestant, as in England and Holland; or Atheist, as in France and Russia; or Racial, as in Germany; yet only with its sanction and within the limits of its laws can the Church organize itself, fulfil its spiritual mission, and hold possessions. Establishment may be nothing more than the sum of the relations with the State which are thus created and defined. The Roman Catholics, the Nonconformists, and the Jews are in this general sense established in England. When, however, the Church of England is described as an Established Church something more is meant.

It is with the actual Establishment of the Church of England that this book is concerned, though it is not unimportant to remember that, if that Establishment were ended by an Act of Disestablishment, the Church of England would still, in the sense which has been indicated, remain established. What then is meant when the Church of England is called the Established Church, and sometimes spoken of shortly as "the Establishment"?

In his well-known *Defence of the Church of England against Disestablishment*, published in 1886, the late Lord Selborne was at considerable pains to provide the answer to this question, which at the time was being much debated. He examined the nineteen heads under which Mr Gladstone in his early essay on the *Relations of Church and State* (1838) had enumerated the things which in his view constituted "the Nationality of the Church of England"; and, after setting aside most of them "as separable accidents of greater or less importance, significant of, or consequential upon, the relations otherwise constituted between Church and State", proceeded to state his own view:

There remain, of his nineteen heads, those which relate to law, legislation, and judicature; viz. the summoning of the Convocations by Royal writs—the part taken by Parliament in Ecclesiastical legislation—the restrictions placed by the State upon the enactment of Church laws—and the authority of the Ecclesiastical Courts.

These, he says, "do constitute the essential terms and conditions of the 'Establishment' of the Church" (*v.*

pp. 68, 69). Elsewhere in his book he defines the Establishment thus:

The Establishment of the Church by law consists essentially in the incorporation of the law of the Church into that of the realm, as a branch of the general law of the realm, though limited as to the causes to which, and the persons to whom it applies; in the public recognition of its Courts and Judges, as having proper legal jurisdiction; and in the enforcement of the sentences of those Courts, when duly pronounced according to law, by the civil power (p. 10).

That distinguished constitutional lawyer, the late Sir William Anson, after stating that every religious society is "in necessary subordination to Parliament, because Parliament may make the profession of its opinions unlawful, may subject the performance of its acts of worship to a penalty, may impose tests which disqualify its members for office or franchise", and pointing out that "every religious society, large or small, which enters into relations of property or contract, must necessarily be liable to have its doctrines discussed in a court of law", proceeds to speak particularly of Establishment as it applies to the Church of England:

But the Established Church has a closer connexion with the State than this necessary subordination to Parliament and liability to have its doctrine discussed and interpreted in courts of law. The King is Head of the Church, not for the purpose of discharging any spiritual function, but because the Church is the National Church, and as such is built into the fabric of the State. The Crown itself is held on condition that the holder should be in communion with the Church of England as by law established. The Convocation of the Church is summoned, prorogued, and dissolved by the Crown, it cannot enter on ecclesiastical legislation without royal permission, nor make canons without the royal licence and assent.

The Crown appoints the great officers of the Church, and

of these the Bishops are not only administrators and judges of ecclesiastical law, but constitute the Lords Spiritual in the House of Lords.

The courts of the Church are not private tribunals for determining the internal differences of a voluntary society; the law of the Church is a part of the law of the land, and the King is over all persons in all causes, as well ecclesiastical as temporal, within his dominions supreme.

For not only is the Church unable to make new canons without the royal assent, but its liturgy and articles of religion have a Parliamentary sanction; though not made by Parliament, they have been accepted by Parliament, and therefore they need the combined action of Church and State for their alteration.[1]

Sir William Anson wrote some years before the passing of the Enabling Act, but his language requires no alteration to make it apply to the situation as modified by that Act.

These statements of eminent lawyers are very suggestive. They disclose a situation which can only be reasonable for the State and tolerable for the Church on the supposition that the law of the realm is Christian, and the State which includes the Church as "built into its fabric" is Christian. This is the order of history. The conversion of the English people preceded the establishment of the English Church. Far into the nineteenth century the Judges assumed Christianity to be part of the law of England, and, on that assumption, administered the laws against those who blasphemed religion, attacked Christianity, and profaned the Sabbath. Anti-blasphemy and Sabbath observance laws command small respect to-day. How could it be otherwise since it is notorious that the great majority of the citizens have ceased in any effective sense to acknowledge the authority of the

[1] *V. Law and Custom of the Constitution*, 3rd edition (1908), vol. II, Part ii, pp. 217, 218.

Christian Church? The strong but waning tradition of Christian feeling still obscures the general abandonment of Christian principle, but nothing can finally avert the effect of de-Christianized national habit. Democracy can only express the general will; it cannot restrain it. Christianity cannot, even in the interest of its own message, use "the arm of flesh". As the secular spirit colours the national life, and determines the nation's policy, the Establishment of the Church must needs become ever more unmeaning and anomalous. It is a survival which has outlived its original *raison d'être*, and is confessedly an anomaly. "We have long rid ourselves of all the secular burdens imposed by what we call the Tudor dictatorship," wrote Bishop Stubbs, "but we are still living under religious or ecclesiastical conditions that owe very much even of their present form, to the hand of Henry."[1] Indeed, it is very difficult to define, still more difficult to defend, a situation in which Establishment implies no restraint on the State and no liberty in the Church. For all practical purposes the Church of England has already been disestablished. The tenure of the ancient endowments may, perhaps, be regarded as conditioned by establishment, but since the ancient endowments were ecclesiastical in origin, and since the State has long ceased to admit any responsibility for providing any additions to them, the argument, however valid in law, must be pronounced to be lacking in equity. For generations the Church has been left unhelped by the State in its effort to provide for the spiritual needs of the nation, and if the provision is admitted to be grievously inadequate, the reason must be found in the smallness of the Church's resources, not in the absence of will, or of effort, or of sacrifice.

The notion that the Establishment might be so transformed as to enfranchise the Church of England, and

[1] *V. Lectures on Medieval and Modern History*, p. 262.

remove from its constitution every taint of Erastianism, has been earnestly pressed by some English Churchmen since the rejection of the Revised Prayer Book by the House of Commons (1928) forced even the most ardent champions of "national" Christianity to re-examine their assumptions. It has received encouragement, and even gained a delusive plausibility, from the course of events in Scotland. There the union of the Presbyterian Churches led to the passing of the Church of Scotland Act (1921) by which, it is confidently affirmed by its apologists, there has been created a frankly non-Erastian Establishment. The united Presbyterian Church was given complete autonomy, and at the same time clothed by statute with the character of a national church. Why, it is asked, should not the Church of England be in like manner autonomous and established? In theory there is no reason why such liberty should not be granted to the established Episcopal Church in the one country as has already been granted to the established Presbyterian Church in the other; but in practice there are differences between the ecclesiastical situation in the two countries so considerable as to make much possible in the one which is not possible in the other. The past history, the national temperament, the social circumstances, the religious outlook in Scotland are curiously unlike those in England. Of all the Protestant nations the Scots are the most religiously united, and the English the least. Dissidence has been as conspicuous in Scotland as in England, but in Scotland there has been nothing properly equivalent to English Dissent. Separations within the common Presbyterian description have been many north of the Tweed, but not dissenting denominations organizing their systems according to their own will. The Westminster Confession and the Presbyterian polity have held Scottish Christians in a fundamental agreement, but between the English Dissenters and the Established Church there are no such strong and recognized links.

Moreover, the Establishment as it now exists in Scotland hardly accords with the English notion of what Establishment properly includes. An established Church which has no legal share in the national government is not from the English point of view an established Church at all. The Church of Scotland, save for the picturesque ceremonial connected with the annual visit of the High Commissioner who represents the sovereign, but has no ecclesiastical function except to sit in the Assembly and deliver an address, is as completely severed from the process of government as a non-established Church. In Article III of the "*Articles Declaratory of the Constitution of the Church of Scotland in Matters Spiritual*", which forms the Schedule of the Church of Scotland Act (1921), it is declared that

as a national Church representative of the Christian Faith of the Scottish people it acknowledges its distinctive call and duty to bring the ordinances of religion to the people in every parish of Scotland through a territorial ministry.

But it may fairly be pointed out that every Christian Church, whether established or not, acknowledges as much; and that an established Church in common with every other Church can only give practical effect to this acknowledgment in so far as its resources of men and money admit. For these resources the Church of Scotland, albeit an established Church, is as solely dependent on the voluntary gifts of its own members as are the non-established and disestablished Churches. Establishment cannot, of course, create or add anything to the spiritual obligation which inheres in the very character of every Christian Church.

The Church of England is otherwise established. Although, as we have said, its functions have been drastically curtailed, so that its opportunities of national service have been greatly lessened, it is still an integral part of the political system. The king must be in communion with it: its bishops sit in the Upper House of Parliament: its clergy serve as chaplains in the army, navy, and national institutions; it has some control of the schools and training colleges. No doubt all this is but the shadow of the shade of its former importance, but it enshrines a principle, and is not wholly ineffective. Establishment on the Scottish plan would be equivalent to disestablishment without disendowment, which indeed is probably the truest description of what has been effected in Scotland.

The endowments of the Church of England, though woefully insufficient for the needs of the Church, are by comparison with the exiguous possessions of the Church of Scotland considerable; and they include the cathedrals and parish churches which are justly reckoned to be the most precious monuments of the national history. The State would certainly and most rightly insist upon effectual guarantees for the due upkeep of these glorious fabrics. Nor could it be a matter of indifference to the English people what were the religious uses to which they were applied, when the control of the law has been withdrawn, and they were left to the unfettered treatment of the disestablished Church. Secularization of consecrated buildings would certainly be abhorrent to English public opinion; but, it has been suggested, the nation might take security against the extremer developments of "Anglo-Catholicism", at least in the case of the cathedrals. Since, however, a genuine autonomy could not but ensure effective domestic discipline, and since it would be absurd to expect the disestablished Church to surrender its liberty at the moment of securing it, there is small likelihood that the Church of England would either be deprived of the sacred fabrics, or re-

strained in its use of them. The risks of unchecked
Anglican control would be seen to be negligible compared with the scandals of any other. Moreover, there
would be a general reluctance to do so grave an outrage
to equity and religious sentiment as would assuredly be
involved in depriving the Church of the sacred buildings
which at such great cost it has maintained, and which
have from time immemorial been used for its worship.
In the case of Westminster Abbey, indeed, it is neither
improbable nor unreasonable that an exception should
be made. The unique character of that famous church
might fairly be thought to require recognition. As a
national church it might be kept under the direct control
of the State.

The root of limitless confusion in the protracted
controversy about the relations of Church and State lies
in the failure of the disputants to agree on the meaning
which they attach to the crucial term, Church. What is
properly implied by the national character of a Christian
Church? To say vaguely that it is the nation in its
spiritual aspect is plainly to beg the question, for
spiritual and Christian need not mean the same thing.
There are other religions than Christianity, and these also
may be "national" and, as such, established. The Church
of Scotland Act describes that Church more carefully as
"a national Church representative of the Christian Faith
of the Scottish people", meaning apparently that version
of the Christian religion which is set forth in the Westminster Confession in such form as it may come to be
accepted by the Presbyterian Church. But there are
many other versions of the Christian Religion which
command acceptance in Scotland, and it is not inconceivable that one or other of them might in the future
oust Presbyterianism from its present supremacy, and
have better title than the established Church to be
described as "representative of the Christian Faith of

the Scottish people". In any case the description is inaccurate for it fails to cover the facts.

What obligations does national character impose on an established Church? All churches, whether called "national" or not, are bound to obey the laws in so far as they do not conflict with their religious allegiance; what, beyond this common duty, is implicit in national establishment? Dr Headlam, the Bishop of Gloucester, in his well-known volume, *The Church of England*, addressing his fellow Anglicans, writes:

I would suggest to you that our primary duty is to remember that we are a national Church and that our first duties are to the nation. . . . We are appointed not to minister to one section of the people or to those who are most anxious to receive our ministrations but to the whole of the people in the parish to which we are assigned, and we should never allow the interests or tastes of a section of the people to hide from us our duty towards the whole. And if that is our duty, it imposes upon us also the obligation of so presenting the message we have to tell that it will appeal to those people to whom we are going. We have to preach the Gospel of Christ, and we must be certain we are preaching that Gospel truly, that we preach it in the way which will appeal to the people to whom we come, and our earnest care should be to adapt it to them. That is our main duty (p. 191).

This is excellent advice which all Christian ministers whether belonging to established Churches or to disestablished or non-established may well take to heart, but it has no exclusive relevance to English churchmen. It was not to the members of a "national" Church that St Paul addressed the admonition, "*take thought for things honourable in the sight of all men*"; nor was it as one who held a "national" commission that he "*became all things to all men that he might by all means save some*". The national character can add nothing to the spiritual obligation of a Christian Church, though it may, or may not, facilitate its effective fulfilment. The bishop's language suggests a somewhat antiquated view of the religious situation. He does not take account of the change effected by the Enabling Act (1919). "The whole of the people in the parish" possess no longer voice and vote in the ecclesiastical affairs of the parish, but only so many of them, generally a petty fraction of their number, who have their names on the parochial roll of electors. As matters now stand in England, where confessedly the great majority of the people have ceased to be practising members of any Christian Church, to "adapt" the Gospel to their preferences might involve the complaisant minister in grave spiritual treason.

Disestablishment is sometimes represented as equivalent to an act of national apostasy, and, of course, if it were effected in the teeth of the Church's protest, if its conditions violated the Church's equitable claims, and if it were conceived in an anti-Christian spirit, it could hardly be denied that national apostasy would be no excessive description. But if, as would almost certainly be the case in England, Disestablishment were readily accepted, even welcomed, by the Church itself; if its conditions were just and, as might fairly be expected, generous; if it were passed in a spirit of goodwill, and in the interest of Christianity itself, there could be no reality in the parrot-cry of national apostasy. In Ireland and in Wales the Church has been helped and not injured by Disestablishment. This is freely admitted even by those who were most strongly opposed to the change. Why should it be otherwise in England?

In any case, the losses involved in Disestablishment would be material and sentimental. Much property would be lost, and some social and political prestige would be taken away. But the gains would be moral and religious. The Church would at last be free to direct its own course in spiritual policy: it would be able to determine its own rules of discipline, and to enforce them: it would be able to cut itself free from the degrading tradition of clerical ill-faith which, however excused and extenuated by sophistries, has in the past done so much to enfeeble the influence of the clergy, and to alienate the public conscience: and it would be relieved from the embarrassment and disadvantage of the State-connexion when it seeks by negotiation with other churches to restore the broken fellowship of the Christian society. Disestablishment would inflict on the Church of England the strain and sacrifice of the difficult transition from Erastian subordination to spiritual independence, but it would restore the Church's self-respect, and once more secure from the nation an audience for its message:

To churches, as to men, the Divine Challenge is spoken—"*What doth it profit a man if he gain the whole world, and lose or forfeit his own self?*"

CHAPTER 3

THE VIA MEDIA

In a remarkable address delivered in 1899 the late Bishop Creighton discussed the position of the Church of England. After stating and rejecting the prevalent views on the subject, he proceeded to set forth his own conclusion in these words:

The formula which most explains the position of the Church of England is that it rests on an appeal to sound learning.

He went on to justify a claim which he admitted had an aspect of arrogance. The Church of England, he said, "though a portion of the Western Church sharing in all its movements" had ever maintained "a certain aloofness owing to its insular position". There, as in the rest of Christendom, "two somewhat different lines of thought can be traced, the one maintaining and explaining popular devotion, the other the principles of the Catholic Faith". As time passed these two tendencies had "become conscious of antagonism", so that, when "the revival of learning had led to a more intelligent study of the records of early times", the conflict between the two had become insupportable. Many efforts at reconciliation had been made, notably in the fifteenth century, but all had failed: it had become apparent that "reform was only possible by returning to the principles of sound learning":

It was just this principle that was applied in the changes made in the English Church in the sixteenth [century]. It was not that England alone possessed the necessary learning; that learning and its conclusions had long been the common property of serious and thoughtful men. But England had the unique opportunity of applying it calmly and dispassionately. In foreign countries the Reformation movement was inextricably mingled with grave political disturbances. It wore a revolutionary aspect. It needed popular leaders whose opinions were necessarily coloured by the conflict in which they were engaged. The new theology had to be adapted to the purpose of attack and defence. This was not the case in England. There was no great leader whose personality impressed itself upon the changes that were made. There was no motive to attend to anything save the long record of the aspirations of sound learning. Our Prayer Book is the standing record of the result of this process.

Every historical verdict which has the authority of Bishop Creighton must command respect, but few students of the English Reformation will be able without very large reservations to endorse his claim that the servants and agents of Henry VIII and his children had "no motive to attend to anything save the long record of the aspirations of sound learning". Something very different from a zeal for sound learning covered England with ruined monasteries, raised no less than three revolts, and added to our national history a long list of judicial murders. Moreover, it is difficult thus sharply to differentiate the Reformation in England from the Reformation on the continent. We have in an earlier chapter pointed out the predominantly political character of the religious changes effected by Henry VIII, and the difficulty of the correlation of the medieval framework, which he bequeathed to his successors, with the drastic doctrinal revolution effected under Edward VI, and substantially included in the Elizabethan Settlement. Neither sound learning nor a zeal for true religion swayed the Tudor sovereigns, but their personal predilections and the cold sagacity of their cynical statecraft. Happily they served the interest of a nobler cause than their own when they placed such men as Cranmer and Parker in positions of decisive influence.

The Church of England, with its medieval framework, preserved by the policy of Henry VIII, and its reformed doctrine, formulated by Archbishop Cranmer under Edward VI, was obviously open to criticism in both respects. Both Papists and Puritans challenged the ecclesiastical system: the Papists challenged also the formulated doctrine. Both Papist and Puritan had alternatives for which they claimed Divine authority. Against the traditionalism of the Papist, the Anglican apologist made appeal to the supreme authority of Scripture interpreted by the primitive undivided Church. Against the unintelligent literalism of the Puritan, he urged a more reasonable application of the sacred text. Jewel and Hooker acquired an almost official character as exponents of the Anglican case. Thus Anglicanism came to stand for a moderation which has become traditional and distinctive. What Bishop Creighton said of the Church of England can more truly be said of the type of Anglicanism which finally established itself as the result of the conflicts and controversies of the seventeenth century. The principle of the English Reformation was, not so much sound learning as such—for every Christian apologist claimed for his own Church the support of sound learning—but a frank acceptance of sound learning as competent to revise the current tradition, both by interpreting afresh the sacred text, and by certifying through independent research the true verdict of Christian antiquity. The Anglican appeal to sound learning was necessarily conditioned by the intellectual conditions of the time, its limited knowledge and its defective methods, but under those conditions it was sincerely made. The via media of Anglicanism is something more respectable than a prudent compromise at a crisis. It implies a principle which ought at all times to determine the procedure of a Christian Church. Bishop Sanderson, who composed the Preface to the Restoration Prayer Book, claimed that that Book represented the same reasonable attitude towards change as that which had been adopted by its original compilers, the authors of the English Reformation. His words may be taken as an official formulation of the Anglican via media:

It hath been the wisdom of the Church of England, ever since the first compiling of her Publick Liturgy, to keep the mean between the two extremes, of too much stiffness in refusing, and of too much easiness in admitting any variation from it. For, as on the one side common experience sheweth, that where a change hath been made of things advisedly established (no evident necessity so requiring) sundry inconveniences have thereupon ensued; and those many times more and greater than the evils, that were intended to be remedied by such change: So on the other side, the particular Forms of Divine worship, and the Rites and Ceremonies appointed to be used therein, being things in their own nature indifferent, and alterable, and so acknowledged; it is but reasonable, that upon weighty and important considerations, according to the various exigency of times and occasions, such changes and alterations should be made therein, as to those that are in place of Authority should from time to time seem either necessary or expedient.

With the development of theological controversy in the churches of the Reformation, the Church of England was compelled to extend this principle of reasonable moderation from rites and ceremonies to the Church's doctrine. In 1618 the Synod of Dort had pronounced

Thomas Cranmer

in favour of uncompromising Calvinism. The Church of England, which was then generally included in the number of "reformed" (i.e. Calvinist) Churches, was represented by five English ecclesiastics nominated by James I. One of these, Joseph Hall, afterwards the famous bishop, first of Exeter and then of Norwich, put forth in 1622 a volume which may, perhaps, have given currency to the description of the Church of England as the Church of the via media. The title of this volume sufficiently indicated its argument and purpose: *Via Media: the Way of Peace. In the five busy Articles, commonly known by the name of Arminius:* 1. *Predestination.* 2. *The extent of Christ's Death.* 3. *Man's Free Will and Corruption.* 4. *The Manner of our Conversion to God.* 5. *Perseverance.*

Interest in the Calvinist controversy had died down long before the Oxford Movement transformed the Anglican outlook. In 1837 Newman published his famous Essay on *The Via Media of the Anglican Church.* It described, not a moderate Calvinism, such as Hall defended, but a conditioned acceptance of the grand principle of Protestantism, Private Judgment. The "via media" is the middle way between the Protestant and the Roman views of Private Judgment.

The English Church...considers that on certain definite subjects private judgment upon the text of Scripture has been superseded, but not by the mere authoritative sentence of the Church, but by its historical testimony delivered down from the Apostles. To these definite subjects nothing more can be added, unless, indeed, new records of primitive Christianity, or new uninterrupted traditions of its teaching were discoverable.[1]

More recently the term has been carried outside the sphere of ecclesiastical and dogmatic controversy, and

[1] Vol. I, p. 128 (London, 1877).

extended to the deeper issues raised by the conflict between Science and Faith, Criticism and Tradition, which became acute in the middle of the nineteenth century, and still continues, though with a lessened acerbity of temper on both sides, and a larger measure of mutual understanding. That conflict, under ever-changing forms, does not appear likely to cease in the future. In the well-known *Prayer Book Dictionary*, published in 1912, Canon Harford, the Assistant Editor, describes "the Prayer Book conception of the Christian Religion" as

a *Via Media*, not in the unworthy sense of a safe and easy path (escaping difficulties, indeed, but by sacrifice of principles), but as the carefully surveyed central road, avoiding the dangerous detours of superstition on the one hand, and the seductive short cuts of fanaticism on the other (p. 193).

Neither superstition nor fanaticism is now so likely to lead the Church astray as a timid conservatism which takes refuge behind the letter of creeds and confessions, on the one side, and a precipitate receptiveness of doctrinal innovation on the other. Theories, albeit advanced in the great names of science and criticism, are not always either scientific or soundly critical. The tendency of dogmatism to outrun knowledge and obscure truth is not limited to theology. "*Prove all things*" is the wise counsel of St Paul, "*hold fast that which is good*". This is the very temper of the Anglican via media rightly understood. Sound knowledge may confirm, as well as disallow, traditional beliefs; and novelty can never be itself a sufficient title to acceptance. Scientific theories, which once had the aspect of unquestionable truths, have been finally cast on the slag-heap of abandoned errors; and the history of Biblical criticism is filled with warnings against a too precipitate Modernism. The via media of a cautiously conditioned revision

f credenda is not merely consistent with the temper and
enor of the English Reformation, but is in itself reason-
ble and religious. The Prayer Book was composed and
ompiled in relatively remote ages, long before the
listinctive problems of the modern epoch had emerged.
t cannot therefore be reasonable to look to the Prayer
3ook for direct guidance, when the solution of those
roblems is in debate. Nevertheless, it is no mean
dvantage which English churchmen possess in the
ssurance, that both the tradition of their Church, and
he binding precedent of its reformation, require them
o face their difficult duty with tolerance, candour, and
resolute loyalty to sound learning and the teachings of
xperience.

When we enquire what may have been the causes of
his tradition, and how it came about that this precedent
vas created, we are obliged to admit that the happy
oincidence which matched the men to the crisis, rather
han deliberate purpose, shaped the history. The prin-
ipal reason why a moderate catholicism developed in
England, and nowhere else in Christendom, as the out-
ome of the religious revolution of the sixteenth century,
vas the remarkable combination of ecclesiastical con-
ervatism in the Tudor sovereigns with patristic learning
nd Christian character in the primates whom they
ppointed. Henry VIII and Archbishop Cranmer seemed
o live again in Elizabeth and Archbishop Parker. To
he masterful monarchs the Church of England owes the
etention of the episcopal polity: to the learned and
arge-hearted primates the Church owes the Prayer Book
nd Thirty-nine Articles. Both episcopacy and the
Prayer Book were vehemently assailed by the opponents
f reformation on the one hand, and by the advocates of
eligious revolution on the other. Papist and Puritan
vere at one in their antagonism to a Church which
laimed to be catholic, national, orthodox, and reformed.

The English theologians perforce observed the limits imposed on them by their opponents. Against Papist and Puritan alike the Anglican appeal lay to that Christian antiquity which preserved the picture of an undivided Catholic Church, everywhere governed by bishops, and everywhere worshipping by means of liturgies. There could be no specifically Anglican theology, for it was the essential meaning of the English Reformation that it reaffirmed the pure theology of the Catholic Church against the corrupt perversion of that theology which the Roman Church maintained.

Something must certainly be allowed for the English temperament, which seems to be naturally suspicious of logic and theory. So long as practical needs are adequately satisfied, the oddest arrangements may be tolerated. Moderation in Church and State is the distinctively English note, and it explains both the stability of English institutions, and the failures of foreigners to understand them. In the most famous of English political pamphlets, *The Character of a Trimmer*, a singularly acute thinker, Lord Halifax, pictured the moderation of English religion as one illustration of a general feature of English phenomena:

Our Trimmer, therefore, inspired by this Divine virtue, thinketh fit to conclude with these assertions: That our climate is a Trimmer between that part of the world where men are roasted, and the other where they are frozen; that *our church is a Trimmer between the frenzy of fanatic visions and the lethargic ignorance of Popish dreams*; that our laws are Trimmers between the excesses of unbounded power and the extravagance of liberty not enough restrained; that true virtue hath ever been thought a Trimmer, and to have its dwelling in the middle between the two extremes; that even God Almighty Himself is divided between His two great attributes, His mercy and His justice. In such company, our Trimmer is not ashamed of his name and willingly leaveth to

the bold champions of either extreme, the honour of contending with no less adversaries than nature, religion, liberty,
prudence, humanity and common sense.[1]

Lord Halifax wrote his famous pamphlet in 1684,
when the nation was yet shaken by the violent passions
which the Popish Plot and its reaction had stirred, but
he places his finger on a normal characteristic of the
English mind—its dislike of pushing principles to their
logical conclusions, its almost limitless acquiescence in
anomalies which are practically convenient, its ready
condonation of admitted abuses which serve material
interests. Foreigners do not share this dislike of logic,
and this indifference to consistency, and accordingly
they find it difficult to understand English political and
religious professions and procedures.

Writing in 1850, when the nation was much excited by
the controversies stirred by the Tractarians, Dr Martineau
drew a vivid picture of the normal Englishman's attitude
towards the Established Church. *Mutatis mutandis* his
words may still serve as a true description of the facts:

He (*sc.* the English layman) looks no further into theology
than the demeanour of the parish clergyman. Let the vicar
and his curate read the service impressively, preach no
novelties, light no candles, look after the village schools,
make themselves useful at the board of guardians, and keep
the neighbours on pleasant terms with one another, and, for
aught he cares, they may suit themselves with any doctrine
between Whitgift and Grotius, Laud and Tillotson. He
looks on the clerical eagerness about dogma as he does on
his wife's gossip and voluminous correspondence—as inherent in the genius of the class, and somehow related to the
nice perception and voluble enthusiasm of which he himself
feels the fascination. Only you must not ask him to take a
part: his businesslike habits are apt to bruise the graces:
and his plain understanding rubs out all the fine distinctions

[1] *V. Life and Letters of Sir George Savile, First Marquis of Halifax*,
by H. C. Foxcroft, II, 342.

of the creeds. He leaves these things to ecclesiastics, and with so free an indulgence that there is scarcely any intensity of bigotry that may not have its way, provided he and his church are not positively committed to them. Folly and narrow-heartedness in one priest are counterbalanced by the wisdom and charity of another; the Calvinism of a Simeon by the Arminianism of a Maltby; the sacramental doctrine of Pusey by the ethical theology of Arnold. The English are not a speculative people. And so long as they see such men as Whately, Thirlwall, and Sumner amicably seated on the same bench as Blomfield and Phillpotts, no religious Churchman will miss there a representative of his faith, and the Established Church will gain the credit of being reasonably open to varieties of opinion. The decisions in the Articles may be stringent, the pretensions of the ordination service arrogant, and the imprecations of the creed unflinching, but while they are not pressed into any visible form of ecclesiastical action, the persons of a few mild and charitable bishops suffice to counteract their effect, and to persuade men, fresh from the very sound of her anathemas, that they belong to the most liberal of churches.

Dr Martineau was not himself an Anglican, and his language must to that extent be discounted, but he was a singularly candid, keen-sighted, and just-minded man, whose opinions must always command respect. We have said that his description is *mutatis mutandis* still true, but there are two important distinctions between the situation in 1850 and that in 1938. *Then* the Tractarians were an unpopular and powerless minority of English churchmen, dismayed and discredited by the recent secession to Rome of Newman and a crowd of his followers. *Now* they are unquestionably dominant among the clergy, and strongly supported by a small but well-organized section of the religious laity. The nation as a whole has lost interest in ecclesiastical matters, and largely abandoned the traditional religious observances. In an atmosphere of indifference controversy flags, and intolerance is ridiculous. If the violent excitements aroused by the Tractarians are hardly intelligible in modern England, the explanation must be sought, less in the larger charity of the Church, than in the lessened religion of the people. Nor may we forget that there are slumbering bigotries which can be wakened, and once wakened can disclose much of the old intractable obstinacy. Normally, however, these latent passions cause no disturbance of the prevailing calm.

The continuing conflict with Rome changed its form in the new intellectual climate of the modern world. As the doctrine of development was carried from physical science to history and theology, it told with decisive effect on the authorized Anglican apologetic. The appeal to antiquity was seen to be plainly irrelevant. Not the earliest phase of Christian history must be held to disclose most fully the content and meaning of the original Gospel, but the latest. Newman's bold sophistry, which began by postulating as the necessary marks of legitimate development the distinctive features of modern Romanism, and then proceeded to argue triumphantly that, since beyond question modern Romanism possessed them all, its title to be the true development of primitive Christianity was apparent and indisputable, could not be effectively met by Jewel's famous apology, which had been irresistible when ecclesiastical history was regarded as a treasury of authoritative precedents. If development were allowed to be the providential method, it was vain to search the ancient Fathers in order to discover in them the Divinely ordained norms of ecclesiastical doctrine and discipline. The validity of all systems, theological, ethical, and disciplinary, must be determined in the light of the conditions under which they were constructed, and the specific objects which they were designed to secure. Truth in a living Church could not finally rest with the antiquarians. It would suffice to show that the original ideas of the Christian revelation, disclosed in the New Testament, were preserved in the systems, theological and disciplinary, which history had shaped, and bequeathed to the modern Church. Could it be reasonably maintained that this National Church of England, as organized and controlled by the English State, was more plainly successful in its wardship, and practical application, of those original ideas of the Gospel than the older and more elaborately ordered Church of Rome? That was the essential question, and its satisfactory answering would necessarily take account of much more than the controversialists of the contending churches drew from their study of the Fathers. The secret of Hooker's persistent relevance, in spite of the apparent obsoleteness which has overtaken his main argument, lies in his appeal, sometimes latent, sometimes manifest, to human reason. Men were everywhere wearying of the controversies of the Schools. They perceived that the tests of ecclesiastical character could no longer be reasonably sought only in the past. Seriously religious men were growing impatient of the attorney-like reasonings of the ecclesiastical champions, and were turning increasingly to another principle of judgment than that which they appeared to regard or require. Churches would be judged by their moral and spiritual achievements. How far was their influence on society congruous with the spirit and teaching of the Founder? It would be remembered that He had said: "*By their fruits ye shall know them.*"

Meanwhile a deeper cause has tended to abate and even silence the civil war of the Churches within Christendom. It is becoming apparent that the religion which all the Churches profess to represent, and in their own way to serve, is itself in mortal danger. The modern world seems to be ever more completely self-absorbed and self-satisfied. It has no use for religion in any form.

Controversy proceeds on a new front, and the older battle-fields are nearly deserted. Sacred learning is no peculium of any single Church. Scholarship acknowledges no denominational frontiers. Research is a common obligation, and a common enterprise of all the Churches. It is a matter of fact that there is a fellowship of sincere students which goes deeper than sectarian differences, and unites them in co-operative effort. The treasure of Knowledge is replenished from every section of the Christian society. Philosophy, criticism, theology, ecclesiastical history, devotional literature—these are the "common fields" of Christianity. Yet in the general effort the Churches follow distinctive procedures, and have distinctive traditions. The Church of England is no exception to the general rule. Dr Hawkins, the famous Provost of Oriel, is said to have summed up the doctrine of the Church of England on the subject of doctrinal proofs in the often quoted formula, "*The Church to teach, the Scriptures to prove*". Another, and not less famous provost, Dr Salmon, the Provost of Trinity College, Dublin, has elaborated this formula thus:

The Church of England, in her Sixth Article, has laid down the principle of her method in the assertion that "Holy Scriptures contain all things necessary to salvation", so that whatsoever is incapable of Scripture proof is not to be required of any man to be believed *as an article of faith*. A profession of belief in this principle of the sufficiency of Scripture is one of the pledges which our Church requires of every priest at his ordination. Nor is this principle merely asserted in one of the Articles, it runs through them all. Everything else, which might claim an independent authority, is made in the Articles to derive its authority from the Bible, and to be authoritative only so far as it agrees with the Bible. The most venerable of all traditions—the Creeds—are said (Art. VIII) to be received only because capable of Scripture proof. Every particular Church, and General Councils of the Church, are said (Arts. XIX–XXI) to be liable to error; and their decisions are said to be binding only when it can be shown that they are taken out of Holy Scripture. Then, in the controversial Articles, one Roman doctrine after another is rejected as a human invention, because grounded upon no warrant of Holy Scripture. Thus you will see that the Sixth Article is not an isolated doctrine, but states the principle of the method which our Church employs in the establishment of all her doctrines.[1]

The Lectures on the *Infallibility of the Church*, from which we have quoted, were mostly written about the year 1870, when the controversy aroused by the Vatican Council was at its height. Their polemical purpose was paramount and confessed, and crowded out every other. As against the claims of the Papacy it was not necessary to consider the limits within which the Anglican theory of Scriptural authority was valid, nor to examine the conditions under which the Creed can justly be regarded as proved by Holy Scripture. These more fundamental questions, however, have to be answered by the modern student who seeks to unite loyalty to his pledges as an Anglican with integrity as a Biblical student. How is he to apply the time-honoured rule—*The Church to teach, the Scriptures to prove*? What Church? Teaching what? What is meant by proof? How is proof by Scripture to be ascertained?

Christianity started, not with a book, but with a preaching, and, when the preachers succeeded in making converts, the essential content of that original preaching was necessarily summarized in a baptismal confession, itself a rudimentary creed. As time passed, and the original preachers died, the preaching acquired a traditional character. The rudimentary baptismal creed gained a quasi-official position, and was stereotyped in authoritative forms. These forms reflected the fortunes of the Church, and were coloured by the influences, intellectual,

[1] *V. Infallibility of the Church*, p. 125.

controversial, and political, by which they were shaped. These influences, however, were by no means wholly favourable to the original purpose which the baptismal creed was designed to serve. As creeds multiplied, and grew longer, their fidelity to the Apostolic preaching became less assured and apparent. There was need for some satisfying test by which that fidelity could be demonstrated. Therefore, from the first, the Church accompanied the Creed with the canonical Scripture, claiming that assurance of truth was to be found in the agreement of the two, the one being shown to be a faithful summary of the other. In the earliest age the Old Testament alone formed the Church's Bible, and the proof from Scripture consisted in the reference to the fulfilment of prophecy. The so-called Nicene Creed echoes the confession of fundamental Christian belief, with which St Paul introduces his famous argument for the resurrection—"*I delivered unto you first of all that which also I received, how that Christ died for our sins according to the scriptures; and that he was buried; and that he hath been raised on the third day according to the scriptures.*" In due course the Church added a Christian supplement to the Jewish canon. The Bible of the Church came to include the New Testament, and this was clothed with the august authority which the Old already possessed. Moreover, when the truth of the Creed was in debate, the Christian supplement could not but take precedence of the Jewish Scripture. The nature of its contents counted for more even than its canonical status. The appeal must needs be to Apostolic authority, since the original preaching, from which the Church took its beginning, was the preaching of the Apostles. Apart from the Apostles the Church could have no knowledge of the revelation of God which Jesus brought to men. The vital concern of the modern Church, parted from the Apostles now by the "changes and chances" of nineteen centuries, is to have reasonable security that the Creed which purports to state the essentials of the Apostolic teaching is trustworthy. Is it a genuine version? The New Testament contains the entire literary output of Apostolic Christianity. It is extremely significant, that the protracted labours of Christian students bestowed on the rapidly accumulating material which comes to Europe and America from the East, has added practically nothing to the witness which the New Testament bears to the Life and Teaching of the Founder of Christianity. A few sayings which seem to be genuine have emerged, but for the rest nothing has come save more or less twisted versions of what the New Testament contains. The New Testament is older than the oldest Creed, and, therefore, it presents a more authoritative version of Apostolic preaching than any Creed can provide. That is Chillingworth's position:

In a word, that all things necessary to be believed are evidently contained in Scripture, and what is not there evidently contained, cannot be necessary to be believed. And our reason hereof is convincing, *because nothing can challenge our belief but what hath descended to us from Christ by original and universal Tradition. Now nothing but Scripture hath thus descended to us, therefore nothing but Scripture can challenge our belief.*

Chillingworth's *Religion of Protestants, a Safe Way of Salvation*, was published in 1637, and we must re-cast its argument into the terms of the twentieth century, if we would appraise its actual value. But, so recast, its essential soundness is apparent. The great theological development which matured in the orthodox theology of the undivided Church, and which still remains without any satisfying alternative, is rooted in the Scripture, which can be shown to stand towards it in the line of a true development. The controversy between the Church of England and the Church of Rome still turns on the Rule of Faith, whether Scripture alone, as the one Church affirms, or Scripture together with another and co-equal authority, Tradition, as the other Church maintains.

Anglicans reject all that fabric of faith and cultus which cannot be shown to be ultimately rooted in the Apostolic tradition preserved in the Scripture. A sufficient example is the Roman belief and practice with respect to the Blessed Mother of the Redeemer. Since the Apostolic Epistles never so much as mention St Mary's name, we cannot be mistaken in holding that the Apostles' version of the Gospel included nothing that could provide a root for such a spreading tree of dogma and devotion as the Church of Rome presents to its members.

Which is the final authority in matters of faith—the Bible or the Church? That is the ultimate question. The Anglican doctrine is understood in two ways. Some hold that it credits the Creed with no more than a contingent authority. It is a summary of Scriptural doctrine, and only finally authoritative in so far as it can be shown to be a faithful summary. If it can be shown to misrepresent the doctrine of the Scripture, it forfeits its claim to Christian acceptance. Others hold that the Creed is the authorized interpretation of Scripture, and as such determines the sense in which the Scripture is to be interpreted. In the one case, the Bible determines the sense of the Creed. In the other, the Creed determines the sense of the Bible.

Both Catholic and Protestants were until recent times agreed in their view of the canonical Scriptures as infallible and verbally inspired. Our Fundamentalists, like the Montanists of the third century, are die-hard theological Tories. Both Catholics and Protestants would subscribe the VIIIth Anglican Article:

The three Creeds, Nicene Creed, Athanasius's Creed, and that which is commonly called the Apostles' Creed, ought thoroughly to be received and believed: for they may be proved by most certain warrants of holy Scripture.

In modern times, however, Catholics and Protestants have gone apart on the subject of the Scriptures, and their divergence has necessarily affected their view of the Creeds. Only a Protestant Church could accept as a true account of its beliefs about the Bible the section on Scripture included in the recently published Report of the Commission on Christian Doctrine appointed by the Archbishops of Canterbury and York. After stating explicitly that "the tradition of the inerrancy of the Bible commonly held in the Church until the beginning of the nineteenth century cannot be maintained in the light of the knowledge now at our disposal", the Commissioners proceed to put forward certain "considerations" by which "the use made of the Bible as an authoritative source of teaching" should be "controlled". The first of these runs thus:

> The authority ascribed to the Bible must not be interpreted as prejudging the conclusions of historical, critical, and scientific investigation in any field, not excluding that of the Biblical documents themselves.

It is difficult to overstate the far-reaching importance of this "consideration". Clearly the epoch of proof-texts and harmonies is over. The sense in which the Anglican articles are to be understood is affected profoundly. The "most certain warrant of holy scripture", which is to justify acceptance of the three Creeds, can no longer be simplified into a mere production of confirmatory texts. Those texts must be weighed in the scales of modern knowledge, historical, critical, and scientific, and only allowed so much weight as is thus disclosed. It is to be noted that the Creed of Christendom, being largely the statement of certain alleged facts respecting the Founder of Christianity, obviously stands in very intimate relation to historical criticism, since only as certified by sufficient historical evidence can the truth of these statements be reasonably affirmed.

If the Church is to offer Scripture as the witness by

whose testimony the truth of its teaching may be proved, then clearly Scripture must be treated as an independent witness. A witness whose testimony was dictated, however in other respects authoritative, could prove nothing in the dictator's favour. Since the Creeds are justly described as "the most venerable of all traditions", and since tradition is notoriously liable to variation and corruption by "the changes and chances" of history, the Church accompanies the tradition formulated in its Creed, by the tradition preserved in the Scripture, and there preserved in a form which is immune from the risks to which creeds are exposed.

The tradition of the Church is no longer suffered to hamper the critical student of the New Testament in his work. In the case of the Old Testament this conclusion was not reached without friction and conflict. The difficulties had been felt from time immemorial, but allegorical interpretation had mitigated the crudity of scriptural teaching, and enabled Christian thinkers, in a measure which moves astonishment, to harmonize the sacred text with the contrariant witness of Christian morality and secular knowledge. The subtlety of the ancient divines has been drawn upon for the relief of modern embarrassments. In the famous essay which the Rev. Charles Gore, then Principal of the Pusey House in Oxford, afterwards Bishop successively of Worcester, Birmingham and Oxford, contributed to the volume *Lux Mundi*, published in 1888, an alert and resourceful intelligence sought to utilize the allegorical essays of Alexandria in the third century for the satisfaction of the intellectual scruples of Oxford in the nineteenth. Two years before the publication of *Lux Mundi*, Dr Bigg, afterwards Regius Professor of Ecclesiastical History in Oxford, had preached a notable course of Bampton Lectures on *The Christian Platonists of Alexandria*. His description of the Alexandrines would serve fairly well for a description of the *Lux Mundi* essayists:

They professed and exhibited the most entire loyalty to the Creed. But outside the circle of Apostolical dogma they held themselves free. They agreed with the Orthodoxasts that Scripture was inspired. But their great Platonic maxim, that "nothing is to be believed which is unworthy of God", makes reason the judge of Revelation. They held that this maxim was a part of the Apostolical tradition, and accordingly they put the letter of the Bible on one side, wherever, as in the account of Creation or the Fall, it appeared to conflict with the teaching of Science. But though there is in them a strong vein of Common Sense or Rationalism, they were not less sensible of the mystic supernatural side of the religious life than Irenaeus. The difference is, that with them the mystical grows out of the rational, that they think always less of the historical fact than of the idea, less of the outward sign than of the inner truth. Their object is to shew, not that Common Sense is enough for salvation, but that neither Faith without Reason nor Reason without Faith can bring forth its noblest fruits, that full communion with God, the highest aim of human effort, can be attained only by those who in Christ have grown to the stature of the perfect man, in whom the saint and the thinker are blended together in the unity of the Divine Love. Hence they represent on one side the revolt of Protestantism against Catholicism, on the other that of Mysticism against Gnosticism. And their great service to the Church is, that they endeavoured faithfully to combine the two great factors of the spiritual life.[1]

Bishop Gore's effort was regarded at the time as an epoch-making venture of theological independence, and,

---

[1] *V. Bampton Lectures*, pp. 51, 52. I was myself one of the large congregation in St Mary's to which Dr Bigg addressed his Bampton Lectures, and they appealed to me with the greater directness since I was at the time approaching the crisis of my own Ordination. I well remember how profound an impression they made in the University. They prepared the way for the more sensational publication of the neo-Tractarian essayists.

s is well known, it provoked the deep resentment and public condemnation of Canon Liddon. But there was worse to come. In 1891, the publication of Professor Driver's *Introduction to the Literature of the Old Testament* caused a considerable disturbance among conservative Christians, who were particularly aggrieved that this bold challenge to the Church's tradition should have proceeded from one who had not only been the assistant of the champion of unyielding conservative orthodoxy, Dr Pusey, but had succeeded him in the Chair of Hebrew. Dr Driver was fully conscious of the breach with tradition which his book represented:

"It is impossible to doubt", he wrote in his Preface, "that the main conclusions of critics with reference to the authorship of the books of the Old Testament rest upon reasonings the cogency of which cannot be denied without denying the ordinary principles by which history is judged and evidence estimated. Nor can it be doubted that the same conclusions, upon any neutral field of investigation, would have been accepted without hesitation by all conversant with the subject; they are only opposed in the present instance by some theologians, because they are supposed to conflict with the requirements of the Christian faith. But the history of astronomy, geology, and, more recently, of biology, supplies a warning that the conclusions which satisfy the common unbiassed and unsophisticated reason of mankind prevail in the end. The price at which alone the traditional view can be maintained is too high."[1]

Nothing has been more emphasized by the Church until recent years than the predictive character of Hebrew Prophecy. The New Testament affirms it: the Creed when it declared that the Holy Ghost "spake by the prophets" has generally been understood to do the same: the principal and certainly not the least effective apologetic method of Christian advocates throughout the Christian

[1] *V. Introduction*, Preface, p. xiv.

epoch has been the appeal to prophecy. A vast literatur
has elaborated that appeal, and its validity is assumed i
Christian art and liturgy. Yet the Report of the Arch
bishops' Commissioners affirms in careful language, bu
with unmistakable intention, that the predictive characte
of prophecy can no longer be emphasized:

> In the past, as a part and consequence of the then curren
> view of Scripture, emphasis was often laid on detailed pre
> diction of facts, especially as concerns the life of Christ. W
> cannot now regard as a principal purpose or evidence o
> Inspiration the giving of detailed information about th
> future; but we recognize, as a consequence and evidence o
> Inspiration, such an insight into the Divine Mind and Will
> and therefore such a general apprehension of the course o
> events to be expected in a world ruled by God, as in particula
> cases resulted in the prediction of events which subsequentl
> came to pass. Nor do we rule out, as possibly a concomitan
> of Inspiration in certain cases, a direct prevision of detaile
> events, though it is not on such prevision that men shoul
> base their belief in the Inspiration of Scripture.[1]

"Prophecy", wrote Bishop Butler, "is nothing but the
history of events before they come to pass."[2] There is a
"far cry" between the author of the *Analogy* and the
Archbishops' Commissioners. "It looks as if it had been
written beneath the cross upon Golgotha", writes De-
litzsch when, in the course of his great commentary, he
has to treat of the 53rd chapter of Isaiah. He does, of
course, but express the pervading assumption of the
Gospels. None the less the Archbishops' Commissioners
do not hesitate to dissociate themselves from that "detailed prediction of facts especially as concerns the life of
Christ" which the inspired Evangelists take for granted.
And the Commissioners are unquestionably right if their
purpose was to indicate the possibility of a working
harmony between Tradition and Modernism.

[1] *V.* Report, p. 29.   [2] *V. Analogy*, ed. Bernard, p. 270.

The premonitory mutterings of the approaching storm were audible in the controversy which arose about *Lux Mundi*. How far was it permissible for an orthodox Christian to reject Christ's statement as to the authorship of the 110th Psalm in favour of the verdict of modern critical scholars? What became of His omniscience, if His opinion were thus to be set aside? The ingenious but abortive kenotic theory was unable permanently to serve the cause of imperilled traditionalism, though for a while it was eagerly accepted, and did undoubtedly serve to mitigate the shock of ultimate discomfiture. It is now everywhere abandoned. The full significance of the Anglican subordination of the Creed to the Scripture was not fully perceived until the argument had passed from the Old Testament to the New. England followed slowly, but inevitably, in the wake of Germany. Dr Sanday played, in the case of the New Testament, the part which Dr Driver had played in the case of the Old. Both men united massive learning and sound judgment with intellectual alertness and great personal courage. They blazed a track for a succession of younger scholars, of whom the most eminent and influential, Dr Streeter, has recently been taken from us. As soon as the New Testament, and herein especially the Gospels, came under critical handling, the question of the Creed could not be avoided. It is, of course, true that this question had been raised in the earlier controversies connected with *Essays and Reviews* and with Bishop Colenso. The publication of Darwin's *Origin of Species*, in 1859, had opened the gates to a flood of Biblical discussion. The opening clauses of the Creed were not easily harmonized with the new theories of human origins, and when at last a *modus vivendi* between the Church and the Evolutionists had been discovered, it rather postponed than ended the main conflict. The Report of the Committee of the Lambeth Conference (1930), which owed so much to the insight and wisdom of that great Christian philosopher, Archbishop D'Arcy, whose recent death has inflicted a heavy loss on the whole Christian society, may be taken to set forth the view which is now generally accepted:

Certain sciences, whose boundaries were for generations indeterminate, have in recent times united to give us a consentient view of the process by which the world as we know it has come into being. From this view has emerged an account of the order of creation upon which all instructed opinion is now agreed. Physics and astronomy, geology and biology, anthropology and archaeology unite to give us a description of the ordered sequence of creation. In view of this revelation, for such it truly is, the popular interpretation of the Biblical account of creation cannot be accepted literally: and it must be remembered that in great ages of constructive theology such a literal interpretation was not regarded as of primary importance.

The battle has passed from the first section of the Creed to the second, from that which declares belief in the Father, to that which declares belief in His only Son. Not the method of Creation is now in debate, but the method of recreation or Redemption. Inevitably the conflict has turned on the miracles which are alleged to have marked the Birth and the Resurrection of the Redeemer. Both claim to be "historical facts", that is, facts certified to be such by adequate historical evidence. There may be many facts which cannot be so certified, but these we do not describe as historical. Now it is not to be denied that, in the judgment of the most competent historical students, the evidence for these alleged "facts"—the Virgin Birth and the Physical Resurrection—is not adequate, and therefore it follows that as "historical facts" they cannot rightly be affirmed. The Commissioners, with commendable frankness, admit that both the traditional and the critical views were represented in their own body, as they are notoriously in the Church. After setting forth "the main grounds on which the (traditional) doctrine is valued", they proceed:

Many of us hold, accordingly, that belief in the Word made flesh is integrally bound up with belief in the Virgin Birth, and that this will increasingly be recognized.

There are, however, some among us who hold that a full belief in the historical Incarnation is more consistent with the supposition that our Lord's Birth took place under the normal conditions of human generation. In their minds the notion of a Virgin Birth tends to mar the completeness of the belief that in the Incarnation God revealed Himself at every point in and through human nature.

We are agreed in recognizing that belief in our Lord's birth from a Virgin has been in the history of the Church intimately associated with its faith in the Incarnation of the Son of God. Further, we recognize that the work of scholars upon the New Testament has created a new setting of which theologians in their treatment of this article are obliged to take account. We also recognize that both the views outlined above are held by members of the Church, as of the Commission who fully accept the reality of our Lord's Incarnation, which is the central truth of the Christian faith.[1]

The Commissioners were unable to agree on a formula which should harmonize the traditional and the critical views: but they certify the co-existence within the Church of England of those who affirm, and those who deny, that the Virgin Birth is a "historical fact".

But, it may fairly be objected, if the Creed be subordinate to the Scripture, and the Scripture be rightly understood, not—as generally in the Church has been supposed —by the steady guidance of an unvarying tradition, but by the changing verdicts of modern Biblical science, what security as to the soundness of his faith can the Christian believer possess? To this objection the answer is implicit

[1] *V*. Report, pp. 81–83.

in the fact that Scripture itself is the product of the Church's Faith, and that the general witness of the Scripture (which Biblical science can never alter, though it may modify it in detail), does undoubtedly authenticate the Creed. No serious student questions that the New Testament was the expression of Christian belief. What the Fourth Evangelist wrote of his Gospel might truly be applied to all the writings of the New Testament: "*These are written, that ye may believe that Jesus is the Christ, the Son of God; and that believing ye may have life in his name.*" The latest critical school, that of the Form-critics, finds the key to the problem of compilation, with which the critical student of the evangelical narratives is confronted, in the desire of the compilers to satisfy the needs of the society of believers. The Church preceded the documents, which were indeed composed in order to record, elucidate, justify, and apply its faith. We cannot reasonably interpret the New Testament in such wise as to stultify the very faith which created it. That the ardour of those first believers did predispose them to accept unquestioningly any tradition about the Divine Lord which accorded with their belief is certain. That we must, as we weigh their records in the scales of a calmer judgment, reject whatever we can clearly perceive is plainly mythical or legendary is apparent. It is not less apparent, that the modern critic who so reads the canonical texts as to transform them from the achievement of Faith into its negation has lost his way. The details of the sacred record may be corrected by criticism, but its central message survives intact. It remains the product and nourishment of Christian Faith. Creed and Scripture are indissolubly united.

It is not without interest that even in the seventeenth century the acute intelligence of Chillingworth had argued from the differences between the several Gospels that not all their statements had the same spiritual importance:

Every one of them (*sc.* the Evangelists) writ the whole Gospel of Christ, I mean, all the essential and necessary parts of it. So that if we had no other book of Scripture, but one of them alone, we should not want anything necessary to salvation. *And what one of them hath more than another, it is only profitable, and not necessary*; necessary indeed to be believed, because revealed, but not therefore revealed because necessary to be believed.[1]

Chillingworth, in common with all his contemporaries, believed in the inerrancy of Scripture, but his argument implies a distinction between what is common to all the Evangelists and what is peculiar to each, which, when applied to the Creed, removes the Virgin Birth from the category of essential Christian beliefs. The single interest of the Christian believer, essaying to bring the Church's tradition to the test of the Scripture, is assurance that he knows what is the true sense of the Scripture. Does the New Testament bear out the statements of the Creed as to the Redeemer's Birth and Resurrection? Certain texts may do so, but does the testimony of the New Testament as a whole do so? The epoch of proof texts is past: we must "search the scriptures", if we would indeed understand them. Here it is important to remove a misunderstanding. Neither the Virgin Birth nor the Physical Resurrection of Christ is challenged because it affirms what is called a miracle, but only because it is not adequately sustained by the Scripture, which is confessedly the only evidence which the Church can offer. Professor Lake misunderstands the issue when he assumes that it is the *difficulty* of the dogma which makes the instructed modern Christian unable to affirm the Virgin Birth. He says truly enough that "the Incarnation is a far more difficult thing to believe than the Virgin Birth", but he ignores the essential difference between the weight of Scriptural support for the one doctrine and that for the

[1] *V. Religion of Protestants*, 10th edition (1742), p. 110.

other. Assuredly the man who believes that God was incarnate in the Man, Jesus, could find nothing *incredible* in the mode of that wondrous Incarnation, nothing save that which was not morally congruous. In any case a special activity of the Holy Spirit would appear to be implicit in an Incarnation, and must therefore have attached to the Redeemer's birth, but whether that activity involved a departure from the normal method of human generation, or not, can only be known to us by such evidence as the New Testament provides, and that, when critically examined, is found to be inadequate. The believer may, of course, hold that a Virgin Birth is the necessary concomitant of a Divine Incarnation, but if he does this, he must not affirm that it is a historical fact, since in default of the requisite evidence it can be no more than a theological inference, or a pious opinion.

If the New Testament may be accepted as presenting a trustworthy account of the faith of the Apostolic Church, we can hardly avoid the opinion that, with respect to the Virgin Birth, its belief might be fairly described in the language employed by the Archbishops' Commissioners when they set forth the state of belief in the Church of England at the present time. All Christians believed in the Incarnation, but as to its method their opinions varied. The Birth narratives in two of the Synoptic Gospels show that there were sections of the Apostolic Church which held that the Incarnate was born of a Virgin Mother, but the majority of the Apostolic converts were ignorant of that supposition, and did not question that His birth was according to the normal manner. Only the coercion of an orthodoxy, more rigid than intelligent, can discover any trace of a belief in the Virgin Birth in the Apostolic epistles.

When, however, we pass from the method to the fact of the Incarnation, we find that the Scripture abundantly confirms the Creed. Somewhat variously conceived indeed, but always implied, the superhuman character of the Redeemer is emphasized in the Apostolic literature. The core of the Gospel from the days of St Paul has been the Lordship of Jesus, and what that Lordship implied is sufficiently disclosed by the fact that Jesus was to the Apostle the Object of Worship, so that he did not scruple to apply to Him passages in the Old Testament which had reference to Jehovah. The reason why the Christian Church cannot but exclude Unitarians from its fellowship lies in their repudiation of its original and essential testimony to the Divineness of Jesus Christ. The Unitarian is not concerned with the pious and necessary task of re-stating the traditional faith of the Church with respect to its Founder, but continues under the conditions of modern society to affirm the original repudiation of the Church's Faith. The Incarnation is, as the Archbishops' Commissioners truly say, "the central truth of the Christian Faith". It is taught by the Church, and proved by the Bible. This "central truth" was variously understood in the age of the Apostles. The New Testament registers these variations. In the ages of Christological controversy which witnessed the gradual working out of the orthodox theology, theories of the Incarnation were many. During the millennium, which intervened between the close of the conciliar epoch and the close of the Middle Ages, theological speculation was arrested, but so soon as the iron yoke of medieval orthodoxy had been broken, the process was resumed, and has continued ever since. With the emergence of the distinctively modern studies which deal with the date, structure, purpose, history, and authority of ancient documents, the treatment of canonical Scripture has entered on a new phase. The Church of England, when it endorses the methods, and accepts the verdicts, of Biblical criticism, is justifying Bishop Creighton's claim that it rests on an appeal to sound learning. When it conditions its revision of traditional doctrine by a tenacious hold of the original Christian belief in the Incarnation (apart from which that original Christian belief is inconceivable), it not merely demonstrates its fundamental orthodoxy, but also affirms the limits within which alone the verdicts of Biblical science can rightly be allowed to determine Christian Faith.

That modern science and criticism of documents have profoundly affected the meaning of the unaltered language of the ancient Creeds cannot be questioned. No one understands the familiar phrases now as they were understood a few generations ago. Between 1800 and 1900 a subtle but transforming change has befallen such expressions as "maker of heaven and earth", "being of one substance with the Father", "came down from heaven", "rose again according to the Scriptures", "descended into hell", "ascended into heaven", "from thence he shall come to judge the quick and the dead", "the holy Catholick and Apostolick Church", "the Resurrection of the dead", or "of the body", or "of the flesh". The cosmic setting of the spiritual revelation has been altered: the conception of the historical process is no longer the same: science, biological and psychological, has wonderfully changed our notions of human nature alike in its slow evolution and in its potential future. We must perforce read into the immemorial expressions of Christian faith meanings which they were never originally intended to bear. From this necessity there is no escape. Theology can never possess more than a provisional or contingent validity. It is the union of two factors, of which one—the Truth as it is in Jesus—is fixed but largely misconceived or unperceived, and the other—the sum of human knowledge—is for ever changing. There can therefore be no fixity in the combination. Theology presents Truth in terms of Knowledge, and its statements must vary with the measure and character of the Knowledge available. But Time clothes creeds and confessions with an authority to which they are not really entitled. In the case of the ancient Creeds there is a special reason why this unwarrantable authority should be abnormally great. In the early centuries, when the Creeds were formulated under political and intellectual conditions which have long passed away, no such awful sanctity attached to them they now possess. They were of comparatively recent origin. They were the products of controversies which long survived their production. Councils had drafted, revised, even reversed them. What Councils had done once they clearly could do again. There was an elasticity in the matter of creed-making which has long ceased. With the downfall of the Roman Empire there supervened the long intellectual eclipse which has been not unfitly described as the "Dark Ages", during which all constructive theological thinking was arrested, and the Western Church, absorbed in its great task of Christianizing the barbarous conquerors of Rome, lived perforce on the intellectual bequest of the older time. When at length intellectual activity revived, and men again reflected on their beliefs, they had in their possession doctrinal statements, the Creeds, so ancient, so long unchallenged, so plainly authoritative, that they were naturally regarded as immune from criticism and incapable of alteration. The rapidity with which Knowledge has accumulated within recent years has undoubtedly created a dangerous chasm between the language of the Creeds and the thought of educated Western Christians. To some extent this chasm has been bridged by the silent transformation of meaning which the language of the Creeds has sustained. The Report of the Archbishops' Commission on Doctrine may suffice to show that this method of relieving the tension is not sufficient, and that nothing short of an explicit acknowledgment of dissentient belief will satisfy the consciences of those devout and educated Anglicans whose acceptance of the Creed is perforce conditioned by their study of the Scripture. They, not less than their more technically orthodox fellow-members of the Church of England, would accord with the Commission's conclusion

that neither can the truth of the Gospel stand unimpaired, nor can any adequate account of its origin be given unless the broad tradition concerning Jesus, to which the Gospels and the Church have borne witness through the centuries, is accepted as historical, and in particular unless it is possible for the Church to proclaim that in the historical figure of Jesus of Nazareth "the Word was made flesh and dwelt among us".[1]

Note

In his notable book on *The Church of England* the Bishop of Gloucester writes:

The Virgin Birth is not the Incarnation (as is sometimes taught), or an essential part of that doctrine.... If it were proved that the story of the birth of our Lord were a myth, or the outcome of religious symbolism, or an attempt to teach abstract truth through concrete images, that would not take away from the reality of the doctrine of the Incarnation or the evidence for it.

It is certainly surprising that the bishop after this candid admission should write with as little accuracy as justice;

But when I turn to the evidence I can find no strong reasons for this scepticism. The arguments against the story are not strong. It is really objected to on *a priori* grounds. Critical difficulties which have been raised have been deprived of authority with increasing knowledge. The belief in the Virgin Birth is clearly older than either of the narratives which relate it. It does not prove the Incarnation: we believe it because we accept the Incarnation and it harmonizes with that belief (pp. 58, 59).

[1] *V.* Report, p. 38.

Many competent scholars who are also devout Christians will not share the bishop's estimate of the weight of the adverse evidence, and many will be disposed to agree with the minority of the Archbishops' Commissioners in thinking

that a full belief in the historical Incarnation is more consistent with the supposition that our Lord's birth took place under the normal conditions of human generation.

Those who wish to see a candid and scholarly statement for and against the Article which affirms the Virgin Birth will find what they want in Canon Quick's recently published volume, *Doctrines of the Creed* (London: Nisbet and Co.).

CHAPTER 4

OF SUBSCRIPTION

The English clergyman at his Ordination, and again when he is licensed to a stipendiary curacy, or instituted to a benefice, is required to make and subscribe the declaration set out in the Clerical Subscription Act of 1865. That declaration, which replaced a more precise and stringent formula, runs thus:

I assent to the Thirty-nine Articles of Religion and to the Book of Common Prayer, and to the Ordering of Bishops, Priests, and Deacons. I believe the Doctrine of the Church of England, as therein set forth, to be agreeable to the Word of God; and in Public Prayer and Administration of the Sacraments I will use the Form in the said Book prescribed, and none other, except so far as shall be ordered by lawful authority.

In addition to making and subscribing this Declaration, the clergyman is required at his Ordination to take the Oath of Allegiance to the Sovereign. After his Ordination every clergyman about to be licensed to any curacy is also required to take the Oath of Canonical Obedience to the Bishop in these terms:

I, A.B., do swear that I will pay true and canonical obedience to the Lord Bishop of — and his successors, in all things lawful and honest. So help me God.

What are the nature and measure of the obligations which the Declaration of Assent and the Oaths of Allegiance to the Sovereign and Canonical Obedience to the Bishop really involve? How far are they found to be effective in securing the clergyman's orthodoxy, loyalty, and submission to episcopal authority? Do they secure obedience to the law, and give reasonable security to the parishioners against individual eccentricities of theological teaching, and unlawful variations from the legally prescribed forms of public worship? These questions raise the more radical inquiry which challenges both the value and the moral legitimacy of doctrinal Subscription. When that inquiry has been answered, there yet remains the question whether the formularies to which Subscription is required are reasonably adequate for the purposes which Subscription is designed to serve.

The ethics of Subscription is a subject of extreme difficulty which has often been debated, and is as far as ever from securing general agreement. Yet the practical reasons why the method of exacting Subscription from the clergy has maintained its ground, in spite of severe and continuing criticism, retain validity, and until those reasons can be removed, there is little probability that *some* form of doctrinal Subscription will not be insisted upon as integral to an official commission. It would appear that something analogous to what philosophers designate an antinomy confronts the ecclesiastical statesman when he seeks to guard admission to Holy Orders from injustice to the individual, on the one hand, and from danger to the congregation and to the Church, on the other. It is, of course, apparent that the obligations inherent in the tenure of ecclesiastical office may sometimes be difficult to harmonize with the insistent requirements of personal conviction, nor may it fairly be denied that the conflict between public and private duty may be so extreme as to make the tenure of office intolerable to a sensitively conscientious clergyman; but the measure of disharmony will vary greatly in extent, and will be negligible if the official formulary which conditions ordination is expressed in largely comprehensive terms; or, if the Subscription imposed is itself confessedly elastic; or, finally, if its character be so understood by recognized and sufficient public authority. The necessary demand of an institution cannot be contracted to the specific needs of its officers, nor can the commissioned teacher of religion be exempt from the limitations of personal self-expression which attach to all commissioned teachers in the fulfilment of their duty. Some discrepancy will necessarily develop between the established dogma and the teacher's private opinion, but this ought not in a well-ordered Church to impair sincerity of teaching, still less to arrest the teacher's fulfilment of his task. A certain tension will always shadow the fact of Subscription, but it need be neither discreditable nor paralysing.

Subscription of creeds and formularies has a twofold object. It is intended to attest the orthodoxy of the individual clergyman, and to secure the Church against false teaching. Can it be fairly maintained that experience has demonstrated the value of Subscription in either respect? Has it been found effective as evidence of individual orthodoxy? Has it protected the Church against the scandal and weakness of teaching which is both commissioned and heretical? To take first the case of the individual clergyman who, as we have said, is required to make and subscribe the Declaration of Assent to the Thirty-nine Articles and the Prayer Book.

The candidate for Ordination is generally a young man, whose self-knowledge must be small, whose learning cannot be extensive, and whose acquaintance with the world is brief and limited. Is it reasonable to require him to make such detailed declarations of theological opinion? How can it be fairly demanded of a young clergyman, on the threshold of his ministry, that he should bind himself, in advance of knowledge, in the absence of experience, never to change his theological opinions? Whichcote's aphorism is relevant:

> He that never changed any of his opinions, never corrected any of his mistakes; and he who was never wise enough, to find out any mistakes in himself; will not be charitable enough to excuse what he reckons mistakes in others.

At his Ordination the clergyman is pledged to

> be ready with all faithful diligence to banish and drive away all erroneous and strange doctrines contrary to God's Word.

How can he fulfil his Ordination vow if he must bring to the treatment of such novel opinions as he may have to examine a mind already closed and settled on every issue?

It is notorious that the influence of the clergy as teachers of religion, and champions of Christianity, is greatly lessened by the knowledge that they are required to decline for themselves the free examination of official credenda which others possess. They are roughly pictured as hired gladiators rather than as free combatants. They are in a false position when they engage in controversy, for they are required to enter the controversial arena as men bound in advance of the discussion to the opinions which have been legally imposed on them. Thus their teaching seems to lack the hall-mark of personal conviction. In all this there is much confusion of thought, and much personal injustice, but it is none the less plausible, largely accepted, and, in its effect on public opinion, widely baleful. The clergyman is rightly required to be a convinced Christian, sincerely believing the Faith expressed in the Creeds which bind all Christians, but ought he, as a commissioned teacher of Christianity, to be less free than the laity to whom he ministers to exercise his private judgment in the difficult questions, moral and theological, which from time to time require answer? Beyond all reasonable question, the Church must insist that the man who seeks the teacher's commission shall give evidence that he is adequately equipped with knowledge for the religious teacher's task, but the legal Subscription goes far beyond this. It is concerned, not with knowledge, but with opinion, and precisely for this reason its moral legitimacy may be and has been weightily challenged. For knowledge is ever advancing, and opinion must needs reflect the fact. Does not the requirement to subscribe doctrinal formularies, which cannot but express opinions, fashioned by other minds under other conditions of time and place, really have the effect of placing the clergyman from the start of his ministry in a situation which must be embarrassing, and may be degrading?

These considerations acquire a special urgency in times of rapid intellectual movement. It is notorious that the morality, the practical value, and the permanent effect of clerical subscription have been much debated in recent years, and do still, in spite of much mitigating casuistry and the relief provided by the Clerical Subscription Act, trouble many consciences.

When we pass from general considerations and examine the formularies themselves, we are immediately impressed by their unsuitableness for their presumed purpose. The union of the Thirty-nine Articles and the Book of Common Prayer in the Declaration of Assent assumes their mutual agreement. The candidate for Ordination professes his belief that "the doctrine of the Church of England" as set forth in these documents is "agreeable to the Word of God". If, however, there be conflict between the two, is it not apparent that he will be carried into a situation of considerable perplexity? Certainly the presumed agreement has been repeatedly challenged, and is not generally allowed. Lord Chatham's

An Act for the Vniformity
of Common Prayer, and service
in the Church, and Adminis=
tration of the Sacraments,
primo Elizabethæ.

Where at the death of our late soveraign Lord King Edward
the sixth, there remained one vniform order of Common Service
and prayer, and of the administration of Sacraments, Rites
and Ceremonies in the Church of England which was set forth
in one Book intituled, The Book of Common prayer, and administration of Sacraments, and other Rites and Ceremonies in the ~~
Church of England, authorized by Act of parliament holden in the
fifth and sixth year of our said late Soveraign Lord King Edward
the sixth, intituled, An Act for the vniformity of common prayer
and Administration of the Sacraments: The which was repealed
and taken away by Act of parliament in the first year of the ~
raign of our late Soveraign Lady Queen Mary to the great decay
of the due honour of God, and discomfort to the professors of the
truth of Christ religion.

Be it therefore enacted by the authority of this present parliament, that the said Statute of repeal, and every thing therein contained only concerning the said Book and the Service, Administration of Sacraments, Rites and Ceremonies contained or appointed
in or by the said Book, shall be void and of none effect, from and
after the feast of the Nativity of St. John Baptist next coming. ~

And that the said Book with the order of Service and of the administration of Sacraments, Rites, and Ceremonies with the Alteration and additions therein added and appointed by this Statute, ~
shall stand and be from and after the said feast of the nativity of

Saint

A page of the manuscript Book of Common Prayer attached
to the Act of Uniformity, 1662

famous description of the Church of England as possessing Calvinistical Articles and a Popish Liturgy has the
measure of truth which belongs to a successful caricature.
It would be broadly true to say that, while the Articles are
the product of the conflicts and controversies which
marked the English Reformation, the Prayer Book utters
the mind of the earlier time, when the visible unity of the
Catholic Church had not yet been shattered. Accordingly, the temper and tendency of the one differ profoundly from those of the other. Controversy determines
the Articles, and Devotion the Prayer Book. Controversy
is ever relevant to factors which have no intrinsic permanence, but Devotion is timeless and universal. Is not
the combination of the two a Mezentian union of the dead
and the living?

Thus, while both the Articles and the Prayer Book are
relatively ancient formularies, the one having been composed, and the other compiled, in the sixteenth century,
it is the Articles which have suffered most from the lapse
of time. Remoteness from the present may not be in itself
a disadvantage, for it can confer a kind of consecration
which prohibits criticism. Cranmer, in his Preface "*Of
Ceremonies, Why some be Abolished, and some Retained*"
which is still included in the Prayer Book, justly rebuked
those eager innovators who would treat the antiquity of
ceremonies as itself a reason for their abolition. He knew
and valued the holding strength of ancient custom. While,
however, this is true in the case of devotional forms, it is
not equally true in that of doctrinal statements. Then
remoteness in time may but too easily involve irrelevance
to actual problems, and the ignoring of real needs. This,
indeed, is confessedly the case with the Thirty-nine
Articles. It is sufficient to recall the fact that they were
composed by men whose modes of thinking and feeling
were still medieval. Cranmer and his contemporaries
were Ptolemaic in their astronomy, fundamentalist in

their view of the Bible, persecutors of what they regarded as religious error, Erastians in their conception of the Church's authority. Many of the questions with which the Articles are concerned were intensely interesting in the sixteenth century, but have wholly fallen out of human concern in the twentieth. Many new questions, such for example as those raised by modern science, by comparative religion, and by Biblical criticism, had not yet been raised. Accordingly, the Anglican statement of doctrine is both partially obsolete and practically unhelpful.

If however we turn from the case of the individual clergyman, and consider the Thirty-nine Articles, not as a statement of personal belief to be subscribed by all Christians, but as the written confession of a particular Church to be loyally accepted by its commissioned officers, we must needs take a more favourable view of their quality and function. In this connexion it is important to have clearly in mind the circumstances in which the famous Confession was originally composed, and the primary purpose which it was designed to serve.

The disruption of the Western Church in the sixteenth century drew in its train the production of a number of theological statements or confessions advanced by the leaders of the fragments, national and denominational, into which the once united Church had been broken. The crisis had raised some formidable questions. Did disruption involve heresy? Did the loss of the old unity of system bring with it necessarily a state of ecclesiastical anarchy? How far did the traditional Christian morality share the fate which had befallen the traditional doctrine? These questions pressed for answer. There was thus a twofold necessity under which the historic Confessions were framed. On the one hand, the revolting sections had to justify their revolt: on the other hand, they had to provide a basis for their own independent organization. Why had they broken away from the immemorial dominion of the Popes? How would they take shape as separated Churches? The times were revolutionary. Grave excesses, doctrinal and moral, marked the course of the Reformation, and damaged its credit. It was plainly requisite that the Reformed Churches should clear themselves of any responsibility for such deplorable developments. The Confessions, therefore, were both apologetic and disciplinary. They proclaimed to Christendom the various "platforms" on which their systems were builded. The Roman Catholic Church, since it also had become but a fragment of the Western Church, albeit in extent the largest, lay under the same compulsion. It too had to accept the necessity of Reformation. The sixteenth century, which witnessed the organization of the Protestant Churches, witnessed also the reorganization of the Church of Rome. Within much restricted limits the medieval tradition persisted in a revised version. The Reformation evoked and largely determined the Counter-Reformation. In the canons and decrees of the Council of Trent the Church of Rome offered its own apology, and provided for its own discipline.

Between A.D. 1530, when the Lutherans presented their famous Confession to the Imperial Diet at Augsburg, and 1571, when the Elizabethan Parliament imposed the Thirty-nine Articles on the English clergy, a succession of doctrinal statements was issued—Lutheran, Reformed, Anglican, and Roman. Political rather than religious causes explain the curious fact that the famous formulary of the Church of Scotland bears an English name, the Westminster Confession, and was not framed until the seventeenth century. All these documents had the same character, and served the same purpose. They set forth to the world the "platform" of the Church which accepted them, and declared the conditions of its membership. The reasonableness of this procedure cannot be disputed. In a divided Christendom there is evident need that every independent fraction should justify its independence, and make plain the conditions of its fellowship. So long as Christendom remains divided, the need for such official confessions will continue. Every Church claiming to be autonomous must declare its "platform". Only those who can loyally accept that "platform" can rightly be commissioned to hold office within the Church.

This character of the Thirty-nine Articles as, not so much a formula of personal belief as the authoritative statement of corporate witness, the basis of common membership, has been frequently recognized. Thus the famous Archbishop Ussher (1581–1656) writes:

We do not suffer any man to reject the Thirty-nine Articles of the Church of England at his pleasure; yet neither do we look upon them as essentials of saving faith, or legacies of Christ and the Apostles; but a mean, as pious opinions fitted for the preservation of unity; neither do we oblige any man to believe them, but only not to contradict them.

Chillingworth (1602–1644) held that subscription to the Thirty-nine Articles meant no more than a general belief in the soundness of the Church of England, and that "there is no error which may necessitate or warrant any man to disturb the peace and renounce the communion of it".[1] This view may, perhaps, be said to be implied in the change of the formula of Subscription made by the Clerical Subscription Act. The formula sets out in broad outline the version of Christianity which the Church of England requires its officials to advocate. It is not designed as a test of personal orthodoxy. But, if this be conceded, what precisely is their present value?

Do they really express the mind of the Church of England here and now? The fact that they were imposed, though with a mitigated form of Subscription, as recently

[1] *V.* Preface to the *Religion of Protestants.*

as 1865, disallows the notion that they may be set aside as obsolete. If, however, they are subscribed in a general sense, authorizing the subscribing clergyman to distinguish for himself between those Articles which he must hold to be binding, and those which he may discount, what guarantee against the gravest doctrinal error does the parishioner possess in the clergyman's Subscription? Would he be worse placed if there were no Subscription at all?

May it not fairly be maintained that the theological laxity, which did not lack practical justification when no alternative to the Established Church was legally permitted, has ceased to be reasonable or morally legitimate now when there is complete liberty of religious self-expression? May not doctrinal incoherence be too heavy a price to pay for ecclesiastical inclusiveness? Is there not a real danger to religious sincerity in continuing a policy which had its sole justification in a situation which has passed away? Why should the comprehensiveness, proper, indeed indispensable, in a National Church, be maintained in a Church which has ceased to be co-extensive with the nation, and has become within the nation but one religious denomination among many? What precisely is the present value of the Thirty-nine Articles, since their original purpose of comprehension has ceased?

The necessity for possessing a "platform" rests indeed on a denomination, not less plainly, perhaps even more plainly, than on a National Church; for, while the latter can base itself on the nation's right to have control of its own affairs, and to be the sole judge of its own interests, the former must rest on the foundation of its own professed principles. Erastianism and denominationalism cannot possibly agree together. Personal belief may be of minor importance in the one case; it is vitally important in the other. Subscription therefore can hardly mean as little in the twentieth century as it may fairly have been thought to have meant in the sixteenth or the seventeenth. What then, it must be asked, is the value of the Thirty-nine Articles at the present time? What is implied in the "assent" which the English clergy solemnly profess?

If, as we have already indicated, the Articles are largely irrelevant, and partially obsolete, what is their precise importance? Who can be trusted to determine where the line is to be drawn between the doctrinal statements which may fairly be pressed as fully authoritative, and those which may legitimately be ignored? Even in the past, when Subscription was authoritatively interpreted to signify rather a profession of ecclesiastical allegiance than a declaration of personal belief, these questions troubled men's consciences, and were anxiously debated. They have continued to be asked ever since, and they are being asked with growing insistence in the strangely altered conditions of to-day. The clergy ask them at their Ordination: the parishioners ask them when their incumbents are instituted, and when they hear them read from the pulpit by a new incumbent, as the indispensable preliminary of his official ministry.

The Puritans and Laudians raised them in the seventeenth century, the Deists in the eighteenth, the Tractarians and "Broad Churchmen" in the nineteenth, the "Anglo-Catholics" and "Modernists" in the twentieth. Since the original motive for calculated ambiguity in the Anglican formularies has failed, why should that ambiguity be tolerated? Is compromise a temporary expedient or a permanent feature of Anglican policy? It is certain that the Thirty-nine Articles were in their original intention more politic than theological. The practical wisdom of the Tudor statesmen mitigated the dogmatic ardour of the Tudor divines. Queen Elizabeth was more concerned for civic harmony than for religious orthodoxy. Fuller, writing in the next century, gave a true

account of the conditions under which the Anglican
Articles were finally shaped:

Children's clothes ought to be made of the biggest, because
afterwards their bodies will grow up to the garments. Thus
the articles of the English protestant church, in the infancy
thereof, they thought good to draw up in general terms,
foreseeing that posterity would grow up to fill the same, I
mean, those holy men did prudently prediscover that
differences in judgments would unavoidably happen in the
church, and were loath to unchurch any, and drive them off
from an ecclesiastical communion for such petty differences;
which made them pen the articles in comprehensive words,
to take in all who, differing in the branches meet in the root
of the same religion.[1]

Fuller was both a peace-maker and a jester. His kindly
humorous disposition had little in common with the
severity of Puritan habit, and the meticulous intrusiveness
of Laudian discipline. But men felt too strongly about
their religion to accept metaphors and jokes for arguments. The Anglican children as they grew up found the
prudently ample vestures provided for them both ill-
fitting and uncomfortable. They looked longingly to the
neater garments of Geneva, and the more splendid
habiliments of Rome. Accordingly they betook themselves to the arts and crafts of exegetic casuistry, and
sought to explain away whatever in the Articles they
could not endure. The critics expressed very different
objections. Some denounced the Articles as unduly re-
strictive of theological liberty and therefore inconsistent
with the fundamental principle of Protestantism: and
others urged that they were out of harmony with the
Prayer Book, unduly hostile to much in the religious
tradition of Christendom which was primitive and edifying, and, to that extent, were incompatible with the

[1] V. Church History of Britain, Bk IX, sec. 52.

essential Catholicism of the English Church. On the whole the Protestant sentiment of the nation held by the Articles, while the Catholic-minded churchmen built their case on the Prayer Book. It is significant that the Toleration Act required the tolerated dissenters to subscribe (with some specified omissions) the Thirty-nine Articles, thus indicating that Subscription was held to guarantee loyal Protestantism.

On a fair review of Anglican history it cannot be questioned that the Thirty-nine Articles have to a remarkable degree succeeded in their professed object as stated on the title-page in the Prayer Book. There we read that the Articles were designed "for the avoiding of Diversities of Opinions, and for the establishing of Consent touching true Religion". Many historians have written admiringly of the moderation of theological statement and tolerance of ecclesiastical attitude which distinguished the Anglican Confession from other contemporary statements of doctrine. "The broad touch of Cranmer lay upon them", and the effect of that touch was strengthened by Cranmer's like-minded successor, Parker, under whom the Edwardian formulary was revised and imposed. "Regarded whether as a symbol or a code", writes Dixon, "the English Articles, which had passed thus successively through the hands of Cranmer and Parker, can scarcely fail to move admiration, in comparison with the similar performances of the age."[1]

In the course of the last two centuries, the position of the Church of England has been greatly altered as the result of the notable development of missionary enterprise which has led to the growth of flourishing churches of converts in Asia and Africa, and to the expansion of Anglicanism in the American Republic and throughout the British Empire. How far could the Thirty-nine Articles serve as the "platform", not of an Established

[1] *V. History of the Church of England*, v, 395.

insular Church, but of a Federation of Churches which accepted the Anglican version of Christianity? The Report of the Committee appointed to consider the subject of Authoritative Standards of Doctrine and Worship made to the Lambeth Conference in 1888 combined a lofty estimate of the Articles with an admission of their unsuitableness for the new requirement.

The Thirty-nine Articles served well the purpose for which they were originally imposed. They enabled men of widely divergent opinions and temperaments to accept office in the National Church, and they made possible the development of that liberal version of Christianity which has, in the course of time, come to be recognized as distinctive of Anglicanism. But they could not escape the disadvantages involved in their close relation to the controversies of the age. As these gave place to new conflicts, the Articles tended to fall out of accord with Anglican feeling. The seventeenth century was not as the sixteenth. Theological controversies were largely replaced by ecclesiastical, and the Articles had little relevance to the new questions which were being raised. The violences of the religious revolution had provoked a reaction which went far to enfeeble, and even invalidate, the original arguments of iconoclastic innovation. Under the influence of the Jesuits the controversy with Rome was transformed. The ground was shifted from Scripture to tradition, from the claims of the Papacy to the teachings of antiquity, from the crude simplicity of Protestant systems to the many-sided appeal of the Catholic Church. The Church of England, dignified, comparatively wealthy, and backed by the power of the throne, drew away from the fellowship of the continental Protestants, and developed claims of its own, which they could with difficulty understand, and could in no circumstances admit. The Thirty-nine Articles were increasingly belittled: the Prayer Book was increasingly magnified. In 1634 there appeared a book on the Articles which anticipated the exegetic method of Tract XC. It was written by a convert from Anglicanism to Rome, Christopher Davenport (1598–1680), better known as Franciscus a Sancta Clara, and it was designed to promote a reconciliation with Rome. It was dedicated to Charles I, and if not licensed by the archbishop, was probably published with his knowledge and approval. Its appearance tended to confirm the general suspicion with which Laud was regarded, and it entered into the case for his impeachment. Of it, as later of Tract XC, it may be truly said that it was less a serious effort to explain the Articles than an adroit attempt to explain them away. For it is certain that the Thirty-nine Articles constitute a Protestant confession, which, as such, was rightly included in the *Harmony of Confessions*, published at Geneva in 1581, and referred to in the XXth Canon of 1604.

With all their halting between two opinions, their want of theological originality, their intentional incompleteness, they have been a noble bulwark of Protestant conviction, and possess a simple dignity and catholicity of their own. Against their measured testimony, spoken with the formula of Trent as clearly in view as those of Lutheranism and Calvinism, even the interpretative casuistry and antiquarian imagination of the Oxford Movement urged their forces in vain.[1]

This is the verdict of a scholarly Presbyterian, and states the truth, but not the whole truth. For the Articles have never stood alone, and were never designed to stand alone, as a summary of Anglican Christianity. They have always been received by English churchmen together with the other Anglican standards, the Prayer Book and the Ordinal, which express a version of Christianity far

[1] *V.* Professor Curtis, Article "Confessions" in Hastings's *Encyclopaedia of Religion and Ethics*.

removed from the fears and feuds of the Reformation. Moreover, the development of the nation's religion has been potently influenced by the course of the nation's history. The normal isolation of the island church was intensified by the course of European politics. Religion had little concern with the causes which led England to take part in continental wars through the century which connects the Treaty of Utrecht in 1713 with the Treaty of Paris in 1815. Churches no longer called the tune for statesmen. In modern Europe dynastic and economic interests rarely coincide with ecclesiastical profession. Thus the Church of England fell apart almost unconsciously from the fellowship of the continental Protestants with whom the Protestants of England had been in such close and affectionate relation. Anglicanism developed on lines of its own, and these have carried it far from the normal Protestant type. In effect, the Protestant character of the Articles, which at first commended them to general acceptance, has become in process of time the reason for their general unpopularity. Older and more fundamental elements of Anglican Christianity have been free to develop without the arresting influence of religious panic, or the coercive guidance of public policy.

Mr Gladstone, writing to a Greek archbishop in 1875, gave a fair statement of the facts as viewed by a moderate Tractarian:

In a practical point of view, the Prayer Book represents the Catholic and historic aspect of the Church of England, the Articles the particular phase brought out by the events of the sixteenth century. I speak of both in the main; for some of the most Catholic declarations are in the Articles, and one or two of the most Protestant are in the Prayer Book. Lord Chatham said the Liturgy, or Prayer Book, was Popish, the Articles Calvinistic. No doubt their colour is distinct, but I do not think that, rationally and comprehensively understood, they are in contradiction. Our divines would say generally that they integrate one another, but would assign the greater moral weight and importance to the Prayer Book.[1]

This substantial agreement may be conceded. The composition of the Articles and the compilation of the Prayer Book were parts of a single process, and must be understood as such. They are complementary and may not be severed. Neither can be dispensed with. The Articles do not provide a manual of public worship, nor does the Prayer Book set out the "platform" of the Church of England. Bishop Gore had travelled far from Anglican loyalty when he publicly declared his desire for "the removal of the Thirty-nine Articles from the position of authoritative standards (in any sense) of belief or practice in the Anglican Church". The Declaration of Faith "prepared by a Committee of the English Church Union, approved by the President and Council of that Body, and addressed to the Oecumenical Patriarch and the Holy Synod of the Great Church of Constantinople" included a formal repudiation of the Articles:

We account the Thirty-nine Articles of Religion as a document of secondary importance concerned with local controversies of the sixteenth century, and to be interpreted in accordance with the faith of that Universal Church of which the English Church is but a part.

This Declaration of Faith was signed by 3715 persons, and was translated into several languages. It appears to disclose confusion of mind.

"Local controversies", whether of the sixteenth or any other century, may be concerned with vital religious issues. The Arian controversy began as a "local controversy", but it was not on that account anything less than vitally important to Christians everywhere. Leo X was not

[1] *V. Correspondence on Church and Religion*, selected and arranged by D. C. Lathbury, II, 67.

well advised when he dismissed the Lutheran controversy
as a petty affair of a disorderly German friar. The Thirty-
nine Articles treat of some questions which are quite
fundamental, such as the Rule of Faith and the fallibility
of General Councils. Every particular Church asserts or
assumes that its official doctrinal confession or formulary
is accordant with the faith of the Universal Church. The
suggestion that there may be a conflict between the two is
all one with a claim to substitute some other understanding of the Universal Faith for that which the Church of
England has formulated. Bishop Westcott used to say
that no man could be a loyal member of the Catholic
Church who was not a loyal member of his branch of it.
The *raison d'être* of subscription to the Thirty-nine
Articles is the necessity, in a divided Christendom, of
agreeing on a version of the Catholic Faith. In the
Articles we have the Anglican version of the Catholic
tradition of Faith and Discipline. It is not open to any
loyal Anglican to form any other.

Alike for negotiations with other branches of the
Church, and for the instruction of its own members, *some*
authoritative statement of specifically Anglican teaching
and practice is really indispensable. Such an authoritative
statement is provided by the Thirty-nine Articles, and, if
they were abandoned, it would be necessary to provide a
substitute.

So long as the Christian society is divided on issues so
fundamental as to transcend even the interest of visible
unity, separate Churches must exist, and must show cause
for doing so. It would be manifestly intolerable that men
should be authorized to minister as officers and teachers
who did not assent to the doctrine and discipline of the
Church which commissioned them. It would be not less
intolerable if the parishioners were to possess no security
against mere individualism on the part of the clergy.
Therefore it seems to follcw that Subscription is really

indispensable, as well for the protection of the people as for the security of the Church.

When, however, we pass from theoretical considerations to the actual situation in the Church of England at the present time, we are confronted by a strange spectacle of doctrinal confusion which demonstrates the failure of Subscription to secure either of the two objects for which presumably it was designed. It does not provide any effective guarantee of the doctrinal soundness of the subscribing clergy, and it does not protect the people from heretical parsons. The Church of England, at the present time, exhibits a doctrinal incoherence which has no parallel in any other church claiming to be traditionally orthodox. It is important that the character and extent of this phenomenon should be justly regarded, for it may well be the case that, when so regarded, it will be found less perplexing and indefensible than at first view it appears to be.

The doctrinal incoherence of the Church of England, though it is unquestionably perplexing, practically embarrassing, and not infrequently actually scandalous, has its roots in something far more respectable than an indolent acquiescence in undiscipline or a reprehensible indifference to truth. It reflects the reluctance of considering and responsible English churchmen to thrust the rough hand of authority into the sphere of religious opinion. Not an indifference to truth, but a juster perception of the conditions under which truth must be sought and defended, leads them to shrink from discouraging individual efforts to discover a solution of the problem which now confronts, in various measures of urgency, every section of the Christian Church, namely, how to reconcile the theological tradition expressed in creeds and immutable in theory, sacrosanct by time, and the ever-growing knowledge of mankind. Christian history, as well ancient as modern, does not encourage the notion that error can most effectually be corrected by the action of official authority, nor does the Christian religion harmonize easily with methods of coercion, while its insistence on truth, and on the temper of sincerity, justifies, and even requires, a large acquiescence in the honest blundering of Christian scholars.

It is certain that distrust of coercion as an ecclesiastical policy is widely extended among English churchmen, and especially among the better educated. The existence of Dissent is a standing disproof of the practical value of coercion in the religious sphere; and the increasing knowledge of the challenges which science and criticism are advancing against the orthodox theological tradition is creating in the minds of the more serious and cultivated Anglican laity a disposition to encourage, rather than to prohibit, the efforts of the clergy, as commissioned religious teachers, to understand those challenges, and frankly to meet them.

The national Establishment of the Church has favoured the growth among its members, both lay and clerical, of a latitudinarian temper, which, albeit shadowed by grave dangers of its own, is not without value, and has certainly saved the Church of England from grave misfortunes. Indifference to doctrinal orthodoxy is the natural temper of an established Church which claims in some sense to be national, and as such broadly representative of the nation's Christianity. That national Christianity is certainly far more various and many-sided than the clear-cut requirements of traditional orthodoxy can tolerate. It is often urged, and not without plausibility, that the Church of England, in accepting the considerable material advantages of its national establishment, has renounced or forfeited the perilous franchise of denominationalism; but it must be answered, that such a price might be too great for rightful acceptance. Yet it may not be fairly denied that the tolerance fostered by Establishment has a value of its own, which should not be ignored or belittled.

It is sometimes objected against the English clergy that they are singularly lacking in exact knowledge of theology, and therefore little disposed to value that dogmatic precision which might fairly be looked for in the trained and commissioned teachers of the Christian religion. This circumstance, it is suggested, fosters an easy acquiescence in a doctrinal individualism which may, and often does, express itself in dangerous error. It cannot fairly be denied that in this objection there is an element of substantial truth; but the student of ecclesiastical history, who notes the continuing scandals of clerical bigotry, which darken its pages, and the ethical obtuseness of doctrinal scrupulosity, will find considerable counter-balancing gain in the generously tolerant habit which has, for the most part, distinguished the English clergy. "Doctor, doctor," said the large-hearted Tillotson to the learned but narrow-minded Beveridge, "charity is better than rubrics." It has been a happy thing, alike for the nation and for the Church, that the spirit of Tillotson rather than that of Beveridge has generally prevailed among the clergy of England.

All these specific factors tending to develop dogmatic incoherence in the Church of England have been powerfully assisted by the prevailing secularism which is the intellectual temper, the "climate of opinion", of the modern world. Nothing indeed is more remarkable, significant, and widely influential than the decay of religious influence throughout the entire extent of Western Civilization. The internal affairs of the Church of England have ceased to interest "the man in the street". The "Nonconformist conscience" has no value for the politician, and the clergy count for little or nothing at a General Election. In these circumstances, public opinion cannot be counted upon to support any exercise of ecclesiastical authority which has, or can be represented as having, the aspect of oppression. The temper and habit of English democracy are definitely hostile to any interference with individual liberty in the matter of religion, and, though it is perceived that the clergyman's position is distinctive, and must properly subject him to an official control which could not be reasonably applied to the layman, yet it is clearly seen that, since the sincerity of the religious teacher is essential to the value of his teaching, the didactic freedom of the clergy is the interest of the laity. This democratic temper both facilitates clerical individualism, and paralyses official discipline.

We have said that every section of the Christian Church is now faced by the problem of discovering some tolerable harmony between the traditional version of the Christian religion, and the accumulated and accumulating knowledge of mankind. The problem is vital, for upon its solution the existence of Christianity as a living religion, able to command the acceptance of civilized mankind, finally turns. The problem is everywhere the same, but it presents itself in many shapes, and the ability of the different Churches, which in their totality represent the Christian religion, to attempt its solution varies greatly. Here it suffices that we should speak only of the Church of England.

It is to be noted that in the studies which affect theology most directly, history and Biblical criticism, the English Church lagged behind the Churches of the continent. The explanation is not obscure. The course of national history for more than a century had deepened the isolation of the Church of England, and until the protracted war with France had ended in 1815, there was little room in English minds for any other interests than those which that war compelled. "*Inter arma silent leges.*" So long as the entire energies of the nation were absorbed in the conflict, domestic issues were driven into the background. The "Oxford Movement" was rather antiquarian than historical, and its theology took small account of the new factors which were affecting the very postulates of current Christian doctrine. Thus it fell out that the breach between traditional orthodoxy and modern knowledge, which had long been apparent on the continent, was not perceived, still less realized, in England until, in the middle of the nineteenth century, the publication of the volume *Essays and Reviews* (1860) startled the country. The considerable controversy, which that volume occasioned, disclosed the general ignorance of the religious public, as well as its vehement, though unintelligent, theological conservatism. The conflict, which made so boisterous a beginning, has continued without intermission ever since, and shows little sign of reaching a decision.

The Church of England brought to its perilous venture three considerable advantages—its inability to legislate secured by its subordination to the State, the relative moderation of its denominational confession, and the tradition of clerical independence distinctive of its legal system. The first disarmed the orthodox resentment which would otherwise have found expression in coercive action; the second so mitigated the burden on clerical consciences that repugnance to the doctrinal tradition was comparatively slight and infrequent; the third so weakened authority as to secure practical immunity for individual aberrations from conventional orthodoxy. The Erastian establishment, the Thirty-nine Articles as imposed by the Clerical Subscription Act of 1865, and the parish parson's freehold in his benefice, however open to adverse criticism from the point of view of spiritual religion, of intellectual liberty, and of pastoral efficiency, did render the important service to the Church of England of providing a break-water against the impetuous reactions of panic-stricken orthodoxy, and thus securing time and opportunity for the development of liberal studies among the Anglican clergy.

CHAPTER 5

THE ENGLISH BISHOP

I.

Among the Reformed Churches only two—the National Churches of England and Sweden—retained an episcopate which drew its title from the medieval hierarchy. Everywhere else the episcopal succession was lost. The fortunes of the historic episcopate in the two episcopal churches were, however, very different. In England episcopal ordination was magnified in controversy until it became the indispensable condition of ecclesiastical fellowship. In Sweden it never acquired any similar importance. The Lutheran origin of their Reformation seemed in the eyes of Swedish churchmen to outweigh the divergence of polity. No practical hindrance to intercommunion was perceived in the circumstance that, while the Swedish bishops possessed succession from the medieval hierarchy, the Protestant bishops of Germany, Norway, and Denmark did not. Agreement in the true doctrine was the essential condition: and all who subscribed the Confession of Augsburg satisfied that condition, and therefore acknowledged ecclesiastical fellowship. Ussher (*ob.* 1656), the famous Irish primate whose picture of a primitive episcopate seemed to many peacemaking ecclesiastics in the seventeenth century to offer a possible basis for religious agreement, laid down, what was certainly the universal belief of the Reformers as well in England as elsewhere, that unity of doctrine was essential, not unity of government:

> For the agreement or disagreement in radical and fundamental doctrines, not the consonancy or dissonancy in the particular points of ecclesiastical government, is with me (and I hope with every man that mindeth peace) the rule of adhering to, or receding from, the Communion of any Church.[1]

We have already pointed out the circumstances in which the Reformation in England was effected. The obstinate orthodoxy of Henry VIII preserved the medieval constitution of the National Church even in the process of substituting the king's supremacy for the Pope's. Thus, when in England also the inevitable necessity for doctrinal alteration arose, the change in faith and discipline had to be correlated with the traditional ecclesiastical system. Polity in the case of the English Church preceded, and did not as everywhere else follow, doctrinal reform. Moreover the English Reformers did not share the doctrinal conservatism of their royal patron. They recognized frankly the religious solidarity of the Reformation, and regarded themselves as linked with the continental Reformers in a common cause. Cranmer seems to have contemplated the assembling of a Council of Protestants which should meet the decisions of Trent with the counter-decisions of a rival Synod not less authoritative. "Our adversaries", he wrote to Calvin in 1553, "are now holding their councils at Trent for the establishment of their errors: and shall we neglect to call together a godly synod, for the refutation of error, and for restoring and propagating the truth?"[2] When the forces of the Reformation were divided by the great controversy between

---

[1] V. *Life of Ussher*, by R. Parr, D.D., his Lordship's Chaplain (London, 1686), p. 5, Appendix.

[2] V. *Original Letters relative to the English Reformation* (Parker Society), p. 24.

the Lutherans and the Calvinists, the English Reformers, with scarcely an exception, espoused the side of the latter. The absence of bishops in the Calvinist Churches was not thought any obstacle to fellowship. During the Marian persecution the English refugees were welcomed by the continental Calvinists, and roughly repelled by the Lutherans. When the situation was reversed, the refugees from the continent received hospitable treatment in England. An interesting memorial of this hospitality still survives. The visitor to Canterbury Cathedral will observe with astonishment a part of the crypt reserved for the use of a congregation of French Protestants. The Primate of All England is to this day *ex officio* Superintendent of a non-episcopal Church.

In his biography of Archbishop Williams, who in 1624 entertained the French Embassy at Westminster Abbey, where he was dean, Hacket relates an episode which illustrates the English point of view in a very interesting way. One of the Frenchmen, a lay abbé, was curious as to the manner of Anglican worship, and asked for permission to attend the service on Christmas Day. He spoke freely to the dean of his impressions:

"Though I deplore your schism from the Catholic Church," he said, "yet I should bear false witness if I did not confess that your decency, which I discerned at that holy duty, was very allowable in the Consecrator and receivers."

The dean expressed the hope that "he would think better of the Religion", that is, of the Huguenots, for the future. "The better of the Religion!" echoed the Frenchman, whose notion of the Huguenots had been formed in the bigoted atmosphere of France, "I will lose my head, if you and our Huguenots are of one religion."

"I protest, sir," was the reply, "you divide us without cause. For the Harmony of Protestant Confessions divulged to all the world, do manifest our consonancy in Faith and

Doctrine. And for diversity in outward administrations, it is a note as old as Irenaeus, which will justify us from a rupture, that variety of ceremonies in several churches, the Foundation being preserved, doth commend the unity of Faith."[1]

It is then apparent that, to a leading Anglican ecclesiastic of the early seventeenth century, the absence of bishops was no barrier to ecclesiastical fellowship.

At the Synod of the Reformed (Calvinist) Churches at Dort (1618) there were present five divines sent from King James as representing the Defender of the Faith. When we bear in mind the authority which was ascribed to the king, not merely by the Tudor statutes, but by the recently enacted Canons of the Church of England, we must needs perceive in the presence of the English deputies an authoritative declaration of the character of the English Church. The question of episcopacy was raised at the Synod, and Bishop Carleton made a protest against the "strange conceit of the parity of Ministers to be instituted by Christ". He asserted the Divine and Apostolical origin of the episcopal government.

In subsequent discussions with the Dutch divines Bishop Carleton ascribed all the distractions of their Church to the lack of bishops, and warned them that they could have no good order until they restored episcopal government.

To this their answer was, That they had great honour for the good order and discipline in the Church of England, and heartily wished they could establish themselves upon this model: but they had no prospect of such a happiness; and since the civil government had made their desires impracticable, they hoped God would be merciful to them.[2]

---

[1] V. *Scrinia Reserata* (1693), pp. 210–212.
[2] V. Collier, *Ecclesiastical History of Great Britain* (London, 1714), II, 717.

Thus the Dutch ministers, with diplomatic skill, did homage to the king's well-known doctrine, so brusquely expressed at the Hampton Court Conference in his exclamation, "No Bishop, no King". James I was theologically in agreement with the Dutch Calvinists, but his political interests drew him to episcopacy. Not the Apostolic succession of the bishops was insisted upon by Anglican apologists so much as the Divine institution of "imparity of ministers", the continuous practice of the Church "from the Apostles' times", and especially the congruity of episcopacy and monarchy. The idea and method of Presbyterian government were rather republican than monarchical, and, therefore, hardly less than the supernational claim of the Papacy, conflicted with the English conception of a National Church.

The political argument for episcopal government in the Church was impressively confirmed by the fortunes of the monarchy. Puritanism in becoming republican ceased to be national. Henceforward it was inseparably associated with the Great Rebellion. Not even the action of the Presbyterians in assisting the return of Charles II could outweigh the scandal of the judicial murder of Charles I. Laud saved episcopacy by his death, as, in the previous century, Cranmer had saved the Reformation by his martyrdom. The restoration of the monarchy ensured the restoration of the Church. Both had blundered together, suffered together, fallen together. Now they triumphed together. But they returned to a new world. When the first frenzies of the great Deliverance had passed, men discovered that the "climate of opinion" had changed, and the whole political environment had been altered. The work of the Long Parliament had not been wholly undone. With Charles I died also the absolute monarchy which he embodied. The effect of the twenty years of the Interregnum persisted in the ecclesiastical sphere also. There could no longer be any

question of a religiously united nation. The Tudor conception of a genuinely National Church had perished in
the Civil War. Idealists, like Richard Baxter, might cling
to the project of comprehension, and statesmen, like
William III, might favour it, but the division in men's
minds was too deep, their mutual antagonisms were too
violent. The Puritans, in surrendering their effort to
control the National Church, preferred to pursue an
independent course. The failure of Comprehension was
conditioned by the establishment of Toleration. Puritans
were henceforth to be, not as hitherto Nonconformist
churchmen, but Protestant dissenters.

The domestic fortunes of the English people were never
altogether unaffected by the course of foreign politics.
Between the accession of Elizabeth in 1558 and the Treaty
of Utrecht in 1713, English politics were always connected
with, and generally dominated by, the grand controversy
with Rome, which the Reformation had induced. That
controversy was carried on by monarchs and statesmen,
by ecclesiastics and diplomats, by missionaries and
scholars, by fleets and armies. It told potently on the
position of the Church of England, and therein especially
on the English Episcopate.

So long as the Papacy was the normal ally of the
national enemies, the patriotic sentiment of English
people could not but be vehemently Protestant. Under
the great queen this patriotic Protestantism was visibly
and grandly embodied in the sovereign. The passionate
loyalty of the nation to Elizabeth was as much religious
as patriotic. Protestantism in the Church and Independence in the State were for most English folk synonymous
and identical. But the dynastic policy of the Stuarts
destroyed the supposition of English loyalty. James I
and his unfortunate son were seen to be lukewarm in the
Protestant cause and plausibly suspected of being unfriendly to it at the very time when that cause was

apparently in extreme peril. The bishops adhered to the royal policy, and shared with the sovereign the popular suspicion which it aroused. Accordingly both Protestantism and patriotism found in the Puritans more trustworthy champions than the monarch or the Church. The Parliament finally overthrew the king because in the view of the "man in the street" the king had ceased to be either the trustworthy guardian of Protestantism in the Church or the effective exponent of patriotism in the State.

In 1660 the whole outlook had changed. The Thirty Years' War had ended with a treaty which recognized the indestructibility of Protestantism in Europe. The power of Spain had greatly declined, and France had not yet succeeded to the leadership of the Counter-Reformation.

While thus the old political dread of Rome had largely died down, there were strong reasons why English churchmen should view with suspicion and dislike the vehement Protestantism which had overthrown both Church and monarchy. The Great Rebellion which made Puritanism abhorrent to the Royalists had also made Papistry tolerable. They could not soon forget that Roman Catholics had stood loyally by the king throughout the Civil War; nor when, soured and impoverished by exile, they returned to their old half-ruined homes, and saw the havoc wrought on the parish churches by the Puritan soldiers, were they disposed to welcome proposals of union with their former adversaries. They were, indeed, Protestants, confirmed in their Protestantism by the bitter experiences of exile, but they had become Protestants with a difference. They attached a new importance to every element in the Anglican system which differentiated them from Puritans at home and Calvinists abroad. Most odious of all to the returned Anglicans were the Scottish Presbyterians, for they had forced on England their "solemn League and Covenant", given victory to the English rebels in their war with the king, and crowned their offences by selling their sovereign to his enemies, when in his distress he had placed himself in their power. The absence of bishops in Scotland was not, as in France and Holland, the result of necessity, but the achievement of rebellion. Therefore, it was indefensible and unpardonable. Episcopacy was the most conspicuous feature of the English ecclesiastical system, and it was none the less precious for being also the most offensive to the Presbyterians of Scotland. Accordingly, English churchmen were in the mood to accept, and even to enforce, a theory of the episcopal office, which would have been generally rejected before the Civil War. Then the country gentlemen had for the most part been Puritan in sympathy, and very hostile to Laud's notions of ecclesiastical government. Experience had worked a revolution in their minds.

"What Laud had failed to do", writes Dr Gardiner, "the Long Parliament had gone far to accomplish. It had singled out the Royalist gentlemen and the anti-Calvinist clergymen for special penalties with the result that every Royalist gentleman became not only a sworn foe to Puritanism, but a reverent admirer of doctrines and practices which ten years before he had pronounced to be detestable."[1]
All the evidence we possess shows the entire absence of any popular desire amongst the laity, outside the families of the Royalist gentry and their immediate dependents, to bring back either episcopacy or the Prayer Book (Gardiner).

The lack of popular support even in the hour of apparent triumph is the key to the singular position of the English bishops at the present time. They have never recovered the hold on the popular mind which they possessed before the commotions of the seventeenth century. While the fervour of the political reaction which restored the monarchy persisted, the hierarchy, more closely bound to the sovereign than before, remained

[1] *V. History of the Great Civil War*, III, 200.

secure. Even the misgovernment of Charles and Laud seemed tolerable when seen in contrast with the more recent and exasperating oppression of the Interregnum. Charles and Laud had purged their sins by martyrdom, and were thought of now with more reverence than resentment. Only when the personal policy of the Royal Martyr's sons had driven a wedge between the Crown and the Church were the bishops driven, in the teeth of profession and precedent, into the position of anti-monarchical leaders. Restored to their position of Pro-testant champions, they became again and for the last time the accepted exponents of the national mind and conscience.

The Revolution affected the Episcopate in two ways. On the one hand, it bound the bishops closely to the support of the Protestant Succession, and, on the other hand, it isolated them from the general body of the clergy. The Jacobite sympathies of the latter drew them to the gentry, and alienated them from the Whig govern-ments. Toleration of the Dissenters, steadily defended by the bishops, was odious to their clergy. Throughout the eighteenth century the bishops could not but be regarded rather as State officials than as "fathers in God". The interest of the party in power determined both their selec-tion by the State, and their own interpretation of official duty in the Church. Convocation, the normal instrument of clerical self-assertion, was silenced, but in the House of Lords, where the Episcopate formed an important part of the Whig majority, the bishops could express themselves without the embarrassment and humiliation of clerical opposition. The political situation stimulated bigotry in the clergy, and depressed spirituality in their leaders. The Methodist movement was intellectually barren, and its influence on the Established Church was by no means wholly good. Hidebound by its Calvinistic dogma and by its connexion with Dissent, the Evangelical party was never really at home in the Church of England. It achieved much in the sphere of social reform, and in the conduct of foreign missions, but ecclesiastically it counted for little and achieved nothing. History bequeathed to the bishops a position of isolation as little consistent with the theory of their spiritual office as favourable to their official authority.

II.

The Reformation had immersed the Western Church in the great scandal and weakness of disruption. This disaster was not soon or easily acquiesced in. It weighed heavily on the hearts and consciences of the best Christians on both sides of the "Great Divide"; and when, with the reaffirmation of medievalism by the decisions of the Council of Trent, all prospect of reunion with the Papal Church seemed to be for ever destroyed, the smaller object of Protestant Union was pursued with determination. Controversy extended the range of discussion. Apologists were carried into new fields. Not the Scriptures only, but the whole literature of the primitive Church were seen to be relevant, and were laid under contribution by the divines. The effect of patristic study on the theory of the Episcopate could not but be considerable. English bishops were assumed to possess the attributes of the Catholic bishops of antiquity. The authority based on succession from the Apostles stepped into the place of the authority of the national sovereign, when by the Great Rebellion the nation had repudiated the Church and murdered the sovereign. The Non-jurors were driven by the spur of political disaster to emphasize the lesson of the Interregnum; and they, more evidently than Laud's ecclesiastical supporters, were the precursors of the Tractarians, who, after an interval of nearly a century and a half, reaffirmed the inherent authority of English bishops as the successors of the Apostles. The ailure of the Savoy Conference (1661) to conciliate the Presbyterians by a revision of the Prayer Book was followed by the ejection of the clergy who had not received, and would not receive, episcopal ordination. Thus the emphasis, both sinister and unprecedented, was placed on episcopacy.

The Church of England had always been episcopal, it now became episcopalian, that is, what had been a matter of practical policy became the requirement of religious principle.

The ecclesiastical isolation, which episcopalian theory demanded, was stereotyped by the national isolation which the political wars compelled. Insularity became the temper of the island Church. The eighteenth century, at its start, found England in the course of the protracted war with Louis XIV. It closed when England was in the midst of the still more terrible conflict with Napoleon. Anti-foreign prejudice, kindled and nourished by frequent war, could not but colour and corrupt English religion. The Church of England grew to be self-centred beyond all precedent, and developed a self-complacency which, to the modern Anglican, appears both excessive and irrational. When the "incomparable Establishment", which moved the exultant admiration of our ancestors, is calmly examined in the clear light of modern knowledge, the student must surely marvel at the blinding power of prejudice and the indurating effect of custom. The reconstruction of the effete and corrupt Church by the State, and its spiritual revival, first by the semi-dissenting Evangelicals and then by the semi-Roman Tractarians, have filled the ecclesiastical record of the nineteenth century, and that century brought with it new and more formidable problems of its own, economic, social, and intellectual. These problems, which had become pressing before the Great War, received from that tremendous experience fresh and more menacing gravity. Throughout the period the English bishops have played a prominent if not always a dignified or effective part.

For easily intelligible reasons the Episcopal Bench has attracted more public attention, friendly and hostile, than any other part of the Established system. Few in number indispensable in ecclesiastical theory, and forced as members of one House of Parliament to come into the political sphere, the English bishops have been much discussed and severely judged. Their action and their influence have been notably affected by the method of their appointment.

The appointment of the bishops by the Crown is the most important element in that subordination of the Church to the State which is the essential meaning of its Establishment. For so vital are the functions of the bishops, and so quickly does the personnel of the Episcopal Bench change, that power to nominate the bishops carries with it an effective control of ecclesiastical policy. It has already been pointed out that before the Reformation a working arrangement between the Crown and the Papacy secured for the sovereign an effective control of episcopal appointments. The abolition of Papal authority left the sovereign without a rival, but in fact it did little more than give legislative form to the existing practice. There was nothing revolutionary in the new system. Ever since the time of Constantine when first the Christian Church was established by the State, the consent of the prince seems to have been necessary for the due election of the bishop.

The procedure in episcopal appointments was laid down in the Act of 1534. After enacting that none for the future shall be presented to the Pope for appointment, no annates or first-fruits paid to him, the statute provides that disobedience to the royal mandate will immerse the disobedient ecclesiastics in "the dangers, pains, and penalties of the Statute of Provision and Praemunire".

This statute, while preserving the form of election, destroyed its reality. It is, perhaps, not undeserving the student's notice, that from 1534 to 1939 no Dean and Chapter has ever rejected a royal nominee. Since the revival of ecclesiastical self-consciousness in the nineteenth century, there have been four nominations to bishoprics which have been resented, but in no case has the resentment expressed itself in effective action. Probably the apparent futility of disobedience rather than fear of the legal penalties have led the reluctant deans and canons to obey the law. Even brave men will hardly consent to "endure hardness" for the sake of fictions. The late Lord Selborne maintained that even the fictional election which conditions episcopal appointments in England might not be altogether valueless:

Whatever may be thought of the reasonableness, on the part of the State, of enforcing by severe penalties this right of nomination to Bishoprics, while forms of election are retained, those forms are not (as is often represented) a mere mockery, nor could they be abolished without the loss of some real security against improper appointments. The time has not been, and is not yet, when Churchmen worthy of the name may not be found in those electoral bodies, and in the highest places of the Church, ready to suffer loss of goods, or worse evil, rather than elect or consecrate, under secular compulsion, persons known to be disqualified for so sacred an office.[1]

"Impropriety" in appointments to ecclesiastical office will be variously estimated, as interest, or prejudice, or personal preference may colour the mind: but, perhaps, it is not unreasonable to say that experience indicates that the appointments, which have been most vehemently denounced as "improper", are not, on a large view of ecclesiastical history, such as have most discredited the

[1] V. A Defence of the Church of England against Disestablishment, p. 76.

Church of Christ. Lord Selborne allows that the actual nominations which have been "unacceptable (whether for good or bad reasons) to parties within the Church" have not been without justification:

the results of the same nominations go far to justify a state of the law which does not leave that power (of rejecting the Royal nominee) uncontrolled and irresponsible, in the hands of bodies which might sometimes be too much influenced by temporary excitements and passing gusts of opinion.[1]

The absence of any effective control over episcopal appointments tells unfavourably on the authority of the bishops, and is likely to do so increasingly, as the State becomes more frankly secularized in temper and policy. This is particularly unfortunate in the Church of England, since the law is largely incapable of enforcement, and such discipline as exists is due to the bishop's personal influence rather than to his official authority.

It would certainly be an error to assume that the personal influence of the reigning sovereign is even now slight or ineffectual in the ecclesiastical sphere. The royal supremacy could not, indeed, remain unaffected by the Revolution which had raised William of Orange to the English throne, and transformed the personal or auto-cratic monarchy of the Tudors and Stuarts into the limited or constitutional monarchy of their successors. Apart from any general considerations, the fact that neither William III, who was a Dutch Calvinist, nor the two first Georges, who were German Lutherans (although all three were Protestants and, as such, able to satisfy the requirement of the Act of Settlement by willingness to "join in communion with the Established Church"), were members of the Church of England by training or personal belief could not but affect their practical inter-pretation of the royal supremacy. Under William III the

[1] *V. A Defence of the Church of England against Disestablishment*, p. 77

oyal prerogative in matters ecclesiastical was practically
ransferred to his Anglican queen, Mary II; and, under
he two first Georges, it was exercised by the Whig
ninisters in the interest of the Protestant Succession.
Even in secular politics the dominance of Parliament in
principle secured by the Revolution was in practice only
gradually disclosed. William III kept the control of
oreign policy in his own hands. Anne tried, not very
successfully, to pursue a domestic policy of her own.
George I and George II were foreigners, whose ignorance
of the language and constitution of Great Britain, and
absorption in German politics, made their effective
personal government both in the State and in the Church
practically impossible. They could not but place themselves in the hands of their Whig supporters, and regard
the island kingdom as an appanage of their native Han-
over. George III, secure in his position as sovereign,
"born and bred a Briton", young, ambitious, intensely
self-willed and pertinacious, and withal a good man and
genuinely religious, succeeded in breaking down the
dominance of the Whig nobles, and recovering much of
the monarch's direct share in the control of policy both
in the State and in the Church. The Revolution itself
could not be undone, but its character was obscured and
its effect delayed.

The ecclesiastical prerogative of the Crown, the abuse
of which by James II had been the immediate cause of the
Revolution, could not be exempt from the general process
which substituted parliamentary for personal kingship. It
also had henceforward to be exercised through ministers
who were responsible to Parliament. It must not, however, be forgotten that there were reasons why the
personal influence of the sovereign should be more
potent, and more freely expressed, in the ecclesiastical
sphere than in any other.

The tradition which bound monarch and Church to-

gether had been powerfully strengthened, and in some
sense consecrated, by their common fortunes in the
seventeenth century. Together they had shared the
humiliation of exile, and the almost miraculous triumph
of restoration. In Anglican minds two facts were indissolubly connected, the supremacy of the Church of
England among the Protestant Churches, and its dependence on the monarchy. The last explained and conditioned
the first. "The only thing that makes Protestantism considerable in Christendom is the Church of England", said
South, and immediately added, that "the only thing that
does now cement and confirm the Church of England is
the blood of that blessed martyr" (*sc.* Charles I). Phipps
took the same line when he argued the case of Sacheverell
as one of his counsel in 1710:

All learned men that understand our constitution have
always agreed, that there is such a near relation between the
Church and the Monarchy, such a dependence of the one
upon the other, that where one falls, the other cannot stand.[1]

This tradition, rooted in the very circumstances of the
English Reformation, strongly grounded in Scripture and
in the Formularies of the Church, consecrated by the
mingled memories of a yet recent past, facilitated
self-assertion in the monarch, and disposed religious
Anglicans to welcome the direct exercise of the royal
supremacy.

It was powerfully assisted by the personal piety of the
sovereigns. Mary II, Anne, and George III were themselves deeply religious, and could not but take their
ecclesiastical responsibilities very seriously. The piety of
Mary II has been immortalized by Bishop Burnet; that
of her sister has its lasting memorial in "Queen Anne's
Bounty"; and that of George III has been enshrined in
many well-known anecdotes. It went far to outweigh in

[1] *V. Trial*, p. 210.

the minds of his subjects the many public mischiefs which flowed from his political blunders. Episcopal appoint-ments might reflect the religious conscientiousness of the supreme governor, but they also served his secular interest. Mary II promoted Whigs: and Anne promoted Tories. Both were insistent on orthodoxy and virtue in the men whom they nominated to bishoprics. George III paid much attention to episcopal appointments, and on one occasion succeeded in filling the primacy without the knowledge and against the wishes of his prime minister.

During the nineteenth century the situation of the Church of England has notably changed. The great increase of the population, and the extension of the franchise to include practically the entire adult population of both sexes, have destroyed the social influence of the hierarchy, and greatly lessened the influence of the Church. The prodigious increase of the national wealth has dwarfed into pettiness the endowments of the Estab-lished Church, which once moved the cupidity and in-spired the rhetoric of radical politicians. The political weight of the bishops has almost vanished. In an Upper House of Parliament, which now includes nearly 750 members, the archbishops and bishops number but twenty-six, and the Upper House itself has lost much of its former power and prestige. In this situation it is apparent that personal preferences, whether of sovereigns or of their prime ministers, can have a freer course than in the days when great political interests were served by the administration of the Crown's ecclesiastical patron-age. Public opinion is, indeed, much more vigilant and suspicious than heretofore, and it is much better informed. The popular conscience is sensitive, and highly resentful of any subordination of religion to politics. On the other hand, the temper of the time is not religious. The "climate of opinion" is no longer favourable to churches, and in an atmosphere of general indifference sects and factions have their chance.

The century which has passed since the enactment of the Reform Act (1832) has witnessed a notable change in the point of view from which the royal supremacy has been regarded and exercised. A deeper sense of duty has marked the action of the State, and a heightened consciousness of spiritual claim has disclosed itself in the Church. Partly this is explicable by the extension to the ecclesiastical sphere of the new conception of public responsibility which the victorious Democracy insisted upon in all departments of State action. Partly, it has reflected the influence of the Oxford Movement which carried to the public mind and conscience a new understanding of the Church's character and rights as a spiritual society. Partly, again, it is attributable to the personal quality of the sovereigns and their constitutional advisers. Even those prime ministers who cared little for ecclesiastical interests, and even less for theological developments, were honourably anxious to consult the Church's interest in their exercise of the Crown patronage.

In his admirable biography of Archbishop Davidson (1848–1930) the present Bishop of Chichester (Dr Bell) has described the procedure which was followed in the matter of episcopal appointments during the long period of which the archbishop had direct personal knowledge:

The personal interest which Queen Victoria took in ecclesiastical patronage was unique in its degree: and her influence was also of exceptional quality. And though the Archbishop always maintained that the exercise of such personal influence in a perfectly constitutional form was a valuable factor in securing the best nominations, it was clearly a characteristic rather specially personal to the Queen. Her two successors on the Throne, King Edward and King George, were both alive to the importance of the best Church appointments, and careful to weigh the merits of alternative names before their formal submission; but, generally speaking, they had not the same individual interest in each particular case. In any event, while Randall Davidson's counsel to Queen Victoria was rather personal than official as Dean and Bishop and Clerk of the Closet, his own official responsibility increased when he became Archbishop. It was therefore with the Prime Ministers that he was most directly and closely concerned; and it was they who asked for and received his recommendations when particular vacancies occurred.

During his Primacy seven different statesmen occupied the post of Prime Minister of Great Britain—three of them Conservatives or Unionists (Mr A. J. Balfour, Mr Bonar Law, and Mr Stanley Baldwin), three Liberals (Sir Henry Campbell-Bannerman, Mr Asquith, and Mr Lloyd George), and one belonging to the Labour party (Mr Ramsay MacDonald). They were very different men, with very different traditions. Indeed, three of them were Presbyterians and one a Baptist. They all, though some less strongly than others, realized their responsibilities in relation to Church patronage. They all gave careful attention to the Archbishop's recommendations, and never, in the many instances of episcopal nominations during twenty-five years, did they make a single appointment which they knew to be fundamentally objectionable to the Archbishop. This does not mean that they always took the Archbishop's advice about fitness for a particular see, but that, if the Archbishop insisted that a particular person was wholly unsuitable for the office of Bishop, no Prime Minister ever during these twenty-five years persevered with his name. Some appointments were, of course, less satisfactory than others, and some the Archbishop, left to himself, would not have made; but in every case the merits and qualifications of the person ultimately chosen were carefully and conscientiously considered; and there was no instance whatever of what could fairly be called a mere political job.

The method which the Archbishop usually followed when a vacancy occurred was this. He would, without loss of time, either speak or write to the Prime Minister about the particular bishopric. Some Prime Ministers knew much more than others about the work of a Bishop and the needs of the diocese, and about the personnel of Church leaders—and this was notably the case with Mr Asquith. If necessary, the Archbishop would describe the general conditions of the diocese—or indicate the kind of Bishop required at a particular juncture. As a rule he would discuss both the diocese and the possible successors in conversation with the Prime Minister as well as in correspondence. And, in all but quite exceptional cases, he would furnish the Prime Minister with some three or more names of people to be considered—only very rarely concentrating the whole of his strength on a single person. He would also make his own inquiries from various sources as to names which might have been independently suggested to the Prime Minister—whether for his own or for the Prime Minister's guidance. It may indeed be argued that there was a reluctance to suggest or to appoint extreme men in any school of thought, and that the Bench therefore lacked the presence of some eminent figures who were leaders in a particular Church party. But while party leaders did in fact become Bishops (like Bishop Gore and Bishop Knox), Bishops cannot so easily remain party leaders; and on investigation it would probably be found that the number of men *vere episcopabiles* overlooked on such grounds in the twenty-five years was smaller than might have been expected. The two general impressions left on the mind, after reading the extensive correspondence and memoranda covering this quarter of a century are, first, that though like other human beings they might not always succeed, Prime Minister and Archbishop both did their very best to find the most suitable men for the Bench of Bishops; and second, that Archbishop Davidson exercised a predominating influence upon the character of that Bench.[1]

This admirably lucid statement shows that, while the influence of the sovereign on episcopal appointments is certainly not negligible (since the sovereign's personal judgment and preference can never be unimportant, and

[1] *V. Randall Davidson*, ii, 1236–1238.

may in some circumstances and with respect to some positions be even decisive), the choice of the bishops rests finally with the prime minister, and that a custom has established itself within recent years which requires the prime minister to seek the advice of the Archbishop of Canterbury, and never to ignore his definite disapproval. How far this situation can be regarded as satisfactory is a question which will be variously answered.

That the choice of the bishops should be practically delegated by the prime minister to the Archbishop of Canterbury is an arrangement which is both natural and inexpedient. This arrangement removes an anomaly which may even become a scandal, but it creates a situation which is not without formidable disadvantages. It tends to increase the authority of the primate, which many circumstances have in recent years enhanced, but it diminishes the independence of the bishops. Centralization in Church and State is the prevailing tendency, and it is not without disadvantages in both. The responsibility remains with the prime minister. How far, we must ask, can the prime minister, even when assisted by the counsel of the primate, be rightly or reasonably entrusted with the momentous task of selecting the leaders of a Christian Church?

The champions of the Establishment will maintain that the subordination of the Church to the State, crudely expressed in the method by which the bishops are appointed, is inherent in the position of an established National Church: that in no other way can the lay mind find adequate expression in the ecclesiastical sphere: that, however objectionable the method of episcopal appointments may be in theory, it is justified in practice: that the experience of non-established and disestablished Churches does not suggest that any other method would produce superior results. The weight of these considerations will be finally determined by the conception of the

Church's nature and function in the community, by the meaning attached to spiritual liberty, and by the importance attached to its corporate exercise.

Here it may be sufficient to point out that the argument cannot reasonably be simplified into the single issue of the quality of the individuals nominated to episcopal office. Despotisms may for some purposes be more efficient than democracies, for they have a less impeded course, sometimes they choose their policies with more intelligence and knowledge, and, in their choice of agents for achieving their objects, they may have a wider range of choice. Nevertheless, on a larger and longer view of efficiency, the verdict may be reversed. Despotisms tend to lower the civic quality of the subject population. Democracies tend to improve it. Under the one system, interest is stimulated, knowledge diffused, capacity is developed, discovered, and exercised, with the result that political errors can be corrected. Under the other, a lethargic acquiescence extends in the community, individual ability and enterprise are discouraged, and there is no reserve of civic capacity which can be counted upon to repair the blunders of government. Something similar is true of the Church. The Church also is a society, and in some sense a state. There also, government ought not so to be constituted that the members have no direct, acknowledged, and important share in it. Unless they have such a share they will take little interest in the Church's life, will acquiesce unintelligently in the action of the Hierarchy, and in their personal religion will tend to be ill-informed and undisciplined. In the long run it is better for the Church to run the risks of self-government than to enjoy the advantages of even more efficient control by the most intelligent and sympathetic government from outside. Clericalism and Erastianism are ecclesiastical diseases which have at all times shadowed the history of Christianity very darkly, and both are implicit contradictions of genuine self-government. In the case of appointing the bishops, even if, as is so often asserted but never proved, it were true that the State nomination of the bishops places on the Bench some eminent men who would be little likely in a self-governing Church to be chosen as bishops, it is none the less true that even less eminent individuals, who could command the confidence and loyalty of their clergy and laity, might be spiritually more efficient than the more distinguished nominees of the State, who, because they were such, had no secure hold on either confidence or loyalty. Moreover, the exercise of self-government is as educative in the Church as in the State. Experience, unfortunate as well as happy, may be trusted to bring home to a self-governing Church a sound understanding of the true conditions of spiritual efficiency, and gradually to build up among both clergy and laity a high and exacting standard of episcopal duty.

Moreover, when those instances of State appointment which are most confidently adduced as evidences of its practical excellence are carefully viewed, it is difficult to conclude that the qualities which secured nomination to spiritual office were invariably, or even generally, those which from a religious point of view were most creditable. Burnet, Tillotson, Tait, Temple and Gore were confessedly eminent men who, when they were appointed by the Crown to episcopal office, were not popular with the clergy, and would probably never have been freely chosen as bishops, but it may fairly be thought that their unpopularity had its origin less in inability to recognize their exceptional ability, than in a distrust, not wholly unjustified, of their political or ecclesiastical partisanship. Their behaviour in office went far to disallow the fears which their appointment had aroused, and there are few students of Anglican history who would not now admit that they added distinction to the Church's record, but at

the time a less favourable estimate was not either unreasonable or unfair.

It is often maintained that the much-vaunted character
of the Established Church of England as the most comprehensive communion in Christendom is due mainly to
the unrepresentative quality of the Episcopal Bench, itself
the consequence of State appointment. It may suffice to
answer, that the best service of distinguished men has
most often been rendered before they became bishops;
that the Church has lost much, perhaps more than it has
gained, from the cessation of their intellectual output by
such eminent historians as Stubbs and Creighton; and
that strong personality and outstanding intellectual distinction do not always, or indeed often, go along with the
pastoral temper and governing wisdom which belong to
the making of a great bishop. Moreover, the comprehensiveness of a Church may have its origin in the paralysis
of its internal discipline rather than in the charity and
tolerance of its members. The absence of persecution is
common to both a "city of confusion" and a "city at
unity with itself". Comprehension may be less a virtue
than a scandal. In the case of Churches as in that of
individuals moral quality cannot be improvised or imposed. It must be achieved in the difficult school of
experience. The advance to ecclesiastical tolerance has
ever been lighted, like Nero's gardens, by the flames of
martyrdom.

Nomination by the Crown is followed by the fictional
election by the Dean and Chapter, where such exist, and
by the Archbishop's confirmation. Then the consecration
to the episcopate takes place, after which it remains for
the newly consecrated bishop to take the Oath of Homage
to the sovereign, and to be enthroned in his Cathedral.
The Oath of Homage includes an explicit acknowledgment of the royal supremacy, and is taken with much
solemnity. Kneeling in front of the king, and placing his

hands within the king's, the bishop repeats after the home secretary the following Oath:

I, —, Doctor of Divinity, now elected, confirmed, and consecrated Bishop of —, do hereby declare that your Majesty is the only Supreme Governor of this your realm in spiritual and ecclesiastical things, as well as in temporal, and that no foreign prelate or potentate has any jurisdiction within this realm; and I acknowledge that I hold the said Bishopric, as well the spiritualities as the temporalities thereof, only of your Majesty. And for the same temporalities I do my homage presently to your Majesty. So help me, God.

This language is less Erastian than it sounds, for the "spiritualities" mentioned refer to the ecclesiastical revenue arising from other sources than land.[1]

In the case of the two Archbishops and the Bishops of London, Durham and Winchester, appointment to episcopal office carries the right to a seat in the House of Lords. In the case of the rest of the bishops membership of the Upper House is determined by the seniority of their consecration. The order in which the archbishops and bishops must sit on the Episcopal Bench in the House of Lords was fixed by Henry VIII, and is still followed. On taking their seats, and at the beginning of every new Parliament, the lords spiritual in common with the lords temporal are required to swear allegiance to the sovereign, and sign the Roll of Parliament.

The Thirty-nine Articles make no mention of bishops, but refer to them "in very general words" as "men who have public authority given unto them in the congregation to call and send Ministers into the Lord's vineyard". The framers of the XXIIIrd Article, observes Burnet,

had the state of the several churches before their eyes, that had been differently reformed; and although their own had

[1] V. Bishop Stubbs's note in *Constitutional History*, ch. XIX, sec. 77.

been less forced to go out of the beaten way than any other, yet they knew that all things among themselves had not gone according to those rules that ought to be sacred in regular times: necessity has no law, and is a law to itself.

A similar vagueness had marked the Augsburg Confession of which the XIVth Article is content to declare that "no person ought publicly to teach in the church, or to administer the sacraments, without a regular call (*nisi rite vocatus*)". Some of the Lutheran Churches adopted an episcopal government, and some, the majority, were Presbyterian. Public ordination according to a duly established system was everywhere held to be necessary, but the character of the system was not declared. It might, and did, vary with the actual circumstances in which the Churches had been reformed. Burnet expressed the general opinion of Protestants, as well Anglican as continental, when he wrote:

That which is simply necessary as a mean to preserve the order and union of the body of Christians, and to maintain the reverence due to holy things, is, that no man enter upon any part of the holy ministry, without he be chosen and called to it but such as have an authority so to do: that, I say, is fixed by the Article; but men are left at more liberty as to their thoughts concerning the subject of this lawful authority.

The Preface to the Ordinal states the reason why bishops alone are authorized, in the Church of England, "to call and send Ministers into the Lord's vineyard". It declares and explains the rule of the English Church: it does not lay down a law which must bind all Churches. No condemnation is passed on the different procedure of other Reformed Churches. Cranmer's Preface to the Prayer Book declares a principle which certainly was understood to extend to the case of ecclesiastical polity.

In these our doings we condemn no other nations, nor prescribe anything but to our own people only.

We have already pointed out how, under the twofold influences of political development and continuing controversy, the larger temper of Cranmer gave place to the narrower views of Laud, and how these were still further hardened and narrowed by the Non-jurors and their later disciples, the Tractarians. It is important now, when so many influences are forcing the practical importance of reunion upon the Churches, to recall the generous attitude of the English Reformers, and to insist on its practical implications.

How far, it must be asked, are the bishops controlled by the law in their fulfilment of their duty in the matter of Ordination. The Preface to the Ordinal states the limit of age and gives a general statement of qualifications:

And none shall be admitted a Deacon, except he be twenty-three years of age, unless he have a Faculty. And every man which is to be admitted a Priest shall be full four-and-twenty years old. And every man which is to be ordained or consecrated Bishop shall be fully thirty years of age.

And the Bishop, knowing either by himself, or by sufficient testimony, any person to be a man of virtuous conversation, and without crime; and after examination and trial finding him learned in the Latin tongue, and sufficiently instructed in holy Scripture, may at the times appointed in the Canon, or else, on urgent occasion, upon some other Sunday or Holy-day, in the face of the Church, admit him a Deacon, in such manner and form as hereafter followeth.

The Canons of 1604 prescribe in much detail the conditions under which the bishop may administer Ordination, but so considerable have been the changes in the conditions of English life, which have befallen in the course of more than three centuries, that these canons are of little assistance to the modern bishop. They are not on that account without value, for they disclose the unalterable principles of ecclesiastical administration. The objects to be gained do not vary with time and place:

but the methods employed in order to gain them must vary if they are to match the changing circumstances of society. The XXXVth Canon provides for the examination of candidates for Ordination:

The Bishop before he admit any person to holy Orders, shall diligently examine him in the presence of those Ministers that shall assist him at the Imposition of hands. And if the said Bishop have any lawful impediment, he shall cause the said Ministers carefully to examine every such person so to be ordered. Provided that they who shall assist the Bishop in examining and laying on of hands, shall be of his Cathedral Church if they may conveniently be had, or other sufficient preachers of the same diocese, to the number of three at the least. And if any bishop or Suffragan shall admit any to sacred Orders who is not so qualified and examined, as before we have ordained the Archbishop of this province having notice thereof, and being assisted therein by one Bishop, shall suspend the said Bishop or Suffragan so offending, from making either Deacons or Priests for the space of two years.

The Rubrick in the Prayer Book requires that the archdeacon or his deputy is to present the candidate for Ordination to the bishop, and in answer to the bishop's enquiry as to their fitness for the Ministry "for their learning and godly conversation", to declare that he has "enquired of them and also examined them and thinks them so to be". The examination, according to Lyndwoode, belongs of common right to the archdeacon and in the canon law it is declared to be one branch of his office. It would appear, therefore, that the bishop's authority in the matter of Ordination is not unconditioned at least as respects the intellectual fitness of the candidates.

"With regard to the moral and personal qualifications of the candidate," says Cripps, "it appears that the bishop in

is discretion is the sole and proper judge, unfettered in the
xercise of his judgment by any particular tests which
ormerly have been imposed."[1]

In recent years much thought has been devoted to the
ubject of clerical education. The bishops have insisted on
period of theological study generally at an approved
heological college, and they have required candidates
ither to pass the General Ordination Examination, or an
quivalent. Examining chaplains, carefully chosen from
mong the best educated clergy, academic and parochial,
ave been appointed in every diocese, and their reports
re generally accepted by the bishop as conclusive. So
ar as organization of teaching, and tests of teaching, can
ecure adequacy of knowledge and the discipline of
atural faculty, there would seem to be little improve-
ment possible. But the principal element in all successful
ducation lies outside the control of authority, and cannot
e provided by system however perfect. The quality of
he human material is the ultimately decisive factor, and
: is precisely in respect of that factor that the bishops find
hemselves increasingly baffled. They are very often con-
ronted with intellectually inferior material. It is matter
f common knowledge that the sterility which lies like
blight on all modern civilized communities is most
pparent in the case of those sections of the people which
y tradition and habit are the most highly educated. The
amilies from which in the past the ablest clergymen have
een drawn are now unable to provide boys to serve the
ation in Church and State. All the professions and the
arious grades of the Civil Service are confronted by the
ame shortage of the best human material. The clergy do
ut exhibit a situation which is general. The candidates for
Ordination are now drawn largely from those sections of
ociety which have hitherto been worst educated, and

---

[1] V. Cripps, On Church and Clergy, 8th edition, p. 25.

whose conditions of life have been least favourable t
culture. In these circumstances of disadvantage even tl
best natural faculty has fallen behind in actual achiev
ment. Intellectual traditions take time to grow, an
culture cannot be improvised.

We may reasonably hope that as social conditions a
improved, educational provision extended and improve
leisure increased, and the intelligent use of it more wide
understood, so the deep division between the culture
and the uncultured classes will disappear, and the level
intellectual quality will be raised throughout the con
munity, but this happy result will not be easily or speedi
gained, and for some while to come the manifold di
advantages of poverty will be grave and apparent.
change for the better is certainly taking place. The gre
secondary schools are so rapidly improving, that it is nc
unreasonable to regard them as destined in the future t
displace the oddly called "public schools" from the
primacy in the educational system of the country. It
certain that a large proportion of the candidates fc
Ordination have received their education in the seconda
schools.

A thoughtful student of English society will discern i
the existing situation the promise of better things. Ult
mately the Church will gain by being compelled to recru
its clergy from a larger area. Not a single class but th
entire community will find its representatives in the rank
of the clergy. The process of emancipation has alread
gone a long way. Nothing could be more misleading tha
the statement, which was so often heard on Churc
Defence platforms in those remote days when Churc
Defence could arouse the enthusiasm of English churcl
men, that the Establishment secures to the nation th
priceless boon of "a gentleman and a scholar in ever
parish". The Anglican Clergy in the twentieth centur
are not generally to be described as "gentlemen" an

"scholars". These almost archaic descriptions are not
itly applied to men who have had no better training than
hat which an elementary school crowned by a theological
ollege can provide.

The present Bishop of Bristol (Dr Woodward) gives a
ery disconcerting account of the quality of Ordination
andidates:

It is rare to-day to find a man who has taken first-class
Honours at his University, and uncommon to find even a
econd-class man, in the lists of Ordination candidates.

The bishop adds that "there are signs that the standard
s improving", but acknowledges that "it is definitely
ower than that of candidates for the Civil Service, or,
ndeed, for most of the learned professions". It is not
nerely intellectual inferiority which explains this deplorable situation, but that this factor is an important
nfluence cannot be questioned.[1]

The bishop is provided with an official house in which
he is rightly expected to reside. This may be an unpreten-
ious building such as a successful retired man of business
might provide for himself, or it may be an imposing castle
or palace, centuries old and richly dowered with historical
associations. His first obligation is to furnish it. To do
his may be difficult, if, as is now commonly the case, he
be a man of small means or even of no means at all. He
may be compelled to borrow the requisite money, and
hus inaugurate his episcopate by the novel and humiliat-
ng experience of getting into debt. Moreover, when by
some device or other he has succeeded in furnishing his
official house, he must face another and perhaps even
more serious problem—upkeep. Large houses require
considerable households. Old and famous buildings are

---

[1] V. The Recall to Religion, by various writers (Eyre and Spottis-
voode, 1937), p. 11.

not kept in repair without considerable expenditure. The question of dilapidations may be hard to answer. There may be extensive grounds attached to the episcopal residence, and these will require the services of gardeners. "The fatal opulence of bishops" looms large in clerical pamphlets and in the rhetoric of popular agitators: but it finds no place in the experience of the bishops themselves. They are, almost without exception, not opulent, but financially embarrassed. The official episcopal incomes vary from £2500 in the case of the newest sees to £10,000 in the case of London, and £7000 in that of Durham. These incomes may be so greatly reduced by taxes, rates, mortgages, pension payments, insurance, dilapidation charges and unavoidable official expenditures as to leave a very small sum for house-keeping, diocesan subscriptions, hospitality and personal expenses. If the bishop be married and the father of children, he is in duty bound both to make some modest provision for his wife in the event of his own death, and for the education of his sons and daughters. Unless he be possessed of private means, the bishop has no other source from which to procure the not inconsiderable amount of money required for such unavoidable expenditure than the income of his see. Many of the bishops are unmarried or childless, and few are wholly without some small income of their own. These circumstances tend to conceal the fact and the gravity of episcopal poverty. In these circumstances it is not surprising that the possession of private means tends to become an important qualification for appointment to an English bishopric. No one who has had any knowledge of the considerations which have determined the appointment of the bishops during recent years will be disposed to deny that among them no unimportant place must be assigned to the possession of private means. Money has told, does still tell, indirectly indeed, and without ill motive, but none the less potently and mischievously, in episcopal appointments, and the sin of simony, which has lain so darkly on the record of Christ's Church since the Apostles' time, and which the clergy are required by law formally to disavow, has crept back in disguise. The English bishop in the twentieth century is required to suffer both the inconvenience of "straitened circumstances" and the odium of excessive wealth. He is through no fault of his own in a false position, which compels him to be always making excuses and offering explanations. The "man in the street" imagines that the noble castle or palace in which his diocesan resides, the fact that he is a member of the House of Lords, and the traditional deference which is still commonly shown to him in public, imply and certify the possession of ample revenues, and the custom of prelatic luxury. He notes that the great houses of the laity are often unoccupied and even dismantled because their owners cannot afford to live in them, while the bishops continue to occupy the immemorial homes of feudal pride and Erastian pomp. Is it astonishing that he finds it hard to believe that within the great houses financial embarrassment shadows the attenuated hospitality and frugal housekeeping of the diocesan?

Two arguments, which have often in the past been urged with force and eloquence, have been emptied of relevance by the course of social and political development. It may have been true, when the landed aristocracy dominated the country, that religion gained by the fact that the bishops, as themselves great territorial magnates, were able to meet on equal terms their secular equivalents in county and Parliament. But now the landed aristocracy, broken by taxation and largely absent from its immemorial homes, counts for little. It is fading out from rural life. England is overwhelmingly industrial, and popular opinion is ceasing to be tolerant of any form of social inequality. The spiritual authority of the English bishop would probably be increased rather than lessened if the circumstances in which he lives did not perplex and offend the popular conscience.

It has been pleaded that the presence of the bishops in the House of Lords has more than justified itself by the public witness which they are thus enabled to bear to principles and causes which, apart from their advocacy, might easily be neglected or forgotten. But reflexion will make evident that in this plea there is really little validity. Even if it could be shown that episcopal activity in the House of Lords has been sometimes serviceable to those high concerns which are confessedly congruous with the spiritual character, can it be denied that such occasions have been few, and that for the most part the bishops in the House of Lords have followed the conventional lines of secular politics? Is it not notorious that few arguments against the Establishment are more effective with the multitude than a cold recital of episcopal action in Parliament? " *The fathers have eaten sour grapes, and the children's teeth are set on edge.*"

The modern bishops are paying for the class-conscious selfishness of their predecessors, for whose conduct they cannot equitably be held responsible. But the fact remains that their spiritual influence now is not assisted by their parliamentary reputation in the past. Moreover, there is no longer any apparent need of bishops to champion in Parliament the cause of social reformation. That cause commends itself readily to popular favour, and therefore none can count so securely on patrons and spokesmen. There is no lack of generous lay peers, able, ambitious, and variously distinguished, who can be trusted to express public opinion, and to promote social reform. In this matter it may be said that " *all the Lord's people are prophets*". The bishops need not be in Parliament in order to promote good causes. The pulpit, the platform, and the press are ready to their hand, and these are more effective than discussions in Parliament for the championship of good causes.

The English bishop, then, by living more simply, and losing his traditional state in society and his privileged position in Parliament, might well be better placed for the performance of his primary task of carrying religion effectively into the national life.

CHAPTER 6

THE ENGLISH CLERGY

In this chapter we are concerned with the clergy, and we shall consider both their social type and their intellectual equipment.

It is probably true that the majority of English clergymen have always been drawn from the humbler ranks of society, not often from the humblest, but mostly from that great intermediate class which now includes the superior artisans and the lower middle class. In the Middle Ages this would appear to have been the case. If it be true that the greater positions in the Hierarchy were in that age of dominant privilege almost monopolized by nobles and officials, yet Ordination was withholden from none, and the door of preferment was never wholly closed to humble merit. The clergy were a reflexion of the nation itself.

The Reformation affected the position of the English clergy in several respects. It lessened their spiritual authority, greatly reduced their number, and by abolishing the rule of celibacy tended to make the clerical profession hereditary. The marriage of the clergy has not been an unmixed advantage. In the adverse scale of the balances must certainly be placed the secularizing influence of wife and family. When, at a later period, religious denominations were multiplied, and the clergy lost their monopoly of education in the universities, their public importance declined. These consequences of the Reformation have been momentous in their cumulative effect on the position and influence of the Church of England.

I. LOSS OF OFFICIAL AUTHORITY

The loss of consequence involved for the ordinary clergyman by the substitution of the pastoral for the sacerdotal conception of the Christian ministry can hardly be overstated. His time-honoured functions were drastically reduced. Between the medieval priest and the modern parson there is a chasm which cannot be bridged. A different hinterland of religious suggestion lies behind the one, and behind the other. The sacerdotal aspect of the ministry was not in express words disallowed, but it was so effectually obscured as to fall out of general acceptance. The word "priest" remained, but it was carefully explained by Archbishop Whitgift to mean no more than presbyter, and it is carefully avoided in official documents. Except when referring to the Ordinal, the Canons of 1604 invariably employ the word "minister" instead of "priest". The suggestion of the official usage was emphasized by the destruction of the altars in the parish churches, the disappearance of the confessional boxes, and the abandonment of the Eucharistic vestments. In abolishing the Mass the Reformers had removed the central feature of the medieval system. In abolishing the Confessional, even while in common with most of the continental Reformers retaining confession, the direct contact of the priest with the parishioner was removed.

It is, of course, true that the English Reformers, while thus they drastically changed the traditional system, never dreamed of creating a new Church. The Preface to the Ordinal is on this point explicit and final.

At a later period this conservative attitude on the

subject of ecclesiastical polity led to consequences of great importance, but its full implications were not at first perceived. The Reformed Churches stood together on doctrinal issues which in their judgment pertained to the essentials of religion. Forms of polity were thought of as relatively unimportant matters which lay within the control of the independent churches. The Apostolic claim for the episcopal régime neither conciliated the Papist, nor persuaded the Puritan; the one stood by the nearer precedent of the medieval church which owned the Apostolic authority of St Peter's successor, the other stood by the text of Scripture which they agreed to regard as authorizing the rule of presbyters.

That the English clergy received episcopal ordination after the fashion required in the revised Ordinal did nothing to avert the impoverishment of the clerical office which the Reformation involved. For the layman judged the priest, not by the theory which validated ministry, of which indeed he knew little, but by the powers which that Ordination conveyed, and most of these, he was now authoritatively assured, had been taken away.

II. REDUCTION IN NUMBER

The Reformation reduced greatly the number of the clergy. Not only did the dissolution of the monastic foundations get rid of the entire multitude of the regulars, but the changes of doctrine and discipline destroyed the *raison d'être* of many others. Mass priests could not survive the Mass. The cathedrals and parish churches, emptied of their shrines, altars, and confessional boxes, needed the services of comparatively few clergy. It is true that the theory of pastoral ministry was in the new Ordinal set forth in lofty and moving language, but the expression of that theory in pastoral practice was left mainly to the voluntary efforts of the parish clergy, since their statutory obligations were sufficiently meagre. In any case, the clergy were now so few and scattered that their importance visibly dwindled, and their influence as a factor in the national life became comparatively slight.

Here it is, perhaps, important to interpose a note of caution. The number of the clergy is no secure indication of the power of the Church, for the process of limiting the functions of the ordained clergy, which had already begun, was by the Reformation notably stimulated, and still proceeds. Any serious attempt to estimate the influence of the Church before and after the religious revolution of the sixteenth century must make full allowance for change in the meaning of the Spiritualty.

The vast hierarchy of officials, commissioned indeed by the modern State, but charged to carry on the manifold labours of the medieval Church, which is concerned with the education, health, relief, recreation, and discipline of the nation, is a relatively greater factor in the community than was the Church in the medieval State during what are called the Ages of Faith. The articulated system of modern civilization in becoming secularized has unquestionably gained in practical efficiency. The State has access to resources of knowledge and strength which the Church in its proudest dominance has never possessed; and, within the secular sphere, it is able to achieve much that the Church could never have reasonably attempted. The clergy, ousted by lay competition from one sphere of activity after another, have inevitably suffered a great and apparent diminution of social consequence.

The process, which the Reformation by lessening the religious importance of the clergy so powerfully stimulated, has continued, and has now almost reached conclusion. The great secular professions have developed independently of the Hierarchy which once contained and controlled them all. Laud (*ob.* 1645) ended the famous succession of ecclesiastical statesmen, and Robinson (*ob.*

1723) was the last of the long succession of ecclesiastical diplomatists. The medical profession, inheriting its principles and ideals from the great masters of ancient Greece, and in the Middle Ages borrowing its methods from Jews and Saracens, was regarded with suspicion by the medieval Church. Its association with infidels and heretics was too apparent, and its dabbling in the proscribed pseudo-sciences of magic and astrology was too frequent. Only with the emergence of modern science in the sixteenth and seventeenth centuries did medical and surgical practice enter on that triumphant progress which has contributed to modern civilization its clearest title to supremacy. Education has retained longest its ancient connexion with the Church, but in this sphere also the secularizing tendency has been present, and now appears to be prevailing. The abolition of religious tests in the universities, and the establishment of a system of compulsory national education in the parishes, went far to destroy the privileged position of the English clergy. Whatever may have been the gain to the nation, there can be little doubt as to the nature and extent of the loss to the Church. To this point we shall return. Here it is sufficient to indicate the effect on the position of the clergy.

One modern profession, the influence of which it is difficult to overstate, has passed from complete subordination to the Hierarchy to complete independence— Journalism. The Press, as we know it now, may fairly be described as a product of the Reformation. How far it can rightly be regarded as the auxiliary of the Church, and how far as the Church's unfriendly critic, will be variously decided. One thing is certain. The Press has almost completely replaced the Church as the instrument by which public opinion is fashioned. Governments now have no need to "tune" the pulpits: they get better results by "inspiring" the newspapers. The political importance of the parochial clergy has almost completely disppeared; and this fact has told on their general influence. Other causes, social and economic, have tended in the same direction. These we must discuss later. The clergy, some 16,000 in number, distributed through a population of nearly forty millions, and limited to functions which lie outside the normal concern of most of their parishioners, are seen in modern England as a small and rather enigmatic profession, not sufficiently powerful or wealthy to be politically important, and too obscure and disorganized to be socially considerable. In history and literature the Hierarchy looms large, but it has ceased to rank among the greater elements of the national life. It is, indeed, the case that on occasions of national importance, such as the Coronation or the Jubilee Celebration of the reigning monarch, the Hierarchy resumes an almost medieval impressiveness, but these occasions only emphasize the contrast between the archaic splendour of the Establishment and the normal obscurity of the incumbents.

III. MARRIAGE OF THE CLERGY

The Reformation brought with it the liberation of the English clergy from the medieval rule of celibacy. That rule expressed the triumph of pseudo-asceticism in the Western Church, and its enforcement secured the dominance of the Papacy. The priesthood became a separate order of men, bound by an arbitrary discipline, which excluded them from the natural function and duty of mankind, and deprived them of the humanizing influence of domestic life. The prohibition of marriage, as inconsistent with the highest standard of purity, told with disastrous effect on the position of the female sex, and stamped sexual relations as in some sense and measure defiling. Chastity was exalted, but purity was endangered. The history of clerical celibacy includes the most pathetic and the most shameful pages of the Church's record, for it is the story of a relentless conflict between sacerdotal theory and ecclesiastical policy, on the one side, and elemental human instincts and sympathies, on the other. The rule of celibacy had been imposed with much difficulty on the clergy everywhere but especially in England, where it raised against itself, not only the general habit of the insular Church, but also the strong domestic feeling of the people. Monasticism, nowhere stronger than in England, did certainly facilitate the success of the innovation, yet several generations passed before celibacy was generally enforced. The wives of the clergy disappeared, but in many cases they were replaced by the concubines who fill so large a place in the proceedings of medieval councils. It is a miserable story. Nothing is more certain than that the moral reputation of the medieval priesthood was scandalously low. It was not the least element in the strength of the Reformers that they proclaimed a higher morality than that of the medieval Church. The restoration to the clergy of the right to marry was required both by Scripture and by Christian antiquity, and it was insisted on by all the Reformers as well on the continent as in England. Yet this right in the case of the English clergyman was not secured without difficulty and delay. Henry VIII, as might have been expected from so orthodox a monarch, was vehemently opposed to it. The statute of Edward VI which legalized clerical marriages was repealed by Mary, and not revived by Elizabeth. The queen made no secret of her dislike of parsons' wives, whom she humiliated and insulted whenever occasion offered. The Injunctions of 1559 imposed degrading conditions on the marriages of the clergy, which indeed were so legally doubtful that those who married were obliged formally to have their children legitimated. Not even Archbishop Parker was exempted from this humiliating requirement. While thus

he State was lukewarm or hostile, the Church did not
esitate. In the Forty-two Articles it was declared that

Bishops, priests, and deacons are not commanded by
God's law to vow the estate of a single life or to abstain
from marriage.

In 1563 the Edwardian Articles were revised and issued
as the Thirty-nine Articles which are still included in the
standard formularies of the Church of England. The
XXXIInd Article, "Of the Marriage of Priests", runs
thus:

Bishops, Priests, and Deacons, are not commanded by
God's Law, either to vow the estate of single life, or to
abstain from marriage: therefore it is lawful also for them,
as for all other Christian men, to marry at their own discretion, as they shall judge the same to serve better to
godliness.

In spite of these ecclesiastical pronouncements a suspicion of illegality still attached to the marriages of the
clergy. The Millenary Petition addressed to James I at
his accession included a request for the restoration of the
laws of Edward VI as to marriage of priests. This request
was granted, and from the first year of James I clerical
marriage in England has been authorized by statute.

The prejudices of the people long survived the prohibition of the law: and it is more than probable that
these went far to provide their own justification. So long
as public opinion regarded clerical marriage with dis-
favour, and the wives of the clergy found themselves
excluded from respectable society, it is probable that the
clergy were driven to take their wives from the least
estimable of the sex. As the medieval tradition died out,
the prejudice which it had included disappeared. Experience disclosed the moral beauty and social service of
many parsons' wives. It was discovered that whatever

may be the social limitations implicit in their position, i
opens a door to respect and influence greater than falls
to the lot of most women. The only disadvantage under
which the clergyman now stands in the matter of marriage
arises not from the contempt with which the clergyman's
wife is regarded, but from the high estimate which now
commonly obtains as to her character and life. The gibing
description of the clergyman's wife as his "unpaid
curate" only expresses the fact, so honourable to both,
that in his wife the parish priest so often finds his most
effective and understanding colleague, that her loyal
partnership may fairly be taken for granted.

The effect of marriage on the temper and habit of the
English clergy has not been wholly beneficial. Uxorious-
ness, secularity, and nepotism are shadows on domestic
life whether clerical or lay, but these shadows are particularly dark when they are seen to rest on the domestic
life of one who is pledged to be independent, unworldly,
and impartial.

The parson's family has deserved well of the nation,
for it has contributed in exceptional measure men of
character and ability who have served the State on every
plane of public service. It has often been a valuable
factor in the parson's performance of duty, forming a
strong link between himself and his parishioners. He is
seen to be personally sustaining the burden of family
care, and, if (as often is the case) he be living in the spirit
of his Ordination pledge, he is acknowledged to be setting
before his people the example of a Christian home, and
thus strengthening his public ministry by the congruous
witness of his private habit. But the clergy are for the
most part very poor men, and poverty may compel an
anxiety for the family interest which is not easily harmonized with personal duty. The poor clergyman is
tempted to make the needs of his wife and children an
excuse for complaisance, time-serving, place-hunting, and

The Parish Church, Bury, Sussex

even naked and not always honest mendicancy, and thus to compromise, enfeeble, and even paralyse his spiritual influence.

IV. TENDENCY TO MAKE THE CLERGY AN HEREDITARY PROFESSION

One consequence of clerical marriage is that the clerical profession has followed the normal course of all human avocations by becoming largely hereditary; and this circumstance has not been an unmixed gain to the Church. If it be true that many admirable clergymen have been "sons of the manse", it is also true that clerical patrons are not well placed for judging equitably the fitness of sons and nephews for appointment to benefices.

Moreover, the essence of a caste is its hereditary character, and in so far as the English clergy are hereditary, they conform to the character of a caste. The area of society which is directly affected by the tenure of clerical office and property is restricted when the clergy are drawn from clerical households. It is not extravagant to find one reason for the small following in the community which the clergy possess in the fact that they are largely in birth and tradition clerical. This fact, however, is losing importance as the clergy are recruited from the non-professional classes, and are themselves becoming increasingly and disconcertingly childless. How far is there justification for the statement, so frequently made by the critics of the Church of England, that it is a "class Church", i.e. that it reflects the prejudices, serves the interests, and accepts the ideals of a section of the people? It must, of course, be admitted that, as educated men holding property, the English clergy are likely to share the outlook of other educated and property-holding men, but education and the tenure of property are not distinctive of one class, though more apparent in some classes than in others. Are the clergy so closely associated with one class as to be disqualified for genuinely national service? It is worth noting that students of Anglicanism differ as to the particular class with which the Anglican clergy are thought to be associated. Brewer maintained that "the Reformed Church of England has always found its strongest hold in the middle classes of this country".[1] Von Döllinger took a different view:

There is no Church that is so completely and thoroughly as the Anglican the product and expression of the wants and wishes, the modes of thought and cast of character, not of a certain nationality, but of a fragment of a nation, namely, the rich, fashionable, and cultivated classes. It is the religion of deportment, of gentility, of clerical reserve.[2]

Mark Pattison, the famous rector of Lincoln College, Oxford, was influenced as much by his academic experience as by his historical knowledge when he wrote the following description of Anglicanism:

Anglicanism is not, as is often repeated by ill-informed assailants, an artificial creation of Laud and the courtier-bishops of Charles I, but the legitimate and necessary form which the Church intelligence of England took, as soon as it had time to repose from the turbulence and volcanic up-heaving of the religious revolution. Thus it is that Anglicanism has always been the religion of the educated classes exclusively. It has never at any period been national and popular, because it implies more historical information and a wider political horizon than can be possessed by the peasant or the artisan. The masses require an intuitional religion, such as is provided by the grosser forms of Dissent in Great Britain, or a ceremonial of drill and parade, such as the Latin and Greek Churches offer to their subject populations.[3]

[1] V. Henry VIII, p. 470.
[2] V. The Church and the Churches, p. 145.
[3] V. Essays (Oxford, 1889), p. 267.

The late Lord Selborne, in his well-known *Defence of the Church of England against Disestablishment*, published in 1886, discussed the accusation of political partisanship urged with much vehemence against the English clergy. He distinguished between the legitimate conservatism of a Christian Church, and the indefensible conservatism of individual clergymen. Whatever may be thought of his apology for the English clergy, who, when he wrote, had thrown themselves with much energy into the defence of the Establishment, few will dispute the soundness of his main argument.

Lord Selborne was an eminent Victorian, and he was not required to face the questions which now confuse and dominate political conflict. The matters which loomed so large on the statesman's horizon in his day have a petty and almost squalid aspect in ours. None the less his words are not without relevance to the existing situation. Christianity has requirements of its own, which no Church rightly described as Christian can repudiate. The clergy must not be blamed for opinions and sympathies which are determined, not by their own social type and economic interest, but by their character as professed exponents of the Christian religion. Yet it is certainly true that social type and economic interest are powerful influences both in shaping individual opinion, and in determining the direction of individual sympathy. How far is it true in the case of the English clergy as a whole that the influences which bear on them are those which normally belong to a single class? The answer to this question must take account of two considerations, the one general, affecting the Christian Church itself, the other particular, affecting the Church of England. The student of ecclesiastical history cannot fail to observe, with astonishment, and perhaps with repugnance, the parasitic aspect of the Church in human society. Its polity is closely modelled on contemporary secular patterns; its theology accepts, incorporates, and assimilates the current philosophical systems: its science is taken without demur from its age: even its moral standards reflect with disconcerting fidelity the reigning mundane conventions. The strange and startling paradoxes of Christian history have their origin in the principle and process of assimilation which distinguish the history of Christianity, "*We have this treasure in earthen vessels*", writes the Apostle. Christianity always "stoops to conquer": and sometimes it has stooped very low, and gained but a Pyrrhic victory. The Christian clergy have always tended to "worship the rising sun". Erastianism is natural to them. If, therefore, in a democratic age, the clergy also shall become democratic in faith and feeling, they will but exhibit a familiar feature. Democracy will be entering on its heritage, when it garners the benediction of the Hierarchy. The Empire, Feudalism, the Landed Class, the Middle Class, in the past, the organized powers of "Big Money" and "Labour" to-day: perhaps (who knows?), the "Proletariat" to-morrow. Whatever the centre of political dominance may be, it will command the parasitic homage of the clergy.

This general consideration is certainly being afforced by the fact, to which allusion has already been made, that the English clergy are now being largely drawn from the artisan and lower middle class. It is certainly significant that, coincidently with the Ordination of artisan-born clergy, a new note is becoming audible in clerical discussions. There is an insistence on the clergyman's "rights", on the excessive duration of his work, on his claim to increased income, even on the propriety and possibility of combination in his professional interest. This unpleasant phenomenon is most easily explained by the circumstance that many of the clergy, born and bred in the atmosphere of trade-unionism, have almost unconsciously seen their obligations as clergymen in the light of trade-unionist standards and ideals. However explicable the fact may be, it is deplorable, for nothing could be more contrary to the true notion of spiritual ministry than the insistence on professional rights and the practice of close bargaining which naturally, perhaps inevitably, determine the procedure of the trade unions. More commonly, however, the temptation of the humbly born clergyman lies in the opposite direction, not in the retention of his class prejudices, but in his exchanging them for the prejudices of the class into which Ordination has carried him. It is here that a grave problem emerges which, for its solution, demands the anxious concern of the Church. It may be stated thus: Since it is probable that in the future the majority of clergymen will be drawn from the wage-earning class, how, in the actual circumstances of the nation, can integrity of motive be secured, and alienation from the wage-earning class be averted? There is the further problem, how to secure equality of educational opportunity for Ordination candidates who come from the wage-earning class.

It is, perhaps, worth while to examine the three points in order, vocation, education, and professional habit.

(i) Most of the candidates will have been led to seek Ordination by their parish clergyman, who has suggested the possibility and encouraged the hope. The precocious pietism of boyhood is easily directed towards a career which appeals to his emotions and at the same time stirs his ambitions. His family regard with favour a career which, from their point of view, is dignified, easy, and well-paid. It is not always remembered, especially when moving descriptions of clerical poverty are unceasing, that the career of an English clergyman does not *to the eyes of the wage-earners* accord with this picture of his life. The incumbent of an industrial parish is known to live in a good house, to enjoy an income greatly in excess of the normal rate of wages, to have the priceless boon, for which wage-earners vainly long, of secure employment, and to be bound to work which, as they regard it, is neither difficult, nor exhausting, nor excessively prolonged. They note that the clergyman's annual holiday is far more extended than any they can hope for, and that his normal work is so completely under his own control that he can take a day off whenever he pleases. Of course in all this there is much ignorance, and some injustice: but that it is, in the actual circumstances, an almost inevitable picture of the parson's position, can hardly be questioned. In the vulgar phrase, the clergyman has *in the view of his parishioners* a "soft job". This is the picture of the clergyman's life which the average wage-earner's son will be encouraged to form, and its effect on the motive with which he is led to profess a "vocation" for the Christian ministry will hardly be wholesome.

(ii) If the wage-earner's son be intelligent and hardworking, as well as devout—and many are certainly so to be described—he may reasonably hope, with the assistance of county-council scholarships, diocesan grants, and private aid, to get to the university. Has he, therefore, enjoyed that "equality of educational opportunity" which is commonly assumed to be his civic right? Far from it: equality in the cardinal factors of genuine education have not been in his case secured, and without them he must needs be grievously handicapped. For he lacks the "foundation" of a well-directed school training; and (perhaps even more serious) he is without the discipline, the mental stimulus, and the sympathetic support of a cultured home. Examinations which are passed with ease by the public-school boy are formidable to the boy who has enjoyed nothing better than an elementary school training. His toil is out of all proportion to his achievement. That is not all. The vacations go far towards undoing the results of the terms. His mind needs in special measure the stimulus and refreshment of an adequate and wisely-ordered holiday; but when term ends he must go back to the uninspiring and unhelpful environment of his youth. He is dulled and wearied by a bookless, uncultivated home. The benevolent millionaire who would devote some part of his wealth to the provision of a Vacation Fund, to be administered by the College authorities in the interest of the poorer students, would go far towards securing for them that equality of educational opportunity which at present they so evidently lack.

(iii) When the wage-earner's son has been ordained and is settled in his pastoral work, first as stipendiary curate, and, then (after a dangerously short interval) as the incumbent of a parish, he finds himself in a new world which has little in common with that in which he was born and bred. Does he become a reconciling factor between the two? Too often, alas, he is precisely the reverse. He may carry himself in such wise, and so order his family, as even to emphasize the calamitous breach. If he could retain the simple tastes and modest expenditure of the artisan, and combine it with the refinement, the intellectual interest, and the moral attitude of an educated clergyman, his influence as an interpreting and reconciling factor in the class-riven society of England could not but be great and far-reaching.

Perhaps this is too much to expect, and the expulsion of class prejudices and ideals from the English clergy will only be gained as one result of that general transformation of social life which has already proceeded far, and proceeds now at an ever-accelerating pace. The Communist's ideal of a classless society may be unattainable, but it is not excessive to look forward to a far greater measure of genuine economic and social equality than exists at present. Assuredly the Church's spiritual task will be facilitated by the removal of one of the most obstinate of all the stumbling-blocks which now hinder its fulfilment of duty.

CHAPTER 7

THE PAROCHIAL
SYSTEM

The parochial system was not an original feature of English Christianity. First came the monastic mission: then, for the due ordering of the converts, the bishop with his body of itinerating clergy: then, a settled ministry providing for the spiritual needs of the little local communities. This provision gradually took shape in the parochial system, which has remained substantially unaltered for thirteen centuries. The old, and not even yet entirely abandoned, view, that Archbishop Theodore was its author, has no real foundation. In many cases local organization was simplified and facilitated by the manner of the original conversion. When the pagan landowner abandoned his ancestral paganism, and received baptism, he carried with him his tenants and dependents. In that case the Christian priest simply stepped into the place of his pagan predecessor, possessing his endowment, and conducting the new worship in the old temple. "There is no doubt", writes the late Professor Watson, "that parochial glebe passed unchanged, with the same rights and the same liabilities, from the last pagan to the first Christian priest. This needed no public sanction."

As the entire country became Christian, a more general provision was requisite, and this was made by the tithe, which still forms the principal part of the parochial endowment. Its origin has been much debated, but does not appear to be either obscure or difficult to understand.

From the time of St Cyprian (*ob*. 257), who (in the words of Bishop Lightfoot) "treated all the passages of the Old Testament which refer to the privileges, the sanctions, the duties, and the responsibilities of the Aaronic priesthood as applying to the officers of the Christian Church", the notion that Christians were bound in conscience to pay tithes to the clergy had been current in the Church, and had generally established itself in Christian minds long before the Conversion of the English. At first, and for some centuries, the payment was voluntary, or enforced by such moral pressure as could be brought to bear, but as the power and prestige of the clergy advanced, and the law of the State reflected ecclesiastical ideals of civic obligation more closely, the payment of tithe was legally enforced. The tithe-owner long retained his right to allocate his tithe to the church of his choice; but, as time passed, this right was lost, and he was required to pay the tithe to the rector of the parish, or to the rector's substitute, the vicar.

The familiar distinction between rectors and vicars has its explanation in the practice of "appropriating" local tithes to the monasteries. The duties of the cure were performed by the monks, and the tithes were paid to the monastery. This was an arrangement which might but too easily conflict with the spiritual interest of the parishioners, or with the jurisdiction of the bishop, or with both.

Pope Innocent III, by the 32nd canon of the great Lateran Council of 1215, enacted that vicars should receive an adequate proportion of the parochial income, and hold their office in perpetuity:

"This canon", observes Mr Hartridge, "may be termed the Magna Carta of the parish priest. Often ignored, often overridden, often misinterpreted, it stood firm throughout the Middle Ages, as the bedrock of the vicarage system. The *perpetual* vicar, to whom it refers, that is, the vicar who was instituted by the bishop and who could not be removed save by force of judicial procedure, and who had a separate endowment of his own, is the typical vicar of that system. A *perpetual* holder of any benefice could only be removed by the proper authorities for crimes and misuse of his office, and could not even resign his benefice without special permit. He was wedded to it for life.[1]

The monasteries as rectors of appropriated parishes kept to their own use the larger part of the income. "Within three hundred years from the conquest more than a third, and among them the richest, of all the parishes of England were appropriated."[2]

The incumbent of an English parish enjoys a measure of independence in the exercise of his ministry which is probably both unprecedented and unparalleled. Neither the Roman priest nor the Protestant minister is so little controlled by authority as the Anglican parson, for while the priest is subject to his bishop, and the minister to his congregation, the parson, within the large limit of the law, which regards his cure of souls as his personal property, can ignore both. This singular situation, as irrational as it is irreligious, is the result of a long history, and now gives distinctive character to the parochial system. The problems of personal belief implicit in Subscription must have been faced, and in some sense and measure solved, at Ordination, but his institution to a cure of souls confronts the incumbent with a practical problem which cannot be avoided. How will he interpret his definite pledge to "use the form in the said Book (*sc.* the Book of Common Prayer) prescribed, and none other, except so far as shall be ordered by lawful authority"? Nothing, it might well be thought, could be simpler or more

[1] *V.* Hartridge, *A History of Vicarages in the Middle Ages*, p. 21.
[2] *V.* Makower, p. 329.

explicit. The Book is in his hand: the services are straight-forward; the ceremonial is neither elaborate nor com-plicated; the directing rubricks are apparently lucid enough. What can he desire more? If he find himself in doubt as to the meaning of the authoritative text, the rubrick bids him have recourse for guidance to the ordinary, that is, to his bishop, or, if he shall still be unsatisfied, to carry his difficulty to the archbishop of the Province. Surely in these circumstances he can never be in any real doubt as to his duty. But the position is not so simple.

The actual procedure in the parishes varies wonder-fully. Not ecclesiastical uniformity but congregational particularism is now the prevailing aspect of the Estab-lished Church. The Act of Uniformity has somehow been made to authorize an astonishing variety of parochial worship. The rubricks of the Prayer Book, as read by the incumbents who are pledged to obey them, do not appear to be either adequate in their range, or lucid in their direction. The bishops are known to differ widely in their interpretations of the law, and their legal advisers, the diocesan chancellors, exhibit a puzzling variety of exe-getic method and official determination. The subtle casuistry of party is ever adding its own contribution to the inevitable confusion.

What, it is asked in the tone of a genuine perplexity, is the "lawful authority" which may authorize departures from the requirements of the prescribed book? Is it some secular authority, such as the Crown, or the Law Courts, or the Houses of Parliament? Is it an ecclesiastical authority, Convocation, or the united Episcopate, or the archbishop, or the bishop of the diocese? Ought we to ignore the unrepealed canons of the pre-Reformation Church, which do confessedly govern the procedure of the modern Church of England in some matters? And what precisely is meant by a departure from the rubrick being "ordered"? Must there be a specific command? or may the incumbent infer approval from absence of prohibition? May he not interpret his diocesan's inaction as acquiescence, or even as approval? Such questions are frequently and keenly debated, and yet it is not easy to perceive any adequate occasion for them.

The utmost precision of language appears to be inadequate to convey to the modern English clergy the intention of the law. Thus in the just-mentioned case of the statutory declaration, it is hard for the plain man to understand how there can be any obscurity. "Ordered by lawful authority" must surely mean "ordered by an authority which is legally competent to override the rubric". Since the rubric is statutory (for the Prayer Book is a schedule of an Act of Parliament), such a competent authority could only be another Act of Parliament. Such an Act was passed in 1872, but it has been as unsuccessful as its predecessor in making its meaning clear. The Act of Uniformity Amendment Act authorized the use, in certain circumstances, of a special or additional form of service, approved by the ordinary, but required that such service should contain nothing (with the exception of anthems or hymns) which does not form part of the Holy Scriptures or the Book of Common Prayer. It would seem impossible to devise a clearer statement, yet no less a person than Archbishop Temple felt free to assume its ambiguity. His biographer records that "he maintained firmly the broad interpretation, namely, that it sufficed that nothing should be introduced that was not in harmony with the spirit of the Book of Common Prayer".[1] A little reflection will make it evident that this is less a "broad interpretation" of the statute than its abrogation; for, since the ordinary himself must determine what is, or is not, "in harmony with

[1] V. Memoirs of Archbishop Temple (London, 1906), II, 274.

the spirit of the Book of Common Prayer", he is really left completely free. Moreover, the words of the Act extend to the Holy Scripture as well as to the Prayer Book, and ecclesiastical history has proved that there is no moral or doctrinal aberration which is not, in the view of its advocates, "in harmony with the spirit" of the Scripture. When such interpretation could find acceptance at Lambeth, it is not surprising that it made its way easily into the rectories and vicarages. That it has done so is indeed notorious.

All this is bad enough, but it is worsened by the fact that neither the incumbents nor the parishioners are properly free agents. Both are affected, perhaps even dominated, by external influences. The immemorial and irremovable dissidence on first principles, which is the congenital weakness of the Established Church, thrusts itself into parochial life; and at every change of incumbency becomes apparent. The solution of the practical problem of his own procedure, which confronts every newly instituted incumbent, has not been rendered easier by the Enabling Act (A.D. 1919), which has set up in his parish a parochial church council possessed of large but vague powers, which he cannot ignore, which he must consult, and which he may not be able to conciliate. He will not always be suffered to find a way through his difficulties without interference from outside. The normally reconciling factors of neighbourhood and good sense may be neutralized by the influence of the party press, and the intrusion of party agitators. By their means controversial mountains may be created out of parochial mole-hills, and public opinion shocked, or amused, or exasperated by intrinsically trivial local disputes. If, as is not infrequently the case, the incumbent be so unhappy as to owe his nomination to a Party Trust, and must needs enter on his sacred task with the doubtful and invidious reputation of a partisan, the normal difficulties will be greatly increased.[1] Even when this specific disadvantage is absent, there are commonly apprehensions and suspicions from which the new incumbent cannot escape, and which he may find it difficult to remove from ignorant and prejudiced minds.

Happily, however, it is still true that, in the majority of parishes, a new incumbent can count upon a friendly welcome from the parishioners. They will regard him with goodwill, and be ready to give him their confidence. His difficulties will commonly have their origin in his own unwisdom and lack of consideration. But whether wise and considerate, or tactless and unteachable, the incumbent will be singularly free from official interference. His position is almost impregnable, for he enjoys the freehold of his benefice. Whether he be conscientious, hardworking, and respected, or indifferent, idle, and despised, his income is secure so long as he avoids conduct which shocks the public conscience and compels episcopal action. His income is not often large, but it is generally sufficient, and almost always both secure and regularly paid. His lawful authority is considerable and unquestioned. He has control of the hours of service, and his pastoral obligations are in practice determined by himself. His parochial church council can protest, denounce, and complain, but it can do little more. The rural dean may report; the archdeacon may visit: the bishop may direct, but neither rural dean, nor archdeacon, nor even bishop, can bring any effective remedy to indifference, idleness, and secularity. The extent of the English clergyman's legal obligation is curiously small: his pastoral duty is indeed solemn and absorbing, but he must needs be his own interpreter of its range and requirement. Legal securities against pastoral inefficiency are little likely to be effective in practice. They are obviously

[1] For some discussion of Party Trusts, see the Essay *Sibbes and Simeon*, published by the late Bishop of Durham in 1932.

superfluous in the case of the good pastor, and, in the case of the bad, no one has any desire to appeal to them. From that dilemma there appears to be no way of escape. The parishioners have no desire for the pastoral ministrations of an incumbent whom they neither love nor respect. In fact the indolence, or indifference, or incapacity of the *incumbent* will normally be acquiesced in because the *man* is distrusted and disliked. Reforming zealots are too apt to forget that, when spiritual issues are at stake, there are strait limits to the possibility of effective legal action. In that sphere it is emphatically the case, that force is no remedy. It is indeed, a supreme misfortune to a parish to have a bad pastor as its parish priest, but the law can only take account of specific legal requirements which can be enforced by legally prescribed penalties, and these do not, and never can, cover the essentials of good pastorate. The parishioners have only one desire, namely, to get rid of the unsatisfactory parson. Expulsion from his benefice is the only remedy for proved pastoral inefficiency, and that is a remedy of such severity that it can only be fitly adopted, when the legal rights of the individual have been carefully secured. It must always be remembered, that natural kindheartedness will generally disincline parishioners to assist any disciplinary action which will bear hardly, not merely on the incumbent, whom they may desire to get rid of, but on his wife and children, whom they may regard with affection and pity. His expulsion will bring them to destitution. It is hardly ever the reluctance of the bishop to exert his lawful powers in restraint of clerical fault that perpetuates even culpable inefficiency and gross personal ill-conduct in the parishes, but the refusal of the parishioners to attest the offences for which they so loudly complain. In *theory* the bishop's disciplinary power is very great: in *practice* it is extremely small, nor is it easy to see how it could be increased without violating principles of equity which the public conscience rightly holds in reverence. In really bad cases of moral delinquency, the bishop may and often does bring such pressure to bear on the incumbent as forces him to resign his benefice: but this extra-legal method is obviously open to grave objection, and may fail to succeed.

Possibly some restriction of the parson's property in his benefice might be serviceable. It may well be the case that the pastoral efficiency of the beneficed clergy would be increased if their tenure of office were more reasonably conditioned. The freehold of the benefice, which secures their present impunity, is a surviving accident of feudal law, not the expression of any accepted principle. It is not right in itself, nor is it congruous with human experience, nor does it satisfy the normal requirement of human nature, that office and its emoluments, work and pay, should be so frankly disconnected as they are in the case of the English beneficed clergy. Idleness and indifference are vices of character of which the clergy enjoy no monopoly. They may be assisted or restrained by the conditions under which men live and work. The incumbent, being necessarily the master of his own time and the organizer of his own work, is particularly well placed for becoming idle and slack. There is no law to compel, and no public opinion to coerce. In the tiny world of the parish he is exposed to the temptations which always shadow autocracy. If, instead of a life-tenure of his benefice, the incumbent were appointed for a term of years, at the conclusion of which his position would be reviewed in the light of his record, is it unreasonable to think that his performance of duty would be improved, and his pastoral character strengthened? A fixed age for retirement would go far to remedy the far-extended failure due to the continuance in office of men who are quite apparently past work.

Even the gravest abuses are never wholly without compensating advantages, to which indeed they owe their

urvival power. The freehold of the benefice, which is
patently both unsound in principle, and mischievous in
practice, is no exception to the general rule. By making
the position of the parish priest irrationally secure, it has
protected him from the pressures of popular opinion and
ecclesiastical authority. These pressures may not always
be exerted in the interest of truth, or of equity, or of
pastoral efficiency. The parson may need to be protected
against parochial prejudice, or against episcopal oppression, or against the unscrupulous zeal of individual
bigotry. In that event the freehold of the benefice may be
the only effective palladium of justice and freedom. In
the case of sincere and devoted clergymen it may clothe
pastoral labour with the dignity and spontaneity of
voluntary work. The parson has been independent in
theological teaching, in moral witness, in pastoral effort
because he has felt, as he addresses himself to his duty,
that he is working without the oversight of official super-
vision, and with no other coercion than that of his own
conscience.

Nor may it be denied that the independence of the
incumbents has sometimes had indirect advantages of its
own. No student of our ecclesiastical record will be
likely to undervalue the contributions to sacred science,
to philosophy, and to devotional literature which have
been made by parish priests who were neither popular
with the multitude nor favourably regarded by their
superiors. It is not wholly unreasonable to think that
these achievements were assisted by the exceptional
security of tenure which they enjoyed.

Nevertheless, when all due allowance has been made
for whatever indirect benefits may be fairly traced to the
practical immunity from discipline which the freehold of
the benefice has secured to English incumbents, it can
hardly be disputed that these benefits have been, and are
still, dearly purchased by a condonation of pastoral

failure which has inflicted grave injury on the spiritua
life of the nation. It is difficult to believe that so gross a
anomaly as is implied in the parson's freehold will be
able to sustain itself much longer against the waxing
resentment provoked by its practical inconvenience, and
the ever-deepening repugnance of the Christian con
science.

While then the freehold of the benefice creates for the
incumbent a legal citadel within which he can maintain
his ground against both the protests of his parishioners
and the mandates of his bishop, the resulting collapse of
discipline has gone far towards emptying of practical
effectiveness the legal securities against his doctrinal and
ceremonial eccentricity. This collapse of discipline is the
result of a twofold development which has disqualified
the State for its ecclesiastical functions, on the one hand,
and, on the other, led the Church to abandon its attitude
of complaisance.

In an earlier chapter we have traced the process of
constitutional development which gradually transformed
the national supremacy of the Tudors and the personal
supremacy of the Stuarts into the parliamentary supremacy of the Hanoverians. We have pointed out the stages
by which Parliament ceased to be in any true sense representative of the English laity. Thus the control of the
Church of England had passed from the Lord's Anointed,
representing by hereditary right the spiritual authority of
the Christian nation, to a Parliament elected by the votes
of an electorate which includes practically the entire
adult population of both sexes irrespective of belief. On
what principle, the question could not but press for
answer, could the control of a Christian Church be rightly
committed to a secularized State? Where was there in the
system of the English Establishment any effective recognition of the character and authority of the spiritual
society?

A national church in the old sense has finally disappeared, since the acceptance of the principle and policy of toleration has secularized citizenship. Hooker's great apology for the Elizabethan Establishment, reiterated in far different circumstances by Burke, with the delusive artistry of his transfiguring rhetoric, is definitely and irrecoverably obsolete. If not the nation as a whole, yet at least its governing element must be Christian, if some measure of significance is still to attach to the Church's national character. The sovereign does indeed communicate with the Established Church as the law requires, but the sovereign has ceased to govern. Can it be said that the majority of the citizens, who through Parliament has replaced the sovereign in the government of the nation, is Christian? The affirmative assumption was generally made by the Anglican champions of the Establishment until the spiritual competency of the House of Commons was definitely challenged after the Great War. The Enabling Act provided for a registration of those members of the nation who could fitly be regarded as professed members of the Church of England. These were to constitute the parochial electors by whom, through a somewhat complicated procedure, the Church Assembly should be elected. It was certainly anticipated that the parochial electors would constitute so substantial a proportion of the nation as would justify the national claim for the Established Church. The actual numbers are disconcerting. It would appear that the professed members of the Church of England form but a petty fraction of the citizens. The maintenance of the Establishment had been clearly seen by its eighteenth-century apologists, Warburton and Paley, to turn on the question whether or not a majority of the people desired it.

"The alliance between Church and State", wrote Warburton, "is perpetual, but not irrevocable, i.e. it subsists just so long as the Church thereby established maintains it superiority of extent; which, when it loses to any consider able degree, the alliance becomes void."[1]

Paley wrote that "if the Dissenters from the Establishment became a majority of the people, the Establishment itself ought to be altered or qualified".[2]

Of course, it is conceivable that, apart altogether from the religious profession of the citizens, a State might for purposes of its own determine to establish a Church, but such establishment is alien to English thought and experience, and in any case would leave the essential issue of the Church's spiritual character and authority undetermined. A Church established against its will would be a Church in bonds.

Opponents of the Church of England, as well Protestant as Papist, are wont to describe it as an "Act of Parliament Church", doubtless designing thus to challenge its spiritual character. The hostile suggestion is sufficiently absurd, but it may not be denied that the invidious description enshrines an element of truth. The character of the English Reformation as the assertion of national independence in the ecclesiastical sphere involved the necessity of accepting Parliament as the instrument through which the nation achieved its purpose. Henry VIII and, in a less measure, Elizabeth were able to make use of Parliament precisely because they were themselves accepted as the supreme embodiments of national independence. The whole process by which the English Reformation was carried through was Parliamentary. The abolition of the Pope's authority, the assertion of the royal supremacy, the subordination of the clergy, the re-casting of the legal system—all were effected by Acts of Parliament. The Prayer Book is a schedule of an Act

[1] V. "Alliance between Church and State", Works, IV, 240.
[2] V. Works, II, 47.

of Parliament. The Thirty-nine Articles have statutory authority. The Church Assembly, created by the Enabling Act, only functions in subjection to Parliament, which at its discretion rejects or approves the Assembly's measures. At no point, apart of course from the actual exercise of the ministry, does the Established Church possess any independence of Parliament. This subjection might be defensible as expressing, in exaggerated form, the essential rights of the Christian laity so long as Parliament preserved the character of the Church's House of Laity; but now, since that character has been abandoned, the spiritual supremacy of Parliament has an aspect of crude paradox which cannot but offend the Christian conscience.

It is not to be forgotten that, apart from the rigidity of Elizabethan policy, there were practical reasons for insisting on uniformity in the public worship. The religious interest of the people required that wherever they passed through the realm they should find the national provision of religion familiar and intelligible. This practical reason, never without some force even in the relatively static society of the sixteenth century, has become greatly strengthened by the mobility which marks modern society. English folk ought to find themselves at home in the parish churches throughout England. This is now so far from being the general experience, that a careful and well-informed student of society would be inclined to assign to the lack of a reasonable measure of uniformity in the public services no slight place among the factors which are breaking down the tradition of public worship.

Uniformity of worship by legal compulsion is certainly more congruous with the mind and habit of the sixteenth century than with those of the twentieth, yet it is not the change of mental and moral attitude which is the principal cause of the failure of discipline in the Church of England. Obsoleteness overtakes all legal systems as well secular as ecclesiastical, and it brings its own remedy, since what is obsolete has ceased to be desired. Why has not the Act of Uniformity passed in normal fashion through obsolescence to acknowledged obsoleteness? Why has its failure to command obedience caused so much friction and confusion? The answer is as notorious as it is complete. Disobedience has not been caused by the normal influence of time, but by the deliberate and sustained effort of discontented men. Uniformity, in short, has broken down, not because it is out of harmony with the modern spirit, but because it hinders the triumph of the policy which essays to remodel the Established Church on lines other than those which the Church generally approves. It is the change which has taken place in the Church of England itself that provides the key to the failure of discipline. The normal see-saw of forces within the Established Church has brought into dominance the anti-Protestant elements which, after long and almost total eclipse, were vehemently re-affirmed in Oxford a century ago, and have gathered strength continually up to the present time. It would certainly be unjust to describe the Tractarians as the advocates of ritual and ceremonial innovation; they stood for a punctilious obedience to rubrics, and a profound veneration for the Book of Common Prayer. Their modern disciples, the Anglo-Catholics of the present day, appear neither to obey the rubrics nor to venerate the Prayer Book.

Reference has been made to the parochial church council which by the Enabling Act (1919) was substituted for the ancient vestry. It is perhaps not generally realized how revolutionary a change in the parochial system was thus effected. The ancient controversy between the "parish church" and the "gathered church", which played so prominent a part in the religious life of the seventeenth century, was now decided in favour of the latter. The territorial basis of church membership (which

The Parish Church, Troutbeck. Windermere

is the necessary assumption of an established national church) was now abandoned, and a statutory definition of Anglican Church membership was agreed upon. Given the necessity for such a definition, it is difficult to imagine any that could have been more broadly inclusive. Every person of either sex who is baptized and above the age of eighteen years may, on signing a simple declaration, be enrolled as a parochial elector, entitled as such to vote for the members of the parochial church council in the annual meeting which has replaced the ancient vestry. The powers and functions of the parochial church council are laid down in the Parochial Church Councils (Powers) Measure, 1921. The general obligations of the council are broadly stated thus:

It shall be the primary duty of the Council in every parish to co-operate with the Incumbent in the initiation conduct and development of Church work both within the parish and outside.

There appears to be a certain ambiguity in the purpose and character of the new councils. Plainly, the autocracy of the incumbent is to be ended. He is to be no longer free to initiate, conduct, and develop Church work according to his own judgment of what the spiritual interests of his people require, but he is to associate himself with the parochial church council, whose notions of spiritual needs may be far different from his own. His "cure of souls" is to be placed in commission. It certainly is not easy to harmonize this version of pastoral duty with that which is embodied in the Ordination vows. The framers of the Measure seem to have confused spiritual duty with business management. Apart from the vague declaration of "primary duty", the Measure is practical enough. It hands over to the parochial church council the "powers, duties, and liabilities" both of the vestry and of the churchwardens, gives it power to acquire property, frame an annual budget, and levy a voluntary rate. All this belongs to the familiar course of parochial business, but it is all subsidiary to the "primary duty" of "co-operating" with the incumbent in "Church work both within the parish and outside". What precisely is meant by "co-operation"? If the incumbent, desiring to initiate some new religious effort, invites the co-operation of the parochial church council, and the council refuses, is the incumbent required to abandon his purpose? This would be to exchange one autocracy for another, the autocracy of the incumbent for that of the parochial church council. Does the council possess a naked veto on the incumbent's pastoral efforts? It is perhaps no mean indication of good sense and good feeling that this vague and pretentious declaration has been almost everywhere ignored. During the "Life and Liberty" agitation, which preceded the passing of the Enabling Act, much was said about the spiritual gain to the parochial clergy implicit in the freedom from financial worry which the creation of parochial church councils charged with responsibility for the parochial finances would provide, but experience has made it plain that the parson's burden in this matter has not been substantially reduced. He still remains the indispensable factor when money has to be raised. His pastoral task has been put in commission but his secular burden has not been lightened.

The feudal lawyers, who transformed the cure of souls into the parson's property, "the freehold of the benefice", also transformed the right to nominate the parson (which had originally a natural and innocent origin) into the patron's property, his ownership of the advowson, or right of presentation. As such it could be sold, left by will, exchanged, and mortgaged at the patron's discretion. Few chapters of ecclesiastical history are so heavily charged with paradox and scandal as that which is concerned with patronage. When, therefore, a serious attempt was made to clothe the national institution with the attributes of a self-governing denomination, it was inevitable that attention should be directed to the method by which the parish clergy were appointed to their cures, that is to patronage. It was seen that, in the long run, everything turned on this point. It was well enough to put an end to the parson's autocracy, and to compel him to run in harness with a parochial church council; but, if the parson himself were undesired and undesirable (a "square peg in a round hole"), or handicapped by physical or intellectual limitations which destroyed his influence, there was little advantage in compelling him to adopt one method of mishandling his parish rather than another. No efforts of the parochial church council, however well considered and well maintained, could improve the quality of the parson's sermons, or make his conduct of the services reverent and edifying, or give some moral effectiveness to his pastoral visitation of the parishioners. The key to the entire problem of spiritual efficiency was felt to lie in the original selection of the incumbent, that is, in the system of patronage.

The parishioners were not unfamiliar with the methods by which the Dissenting denominations, or (as it is the fashion now to style them) the Free Churches, appointed their ministers to office. The contrast between the self-direction of the sectarian congregations, and the helplessness of the parish churches, was as familiar as it was invidious. The disadvantages of the Dissenting arrangement were, indeed, apparent—the canvassing of the candidates, the humiliating experience of the "trial sermon", the inevitable division of the Church into factions, for or against the chosen pastor, the unworthy dependence of the minister on his supporters, the excessive importance attached to merely popular qualities, and the like. The clergy were resolutely hostile to the popular choice of incumbents: and the laity were certainly not enthusiastic in its favour. The opinion finally prevailed that on a balance of loss and gain, the election of ministers was not desirable. Nevertheless, the one prerogative which parishioners, who for some reason, often a very sufficient one, were discontented with their parson, really coveted, was an effective share in the process by which incumbents obtained appointment.

Ultimately a middle way was taken. Patronage was slightly reformed, but not essentially changed. *Some* voice in the choice of an incumbent was given to the parochial church council, but not the deciding voice, and in no case might it suggest a particular name to the patron or to the bishop. Hardly any measure of the Church Assembly has been less successful than that which was designed to improve the administration of patronage. It has caused undesirable delay in appointing to vacant benefices, and it has given the parishioners no right which in substance they had not always possessed. Moreover, it does not extend to the parochial patronage of the Crown, which, for easily intelligible reasons, is particularly unsatisfactory. The measure has, perhaps—though there are high legal authorities who would not allow so much—made an end of the unpleasant and unpopular practice of exchanges. Two incumbents, discontented with their situation, agree together to exchange benefices. If they can secure the consent of the respective patrons and bishops, they have been able to secure their purpose; and the parishioners in both the parishes affected have the disconcerting assurance that their new incumbent's title to appointment was his own consciousness of failure in his last cure. In such exchanges the needs of the parishes and the desires of the parishioners are ignored, and the private interest of the incumbents is alone considered. It is difficult to imagine anything more inconsistent with the spirit and (though this has been challenged) with the letter of the law. One thing is certain. Such exchanges are always regarded with suspicion and dislike in the parishes, and, though experience has sometimes corrected the initial prejudices, they very rarely succeed. Some bishops refuse on principle to permit them, and it is probably the case that the scandal, for such it really is, maintains its place in the Anglican system solely by virtue of its practical convenience. It goes some way towards mitigating the effect of "the freehold in the benefice", while itself illustrating the paradox implicit in the legal theory.

Inseparable from the right to appoint the incumbent, is the obligation to provide an adequate income for his maintenance after appointment. The system of patronage rests on the basis of endowment. In theory the patron of the benefice represents the man who originally endowed it; and, though that title has in the case of most existing patrons been long buried under the accumulating changes in property tenures which have taken place in the course of a long history, it still expresses the only principle on which private patronage can be justified. The "Free Churches" are organized on a voluntary basis. Their ministers are maintained chiefly, if not wholly (for endowments are beginning to appear), by the contributions of the churches, mainly of the local congregations. This circumstance may, and often does, place the minister in a situation of dependence on the people, which is in itself irrational, and which may be consistent neither with his independence as a spiritual teacher, nor with his self-respect as a Christian man. There can be no doubt that one reason why so many Dissenting ministers apply to the bishops for acceptance as Ordination candidates is their natural desire to escape from a situation of intolerable subjection. On the other hand, it is not to be denied that the voluntary system quickens interest in denominational life, deepens the sense of personal responsibility, and induces remarkable measures of personal sacrifice.

Endowment, which has secured an unique official independence to the incumbent, has almost destroyed the sense of financial obligation in the parishioners. From time immemorial the parson's income has not entered into the sphere of the Anglican layman's recognized responsibility. This fact explains the impressively small response made by the Anglican laity to the frequent appeals, often expressed in terms of almost tragical urgency, for an increase of clerical incomes. No doubt there is a widely distributed suspicion that the parochial endowments might be less inadequate if they were more reasonably distributed: that many clergymen are not provided with sufficient employment in the tiny cures which they are appointed to serve: and that large economies of men and money might be effected by the union of superfluous parishes in the towns, and the extinction of small parishes in the country. When, however, all due allowance has been made for all these considerations, the fact remains that English laymen contribute remarkably little to ecclesiastical objects, and that of all such objects none is so little regarded as that which is concerned with the poverty of the beneficed clergy. It may, perhaps, be doubted whether anything short of the sharp crisis of disendowment will be able to break the ill-habit of centuries, and bring home to the generality of English churchmen an adequate sense of a religious obligation which from the time of the Apostles has been held to attach to membership of the Christian Church. Certainly if denominational independence is ever to belong to the Church of England, the English laity will have to face the duty of maintaining the Ministry of the Word and Sacraments.

CHAPTER 8

NATIONAL EDUCATION

The Church of England inherited from the Middle Ages an educational tradition which has been unduly under-rated. Learning was then practically limited to the clerical order, but this included, not merely the ordained clergy, but also a great multitude of others who needed a knowledge of Latin for their work.[1]

The weakness of medieval education must be found, not in the obscurantism of ecclesiastics, nor in the absence of educational opportunities, but in the limits and methods which its ecclesiastical character imposed. "There was nothing that can be called an educational system in the Middle Ages", says Dr Coulton, and this is true, though, as Professor Powicke insists, the medieval lack of system was neither so irrational in itself, nor so barren of result, as its critics often assume, nor does the modern system prove as satisfactory as its advocates often assert.

The education of the individual, on the assumption that he is a responsible moral agent, set by his Creator to fulfil the duty of his station, and thereby to prepare himself for an eternal destiny, is the foundation on which the medieval Church proceeded. The equipment of the individual with the knowledge requisite for secular suc-

[1] *V*. Bishop Stubbs's favourable judgment in *Constitutional History*, vol. III, chap. XLIX.

cess without reference to super-mundane obligations and immortal interests is the modern State's conception of educational purpose. If the one will too easily starve the mind: the other will assuredly mutilate the self. The essential problem of education is to combine in a single scheme the interest both of mind and character, and to do so in such wise that, in deference to the democratic assumption of equality, the harsh differences of natural capacity and secular circumstance may somehow be harmonized with identity of opportunity. Two generations have passed since the State in England definitely put hand to the task of national education, and the results have not been all that was hoped and expected.

The Church of England inherited from its medieval predecessor an educational equipment which the religious crisis had disorganized, and largely destroyed. In spite of the scorn with which Erasmus and his admirers denounced the ignorance of the priests and monks, there was little zeal for intellectual cultivation among the reformers. The religious crisis created a state of educational chaos. The old paedagogic methods and disciplines were largely abandoned; the old standards and classes were rudely cast aside; but there was little attempt to replace them. The dissolution of the monasteries had destroyed many schools, and had deprived the universities of the sources from which a considerable proportion of their students had been drawn. The dispersion and destruction of the monastic libraries had lowered the level of culture in the community, and depleted its intellectual resources. The breach with Rome immersed the nation in a more than insular isolation from the continent. The prolonged dislocation of society caused by the religious revolution was highly unfavourable to educational development. Polemical theology crowded out all other subjects of mental effort, and lowered both the moral and the intellectual temperature of the nation.

If, then, it be certainly true that, in the long run, the Reformation stimulated intelligence, and greatly advanced national education, it must be owned that its first effects were deplorable. The pioneers and first beneficiaries of educational reform were not the Reformers, but the Jesuits, their ablest and most relentless adversaries. Sir Edwyn Sandys justly attributed the rapid progress of the Counter-Reformation to the educational activity of the Jesuits.[1]

Cranmer was almost alone among the English Reformers in caring for the interest of education, and he was temperamentally ill-fitted for restraining the sordid aims and appetites of the rapacious careerists who came to the front in the miserable reign of Edward VI. His noble protest against the arrogant class-feeling which would have shut out the poor from access to educational opportunity relieves the record of philistine rapacity.

When the commission was sitting which turned the monastery of Christ Church into a capitular body, the business came before it of electing children to the grammar school. To some of the commissioners (one of whom was the remarkable Sir Richard Rich) it seemed good that none should be elected but sons or younger brothers of gentlemen. "The children of husbandmen", said they, "are meeter for the plough, or to be artificers, than to occupy the place of the learned sort. Let none be put to school but gentlemen's sons." Cranmer, to his honour, testified proper indignation at this manifestation of the spirit of the revolution. "Poor men's children", he exclaimed, "are many times endued with more singular gifts of nature, which are also the gifts of God: they are often more diligent to apply their study than the gentleman's son, delicately educated. Is the ploughman's son, or the poor man's son, unworthy to receive the gifts of the Holy Ghost? Are we to appoint them to be employed according to our fancy, not according to the gifts of Almighty God? To shut up the bountiful grace of the Holy

[1] *V. Europæ Speculum* (London, 1673), p. 90.

Ghost in a corner, and attempt to build thereon our fancies, is to build the tower of Babel. None of us all here, but had our beginning from a low and base parentage. All gentlemen, for the most part, ascend to their estate through learning." It was answered that the most part of the nobility were made by feats of arms. "As though", said the Archbishop, "the noble captain was always unfurnished of good learning! If the gentleman's son be apt, let him be admitted: if not, let the poor man's child that is apt, enter his room."[1]

Canon Dixon regarded with aversion the whole process of the Reformation, in which he refused to see anything greater than a "revolution of the rich against the poor". "The poor", he says, "had less chance of education after the Reformation than they had before it." If the estimate of consequences be taken on the morrow of the religious revolution, it is difficult to dispute the truth of this verdict: but if a longer view be taken, and the Reformation be judged in the light of its logical and permanent achievements, Canon Dixon's verdict cannot be sustained.

When after the political and religious conflicts of the seventeenth century, the English people "found rest" in the Revolution Settlement, the condition of the poor began to arrest attention. It was their irreligion and immorality rather than their ignorance which caused alarm, and moved compassion. So far as their education was concerned, it must be admitted that Lord Rich rather than Archbishop Cranmer seemed to call the tune for the Church of England. Popular education was conditioned by its utility as a barricade against social and political disaffection. And even so, it was not looked upon without misgiving.

The necessity of a national system of education was not soon perceived even by those who were sincerely attached to the cause of education. Moreover, even when at length the necessity had been perceived, the actual

[1] *V.* Dixon, *History of the Church of England,* II, 228.

stablishment of a national system was hindered by many
bstacles which had their roots in untoward social con-
itions belonging to a past phase of national life. The
roject of popular education was in English minds handi-
apped by its association with the French Revolution.
he ignorance of the masses was thought by the ruling
lass to be the best protection of society against the
estructive idealism of minds which had been so far
nfranchised by knowledge as to feel hardship and to
esent oppression. Even Sunday schools were regarded
ith suspicion. They were "the thin end of the wedge",
nd might create appetites which could not safely be
atisfied. The conception of social responsibility which
opular education implied was assuredly congruous with
Christianity, but it had been so long submerged by class
omination, that, when it was reaffirmed with fierce
mphasis and morbid exaggeration by Rousseau and his
isciples, its essential soundness could with difficulty
ommand the assent of minds scandalized and terrified
y the violence of revolutionary France. The Christian
onscience was paralysed by religious panic, and the
ublic mind hag-ridden by dread of the potential mis-
hiefs of social change.

In England, it is true to say that the education of the
eople had never been wholly neglected, but so long as
nglishmen were obsessed by the sterile passions of
heological controversy and civil strife they had small
oncern for anything else. The mass of the population
ad not emerged from medieval superstition. At the
eginning of the nineteenth century the English people
enerally was illiterate, lawless, and depraved.

The religious revival which followed the Revolution of
688 had led to the creation of many "Charity Schools",
nd these led on to the more ambitious projects of
opular education which are associated with the National
ociety, founded in 1811, and the British and Foreign

School Society, founded in 1814. These two societie
reflected the religious division of the nation, which ha
affected the course of educational development ever since
and affects it still. When the State itself put its hand to th
work, it found the ground already occupied by system
expressing the distinctive and conflicting interests of th
Established Church and of the Dissenting sects.

National education was regarded for the most part a
ancillary to the religious interest of the children whos
morals, it was believed, depended mainly on thei
Christian belief. The essential concern of the State, it wa
held, was bound up with the character of the citizens, and
this was determined by their acceptance of Christia
faith and morals. Education, therefore, was only so fa
important as it facilitated the effective Christianizing o
the people.

Preaching in aid of the "Charity Schools in and abou
the Cities of London and Westminster" in 1745, Bisho
Butler had advocated popular education on ground
which could not but justify a larger conception of educa
tional obligation. In view of "the ingenuous docility o
children before they have been deceived", and thei
helplessness if left to grow up unguided and untaught, h
maintained that they were equitably entitled to be dul
educated. He would not allow the notion that the matte
could properly be left to the natural obligation of thei
parents:

This care of youth, abstracted from all consideration o
the parental affection, I say, this care of youth, which is th
general notion of *education* becomes a distinct subject, and a
distinct duty, from the particular danger of their ruin, if lef
to themselves, and the particular reason we have to expec
they will do well, if due care be taken of them. And from
hence it follows, that children have as much right to som
proper education, as to have their lives preserved; and tha
when this is not given them by their parents, the care o

t devolves upon all persons, it becomes the duty of all, who are capable of contributing to it, and whose help is wanted.

After meeting the objections of those who urged that the poor rate ought to provide for all that was needed, and that education would only disgust the children for the manual work which was their hereditary vocation, the bishop dwelt on the effect of the new conditions under which society was living, and which might well injure rather than benefit the lot of the poor.

This whole discourse is a very noble pronouncement, and discloses a wealth of popular sympathy and practical sagacity which, perhaps, is not often credited to the illustrious author of the Analogy. Bishop Butler took a larger and longer view of popular education than even now many English churchmen are able to accept. The character and range of his appeal for "Charity Schools" in 1745 are precisely those which belong to the more generous policy of national education which belongs to our own time.[1]

It has been already pointed out that, when the State put its hand to the task of organizing the education of the people, it found the ground already occupied, though by no means covered, by two systems, which proceeded on different principles, and embodied different educational traditions. The conflict of the Established Church and the Dissenters which had divided English Christianity almost since the Reformation, and which at the Revolution had secured a more or less satisfying *modus vivendi*, had been carried over from politics and religion to the sphere of education, where it was particularly anomalous and unfortunate. Both the rivals had respectable educational traditions. To take first the case of the Established Church.

[1] The sermon is printed in Bernard's edition of Butler's *Works*, 244–258.

The Church of England had created a network o
"National Schools", supported by voluntary contribu
tions with some assistance from the State, which taugh
the elements of secular knowledge. It was natural tha
the Church of England should assume responsibility fo
the education of the people. It had inherited from it
medieval predecessor, not only the traditional associatio
of religion and education, but also a considerable educa
tional endowment—colleges, grammar schools, an
various types of parochial schools. The Reformatio
continued the first, and developed so much of the last a
had survived the religious revolution. When the Churcl
was reconstituted after the Interregnum, the Act o
Uniformity (1662) was made to cover the case of school
masters and tutors. In fact education, from the parisl
school to the university, was regarded by the State as par
of the function of the Established Church. Religio
continued to determine both the object and the method o
national education. The Christian nation was obviousl
concerned to have its citizens trained in Christian fait
and morals. Orthodoxy was the condition of truth i
every sphere, and its profession was the indispensabl
guarantee of good citizenship. Even the undergraduate
of Oxford University far into the nineteenth century wer
required at matriculation to subscribe the Thirty-nin
Articles, and when the National Society was constitute
in 1811, its avowed purpose was "the promotion of th
Education of the Poor in the principles of the Establishe
Church". The immemorial association of the clergy witl
the education of the people, and the dominance of re
ligion in the scheme of sound education have persiste
in Anglican minds long after they have been abandone
by the State, the one as impracticable, and the other a
irrational. Nevertheless the old assumptions do stil
colour and inflame the continuing controversy betwee
Church and State in the sphere of national education.

The Dissenters from the Established Church, whose existence was legally tolerated by the Act of 1689, were not without an educational tradition of their own. They also associated religion with education, but the circumstances in which their educational tradition had been shaped gave it a character and tendency so sharply distinctive from those which marked the educational tradition of the Church of England that conflict between the two was finally unavoidable. While the Church expressed the ideal of a Christian State which was organically united with itself, the Dissenters found their *raison d'être* in the disallowance on principle of that organic union, and developed their educational provision by voluntary efforts outside the State system. Excluded by statute from the universities, and shut out from the teaching profession, the Dissenters, with admirable courage and resource, established seminaries and schools of their own, in which their youth could be educated in accordance with their own principles. Many of the Puritan ministers ejected from their benefices by the Act of Uniformity turned to teaching in order to gain a livelihood, and no doubt they carried into their new situation embittered sentiments towards the established system. Their labours were remarkably successful. The Dissenting academies, though frowned on by the State, and evilly regarded by the Church, soon acquired a considerable reputation as places of higher education. They contrasted favourably with the ancient universities, which had fallen into a lamentable intellectual somnolence. Scotland and the continent went far to provide the Dissenters with the academic provision which was refused to them in England. Dissent flourished mainly in the lower middle class, until the Methodists succeeded in evangelizing the masses. The "Charity Schools" organized by the Anglican clergy in the reign of Queen Anne affected a section of the people which lay outside

denominational controversy, and the Dissenters assisted
in the creation of these schools until the fierce political
prejudices of the time arrested all co-operation between
the clergy, who were mostly Tories, and the Dissenters,
who were universally Whigs.[1] In an attenuated form this
political prejudice has continued to operate. In recent
years the waxing importance of economic issues has gone
far to obliterate the older lines of political cleavage.
Socialism has affected Churchmen and Dissenters alike,
and the clergy of all denominations are now extensively
leavened by communistic feeling. Still the old political
conflict associated with class divisions, which die slowly,
lingers, and still embitters and confuses the problem of
national education.

Dissenters, not less than Anglicans, regarded the
education of children mainly as ancillary to their moral
and religious interests; but their approach to the practical
problem was different. The Dissenters did not share the
view of childhood as itself a consecrated thing, entitled to
be treated as such, and therefore requiring for its due
development Christian instruction and Christian discipline. Many Dissenters repudiated the ancient Christian
practice of infant baptism, and almost all denied the
sacramental doctrine which infant baptism expressed.
Children were not in their eyes Christian, but only
potentially Christian. Their emphasis was less on the
Incarnation, with its implicit claim that "the earth is the
Lord's and the fulness thereof", and its sublime estimate
of human nature as such, than on the Atonement, with
its sombre presuppositions and implications. The essential thing for the Dissenter was to make sure that the child
was so handled as to facilitate his "conversion", and to
protect him from the disastrous influences of the evil
world. As one who was living consciously "ever in the
great Taskmaster's eye", the Dissenter carried into his

[1] Sykes, *Edmund Gibson* (Oxford, 1926), p. 198.

educational method a lofty sense of moral obligation, and an ascetic dislike of the refinements and indulgences of civilized society. Education was practical and efficient, but severely limited in range, and austere in temper.

The difference of educational method, which grew from distinctiveness of history and theology, has determined the attitude adopted severally by Anglicans and Dissenters towards the educational policy of the State when, at length, in the nineteenth century, the State entered the field of national education, and rapidly marched to a dominance which now clearly approaches monopoly.

With the Reform Act (1832) the nation entered on a course of political and social development, which has recast the constitution and destroyed privilege on every plane of society. The awakened self-consciousness of the English people could not acquiesce in the absence of effective provision for national education. So vast and vital a public interest could not be left permanently in the hands of any lesser authority than that of the State itself. At first tentatively, and on an extremely limited scale, but, as time went on, ever more directly, and with an ampler view of obligation, the State carried the burden of the nation's education.

At first the existing schools were subsidized, and then their efficiency was secured by official inspection; but, as the range and cost of education continually increased, the State was called upon to contribute ever more largely to the cost of the schools. In the urban districts State schools were perforce provided, and maintained at the public cost. Voluntary effort was plainly quite inadequate for the task to which it seemed to be committed, and with every addition to the State's contribution, came a fresh menace to the existence of other than State schools. Nor was this all. The rapid multiplication of schools drew with it the formidable question of providing teachers sufficient in number and adequate in qualification. A sufficient supply of professedly Christian teachers could not be counted upon, for the membership of the Church and the Dissenting denominations was quite unable to satisfy the demand. The nation as a whole had to provide for a new and most important branch of the State service. Democratic principle could not tolerate any form of religious test for the nation's service. Therefore, the State schools must stand outside denominational control. Originally designed to supplement the provision made by the Established Church and the Dissenters, the State schools became very quickly the principal part of the educational system. Moreover, the cost of education increased as well as the scale on which education had to be provided. The voluntary agencies were as little able to find the money as to find the teachers. The State had to make up the deficiency in both. By the Act of 1902 the State assumed responsibility for the payment of the teachers in all schools. But even this could not suffice. Not even the maintenance of suitable buildings was within the shrinking resources of the "voluntary" schools. Speaking at a meeting of the National Society in January 1938, Lord Sankey, the Chairman of its Standing Committee, reviewed the existing situation in a speech of remarkable insight and candour:

There were in England and Wales 10,100 Council schools and 9100 Church schools. The pupils in Council schools numbered 3,661,000, and those in Church schools exactly a third. It was evident that in the Council schools there were a great number of teachers who belonged to the Church of England. Out of a total body of Church children, sixty-five per cent were in Council schools, and only thirty-five per cent in Church schools. One hundred Church schools were being shut down every year, and since 1902 the Church had lost 2620 schools.[1]

[1] V. Church Times, January 14th, 1938.

With characteristic lack of logic the English people have hitherto refused to adopt the naked secularization of the national system which democratic principle appears to require. The official membership of the Established Church and the dissenting denominations provides an untrustworthy measure of the popular mind. Christian sentiment is widely diffused throughout the nation; and a total absence of moral and religious teaching from the school curriculum is not thought by many eminent educational authorities consistent with the requirements of efficient education.

Might it not be fairly assumed that the essential elements of Christian faith and morality could be taught with general acceptance? Could not the State, while avoiding any denominational preference, limit its teaching to the truths which all Christians agree to be fundamental? Did not the Bible provide a manual of essential religious and moral truth on which all Christians were agreed? If, in Chillingworth's famous phrase, the Bible only is the religion of Protestants, was it unreasonable to suppose that a scheme of teaching based on the Bible, and making use of no other authoritative book, might be accepted by the majority of English Christians? This policy was embodied in the famous Cowper-Temple clause of the Education Act of 1870. This clause forbade the use in Board Schools of any catechism or formulary distinctive of any denominational creed, whilst permitting school teachers to expound as well as read the Bible.

There can be no reasonable doubt as to the justice of this interpretation of the national mind. The English, it has been well observed, are indifferent to theory, but kiss the ground before a fact. The fact of the general agreement of the people in a doctrinally vague, but strongly ethical, version of Christianity based on the Bible is apparent and indisputable. What could be more reasonable than to carry it into the State schools?

Experience has gone far to justify the policy of the Cowper-Temple clause. The denominationalism of the English people is more formidable in appearance than in reality. Religion in England is not so chaotic as it looks, and as its critics often describe it. Polemical reasons have given great prominence to the argument for parental preferences in the matter of religious teaching in the State schools. It is assumed that these are overridden by the "undenominational" teaching which alone the law permits. But the implicit assumption that because they ought, as loyal members of their denominations, to insist on the distinctive teachings, which the said denominations affirm, they are therefore offended by the omission of those teachings from the school curriculum, is contradicted by the actual facts. It is, of course, notorious that there are many Dissenting bodies, among which the mass of non-Anglican Christians is distributed, and that every one of these has some doctrine or discipline to which it (theoretically) attaches decisive importance; but what in actual experience is the relation which exists between the members of these bodies? Are they parted by strong differences of belief? Do they follow distinctive modes of religious living? Are they absentees from one another's social intercourse? It only needs to ask these questions in order to answer them. It is notorious that denominational divisions are everywhere fluctuating and unreal. The law prohibits interchange of pulpits between Anglican and Nonconformist clergymen, but the interchange of congregations prevails, and nothing would please the religious folk of the middle and lower classes better than such an alteration of the existing law as would permit the clergy to treat their dissenting brethren as religious equals. The parents of the children who use the State schools are in this sense "undenominational", that they worship without hesitation in church and chapel indiscriminately, use the same religious books, sing the same hymns, share the same standards of duty. It was stated by Sir John Gorst, speaking in Parliament as the representative of the Education Department, that there was no religious difficulty within the schools. This is the natural consequence of the fact that there is no religious difficulty among the parents of the children who use the schools. The protagonists of denominational teaching in the State schools are certainly earnest and estimable men, and include in their number many whose disinterested concern for sound education cannot be disputed, but they do not express the mind of that section of the people which is directly interested in the State schools.

Religious education in the State schools, if it is to continue, must be undenominational in character, and taught by the regular staff of the school. The first condition is required by the character of the national religion, and the other by the reasonable requirements of the teaching profession. It is justly urged that the discipline of the school will not admit the exclusion of the headmaster from so important a part of the teaching as that which is concerned with religion and morality. It is not less justly urged that, if the headmaster is to control the moral and religious teaching of the children, there must be provided some reasonable guarantee that he is himself a religious man.

This is the crux of the practical problem. How can the competence of the headmaster for the control of religious and moral teaching be certified apart from the application of some kind of religious test which would do violence to fundamental democratic principle? The so-called "Dual System" which still survives, though in a moribund condition, implies acquiescence in a curious compromise. While the "provided" schools may insist on a denominational test for their headmasterships, the "non-provided" schools must have none. The victory of the denominationalists was dearly purchased, for the effect of reserving the headmasterships of the one type of schools to denominational teachers has had the natural effect of hindering the appointment of denominational teachers to the headmasterships of the other type of schools. This disadvantage is increasingly serious since the "provided" schools are quickly growing in number and importance. The abler and more ambitious teachers are not unnaturally reluctant to prejudice their chances of service in the schools which are clearly the most important in the country.

The maintenance of the Dual System, which perpetuates, though in an attenuated form, the authority of the Established Church in the sphere of national education, appears to block the way to such a solution of the problem of religious teaching in the schools as, though not theoretically unobjectionable, would satisfy the general feeling of the English people. It is no doubt true that there are other "provided" schools than those of the Established Church. The surviving schools of the Protestant Dissenters present no serious obstacle, since the Cowper-Temple type of religious teaching accords with their own, and if the Dissenters could be assured that in a reconstituted State system the religious teaching would be secured and efficient, they would be satisfied. There remain the schools of the Roman Catholics and the Jews, but these may fairly be left out of reckoning. Neither Roman Catholics nor Jews can be brought into any general system of religious teaching, for both are minorities so largely alien in race and creed, as to be properly accorded distinctive treatment. The National System must provide for certain exceptions from the prevailing type. To that extent denominationalism must remain a feature of national education. Roman Catholic and Jewish schools are genuinely denominational institutions, for they are only provided where there is a definite denominational demand to be satisfied, and their sharply distinctive character renders them unattractive to the general body of English people. The Anglican schools, with few exceptions, stand in a very different case. They are "national" schools, intended for the use of English children as such, and only attached to the Church of England by the accident of history.

To some extent it would be true to say that the Church of England is, in the matter of its schools, the victim of its own privilege. It led the way in national education and the State had encouraged it to essay the gigantic task. It was the established national church, and appeared, as well by its traditions as by its parochial constitution, to be the appropriate instrument of national action. But its resources, even when supplemented by voluntary contributions, and the exiguous grants which Parliament could be induced to vote, were always unequal to the requirements, and, as we have said, failed altogether when confronted by the abnormal demand created by the rapid industrialization of the people. The theory survived the practice, lingering longest in rural parishes and parsons' minds. The very title "National School" perpetuates a claim which, almost everywhere outside the country districts, has lost reality. The schools designed for the general use of the community could not be distinctively Anglican. Dissenters, not less than Church people, sent their children to them, and in many parts of the country, notably in Wales and in the North and East of England, Dissenters were so numerous as to constitute a majority of the pupils. Inevitably the tone of the school and the type of the religious teaching were affected by the mixed denominational quality of the children. The "undenominational" Christianity legalized by the Cowper-Temple clause in 1870 had largely prevailed in the "National Schools" long before, for though the Catechism was taught, its character not as a denominational formulary but as an admirable summary of fundamental

Christian faith and morality had been generally emphasized.

It is perhaps worth pointing out that the rather uncouth word "undenominational" has been largely misunderstood. Polemical zeal has transformed "undenominational teaching" into a "moral monster" by reading into it a meaning which its advocates would generally disavow. If indeed it meant, what its hostile critics affirm, viz. such residuum of Christian faith as remains after every challenged belief has been abstracted, it would need little argument to show that such teaching would be both intellectually contemptible and morally worthless. But when ordinary English folk speak of "undenominational teaching" they mean that fundamental truth which is held in common by all orthodox Christians, which they know themselves to share with their Christian neighbours as well Anglican as Dissenting. Roman Catholics, Jews, and Unitarians stand apart from this general agreement, for they are highly specialized minorities who have set a fence about themselves. They must be separately provided for, but cannot rightly or prudently be allowed to prohibit a recognition in the State schools of the fundamental agreement with respect to Christian faith and morals which happily exists among the people.

The "National Schools" were, for the most part, built at a time when educational requirements were little understood. They are in many cases inadequate, inconvenient, and sometimes insanitary. Only the necessity for drastic economy in public expenditure created by the Great War has preserved these schools from official condemnation. Their disappearance cannot be long delayed when the disastrous (though alas unavoidable) wastage of national wealth on warlike preparations has come to an end. The attempt to give a definitely denominational character to the "National Schools" ignores their original character, and commits the Church of England to a responsibility beyond its powers. Moreover, the claim that these schools represent great personal sacrifices can hardly be sustained. Bishop Gore emphasized this claim in a letter published during the election of 1906, and his words are often echoed by the advocates of "Church schools for Church children" at the present time:

Loyalty to those who have gone before us and the sense of our great duty to the children of Church parents have impelled us to make great sacrifices that we might secure for such children instruction in the faith their parents hold.

Such language will not bear serious examination. At best it is greatly exaggerated. In view of the fact that since the year 1870 the maintenance of the elementary schools has been part of the citizen's duty, the subscriptions to denominational schools have for most of the subscribers been a cheap alternative to the educational rates which, if the denominational schools had ceased to exist, they would assuredly have had to pay. Apart from the clergy, who did in many cases make considerable sacrifices to maintain the schools in their parishes, the subscribers were often, perhaps generally, influenced less by religious than by economic motives. No argument was more effective with landowners, shopkeepers, and shareholders than that which demonstrated that their pockets would be relieved by the maintenance of the denominational school. To subscribe was cheaper than to pay rates. Only that consideration could justify directors in voting away the shareholders' money. The less said about the "great sacrifices" made in the creation of the voluntary schools the better. How petty is the amount of money now contributed by the Church of England to the maintenance of "Church Schools" may be seen by the statement of voluntary contributions for the year 1936. Out of a total of more than six million pounds little more than £130,000 was devoted to the repairs and construction of the day schools of the Church. The Dual System has already fallen in the practical judgment of most Anglican laymen, though there are not lacking enthusiastic "last-ditchers" who are blind to the fact. The real problem which confronts ecclesiastical statesmen is how to surrender the System without injuring the interest which it embodies and in some poor sense serves.

The Dual System, as it now exists, obstructs the complete triumph of the secularizing tendency. It affirms an educational ideal which is larger in range, more intelligently sympathetic in temper, more congruous with human nature, than that which secularism embodies. It is a rallying-point, to which all the higher factors in the community can gather, and by means of which they can affect more or less directly the whole educational process. The advocates of the Dual System, leaving the ground of denominational claim, and arguing their case on the larger plea of educational function, are disposed to apply to the Dual System the words of the prophet—"*Destroy it not for a blessing is in it.*" There can be little doubt that such considerations as these are determining the attitude of many thoughtful persons at the present time.

Shall the national education continue to include instruction in Christian faith and morals? Many tendencies of the time are pointing in the direction of a complete secularization of education. The process of "cutting out religion" has gone far already. The universities are frankly secular institutions. The teaching profession is almost completely secularized. The secondary schools, which are evidently destined to play a very important part in the general scheme of national education, are entirely secular. Religious teaching in the elementary schools is in obvious danger of being reduced to the shadow of a shade by the pressure of the waxing curriculum, and the lack of inspection. It is not easy to avoid the belief that naked secularism is within sight on every plane of educational activity.

The principal danger to education in England at the present time arises less from the secularization of school curricula, which on many grounds might in the actual circumstances of the nation be even desirable, than on the anti-religious tone of a section of the teaching profession, and the widening breach between the State schools and organized Christianity. Both these evil tendencies are strengthened by the desperate efforts, as natural as they are hopeless, to maintain the Dual System. The teaching profession, numerous, well-trained, and professionally enthusiastic, will not consent to accept any subordination, or suggestion of subordination, to the clergy, such as is traditional in "Church Schools", and properly inherent in their constitution. The effort to raise money for the support of these schools compels the adoption of an attitude of suspicion, and even of hostility, towards the State schools. The influence of the teachers is alienated from the parish church, and that of the incumbent is definitely lowered. Popular life is the poorer by the weakening of its highest factors, religion and education.

The high motives which do certainly lead devout Churchmen to cling to the Dual System are obscured by the apparent presence of other motives which are less worthy of respect. No one who has an intimate and sustained acquaintance with English life as it proceeds in the parishes can be in any doubt as to the unfortunate effect of the agitation, which tends to become more exasperating as it is seen to be practically futile, to maintain the Church schools. The educational credit of the Church of England is lowered by its familiar association with inferior buildings, pinched equipment, and (sometimes) inferior teachers. Church schools take in the general view an aspect of inferiority, and though this aspect is often misleading, it is rarely lacking in excuse.

If the Dual System, which has been completely outgrown, could be brought to an end by means of an amicable agreement between Church and State, the door would at length be opened for a happy change in the relations of the two great professions which are historically allied in the work of education, and the most vital interests of the nation might become the realized and anxious concern of Christian people as such. There is no doubt as to the desire of the English people as a whole to ground their system of popular education on effective teaching of Christian faith and morals. There is no doubt as to the fundamental agreement of the great majority of English Christians in the essentials of such teaching. Experience has already demonstrated the willingness of Christians of various denominational descriptions to unite in organizing effective religious teaching in the schools. In many parts of the country agreed schemes have been put forward with general approval. If the national education of England is secularized, it will be because advantage has not been taken of the resources of good will and public spirit which the population contains. Regarded from the standpoint of the national interest, which is vitally concerned with the moral training of its citizens, the problem of religion in the schools is seen to be both supremely important and practically soluble.

If instruction in Christian faith and morals were made compulsory (subject to a conscience clause) in all schools: if the State limited its direct concern to the secular subjects, and entrusted the religious instruction to the local educational authorities, there is little reason for doubting that in a very short time the problem would be happily solved. Dissentient minorities would constitute a distinct issue which the State would have to handle apart from the main project, but the latter would be in essential agreement with the conditions of English life. There are in all parts of the country resources of Christian feeling and an intelligent concern for sound education which, if the opportunity for effective expression were provided, would eagerly come into play. The Dual System blocks the way to a working alliance of men of good will.

CHAPTER 9

THE TRANSFORMATION OF THE ESTABLISHED CHURCH

The century which followed the Reform Act (1832) witnessed a remarkable transformation of the Established Church. What had become in practice, and largely in theory, a Department of State, developed into a highly self-conscious religious denomination, disdaining the limitations, legal, insular, and ethnical, which history had created, and deliberately organizing itself as the centre of a federation of self-governing churches, acknowledging i n England their spiritual home, but jealously regardful of their individual autonomy.

If we contrast the Church of England as it existed on the morrow of the long war with France with the Church of England as it exists now, we cannot fail to observe four institutions which are prominent at present, which then were unknown—the Ecclesiastical Commission (1836), the Convocations (1852), the Lambeth Conference (1867), and the Church Assembly (1919). These institutions may be said to reflect four influences which have borne, with varying measures of pressure, on the Established Church. Public opinion, goaded to effective action by the intolerable anomalies and abuses which disfigured the national Establishment, created the Ecclesiastical Commission in the teeth of vehement clerical opposition. Tractarian medievalism triumphed when, as the result of a brisk agitation, the Convocations, which had been paralysed for 135 years, were suffered to resume some of their immemorial functions. The Lambeth Conference has grown out of ecclesiastical requirements implicit in the amazing expansion of Great Britain, partly by emigration, and partly by conquest, into the British Empire. As the colonial churches developed they presented problems of their own; and, outside the boundaries of historic Christendom, the communities of native Christians which were coming into existence as the fruit of persistent and ubiquitous evangelistic effort, presented questions, doctrinal and disciplinary, which were equally novel, important, and perplexing. The island church, almost in spite of itself, acquired a world-wide character. Finally, the waxing self-consciousness of the Church of England rebelled against the restrictions of its legal establishment, and aspired to the full franchise of denominationalism.

I. THE ECCLESIASTICAL COMMISSION

When, after the crowning victory of Waterloo, the Second Peace of Paris (1815) inaugurated a period of tranquillity, domestic affairs recovered their long-lost prominence in the public mind. The system of government was seen to be intolerably anomalous, anachronistic, and inefficient. This situation was the more resented by public opinion, since the ideas which had triumphed in the French Revolution were widely spread, and the more exacting sense of religious obligation, which the Methodist Movement had embodied, was establishing itself in the public conscience.

Of all the national institutions the Established Church of England was, perhaps, the most grossly disfigured by anomalies and abuses. So soon, therefore, as the Reform Act (1832) had clothed the House of Commons with adequate popular support, Parliament addressed itself to the work of recasting the Establishment. A Royal Commission, appointed within three weeks of the passing of the Reform Act, issued its final Report in 1835. Dr Mathieson has observed that if this document, "the Domesday Book of the Church", had appeared four years earlier, "it would have checked the rise of an apocryphal literature in regard to Church revenues",[1] a literature, we may not forget, which is not even yet entirely extinct, and still does much to colour popular notions about the Established Church.

In 1836 the Established Church Act was passed, and immediately aroused considerable opposition from those zealous Anglicans on whom the Tractarian Movement was exerting a considerable influence.

By far the most violently assailed section of the Act was that which established the Ecclesiastical Commission. This body was denounced because it comprised a majority of laymen, because all its members, except the two Archbishops and the Bishop of London, were either Ministers or removable at the pleasure of the Crown, or, in other words, of the party in power, and because it was unlimited in duration and all but unlimited in scope. Bagot[2] considered it "a power as irresponsible as it is gigantic—an *imperium in imperio* which before long must supersede all authority in the Church". Phillpotts[3] predicted that it would soon be "invested with attributes compared with which the highest authority over the Church claimed by the Tudors or the Stewarts will appear powerless and insignificant". Manning,[4] a recent convert to the doctrine of apostolical succession, declared that it reduced the Church to "a mere secular establishment for popular religious instruction"; and another writer, commenting on the power of the Commission to call for persons and documents and to examine on oath, pro-

[1] *English Church Reform*, 1815–1840, p. 111.
[2] Bishop of Oxford (1829–1845).
[3] Bishop of Exeter (1830–1869).
[4] Afterwards Cardinal.

Archbishop Laud

nounced it "an inquisitorial tribunal of the most vexatious kind". The Bill was received by the Lords late in the session, and is said to have been opposed by all the English Bishops who had not left London. But only four of them have denounced it in their charges.[1]

Though the Ecclesiastical Commission was imposed by the reforming State on a reluctant Church, it was eminently successful. In the course of a century, it has won its way to the Church's confidence so effectually that few, if any, echoes of the original objections are now audible. Partly, this remarkable success has been owing to the ability of the men who, as "Church Estates Commissioners", have guided its course, but mainly it has arisen from the realization by the clergy of the substantial advantages which they derive from the more efficient management of ecclesiastical property. The importance of the Commission has continually grown, and is now so great, that it is hardly excessive to say that the Ecclesiastical Commission provides the backbone of the Church's practical system. The extent of its responsibility is sufficiently indicated by the fact that it now administers an annual income of £3,500,000. It has sometimes been suggested that the centralization in London of the management of estates which are scattered all over the country tends to exclude the "human factor" from the process, and that economic efficiency is sometimes too dearly purchased by the loss of personal contact, but this criticism has been much exaggerated, and is losing whatever force it once may have possessed. As time passes acquaintance with local conditions is acquired and registered, and the methods and officers of the Commissioners become known. Moreover, in the rapidly changing conditions of rural life, the natural conservatism, which resents and suspects all changes, however whole-

[1] *V.* Mathieson, *English Church Reform*, p. 138.

some, is losing hold. The increasing poverty of the incumbents is seen to disqualify them for the rôle of landowners, which the possession of the glebes attached to their benefices imposes on them. It is becoming apparent that the parochial clergy would gain by an arrangement which would transfer the control of the glebes to the Ecclesiastical Commission, and, while securing the incumbents in their net official income, would relieve them of the difficult and incongruous character of landlords. Certainly the tendency among churchmen is to extend, rather than to restrict, the responsibilities of the Commission.

Probably the efficiency of the Church would be increased, if the diocese rather than the parish were made the recipient of the Commissioners' grants. At the time when the Commission was constituted, the most apparent need of the Church was a great extension of the parochial system. To create and endow new parishes was the primary purpose to which the "Common Fund" was to be devoted. Now the problem is rather to reduce than to multiply the number of parishes, for, even if incomes could be provided, suitable incumbents could not always be found. In plain terms the Church of England is no longer able to maintain the national system. The rapidly increasing fluidity of the population has gone far to paralyse the parochial system. It would probably be more serviceable to the spiritual interest of the people if the Commission were free to deal directly with the diocese. A block grant to the diocese, leaving the diocesan authorities free to distribute it in the parishes as seems best to their judgment, would avoid the painful but not uncommon experience of Commissioners' grants to parishes "with local claims" remaining unused in districts where the spiritual penury is apparent and extreme.

II. CONVOCATION

The Ecclesiastical Commission was a modern institution imposed by the State on a reluctant Church, and had to win its way to the general approval. Convocation, or rather the Convocations, owe their survival as operative assemblies to a brisk ecclesiastical agitation, inspired by the Tractarian Movement, which succeeded in wringing from a reluctant State the revival of a medieval institution which had long ceased to possess practical importance.

It is, perhaps, surprising that the agitation for the revival of Convocation was crowned with success, for the public mind in the middle of the nineteenth century was more than usually disinclined to make concessions to clerical sentiment. The Gorham Judgment had occasioned a wave of secessions to Rome; and the Papal Aggression had lashed to fury the latent "No Popery" prejudice of the nation. The State was suspicious, and the Church was divided, for the one dreaded an increase of sacerdotalism, and the other an embitterment of party strife.

On 6 February 1855, the Convocations assembled, and ever since they have continued to meet and transact such business as may be proposed to them. They have discussed with freedom and, under the conditions prescribed by the law, have even enacted canons. Opinions vary greatly, as perhaps might be expected, on the importance and value of their proceedings. Mr Warre Cornish thinks that "the general life of the Church was undoubtedly stimulated by the spectacle of Convocation taking up its ancient functions", but, even if this may have been the immediate effect, can it be said on a review of the last eighty years that that effect has continued? Is it not really misleading to speak of "taking up its ancient functions"? Was it within the power of Convocation to do so? and, even if it had been, could it have done so with effect? Is it not apparent that, in the circumstances of the modern Church, the "ancient functions" of Convocation are not serviceable to any useful end? Convocational condemnations of objectionable books could do nothing to limit, but might do much to increase, their circulation. Decisions on doctrinal and ethical questions, however incessantly clamoured for, could carry no greater measure of authority than that which knowledge and sound reasoning could give them. No considering man now attaches any weight to the pronouncements of authority, however theoretically great, which cannot make good its verdicts in the open court of informed and rational debate. It is certain that Convocational votes command little attention, and less deference, while the importance attached to Convocational debates will be determined by the personal reputation of the debaters. This reputation has sometimes in the past been very high. There are reasons for thinking that it now tends to fall. Outstanding personalities are few, and becoming fewer, in the ranks of the clergy. The Convocations, although often criticized as inadequately representative, do probably reflect very fairly the general levels of culture, knowledge, and opinion among the clergy. The age of erudite and scholarly ecclesiastics has passed. It is not probable that the Anglican hierarchy will again be distinguished by the massive learning of Thirlwall and Lightfoot. The succession of episcopal historians ended with Stubbs and Creighton. The recognized qualifications for high ecclesiastical office reflect the public taste.

In the opinion of the Bishop of Gloucester the abolition of the Anglican monopoly of the ancient universities has not been unattended with ill consequences. "The supply of learned clergymen in the Church of England", he says, "is far less than it was." It may, however, be doubted whether the intellectual indolence fostered by academic privilege did not at all times outweigh the intellectual stimulus of the academic endowments. More potent has been the effect of the increasingly miscellaneous character of academic education, the new direction of public interest, and the changed social traditions of the clergy themselves.

In effect, the debates in Convocation have reflected the intellectual, social, economic, and even political fashions of the day. The members are more interested in social ethics than in theology, in liturgiology than in history, in Biblical criticism and psychology than in classics, mathematics, or pure science. Thus there is nothing to clothe convocational debates with any distinctive interest or importance. The same matters are being everywhere debated by the laity, and discussed in the newspapers, with no less knowledge, often with larger practical experience, and sometimes with superior intellectual equipment. It is not to Convocation that men look when they seek some help in the urgent and painful task of solving the problems, religious, moral, and economic, which bear so heavily on the mind and conscience of modern churchmen.

Moreover, its purely clerical composition is everywhere felt to be a grievous disadvantage. Indeed, it may well be asked, what good purpose Convocation now serves, since its entire personnel has been included in the membership of the Church Assembly, created by the Enabling Act (1919). It is not to be forgotten that the original scheme on which the Enabling Act was based contemplated the transfer to the newly created Church Assembly of that power of enacting canons which has ever been the highest function of the Convocations.

If it be urged that there are matters, from the handling of which it is desirable that the laity should be excluded, it may suffice to point out that by the constitution of the Church Assembly, the House of Clergy (which includes the entire personnel of both the Lower Houses of the Provincial Convocations) can at any time sit separately for discussions, and that the legislative decisions of the

Assembly require the agreement of all three Houses. In these circumstances the maintenance of the ancient Convocations, whose functions have either ceased or been transferred to the Assembly, appears to be an irrational concession to a rather archaic ecclesiastical conservatism. It complicates the machinery of self-government without any compensating advantage. It may be added that the irrational and inconvenient arrangement of two Convocations in one national Church would be ended if the House of Clergy in the Church Assembly replaced the separate action of the clergy in the Provincial Convocations.

III. THE LAMBETH CONFERENCE

The occasion which led to the summoning of the first Lambeth Conference in 1867 was colonial and controversial. In 1853, Colenso, a man of great ability and independence of mind, but tactless and uncompromising, had become Bishop of Natal. The experience of the missionary confirmed and increased the doubts of the theological student. He expressed his mind with characteristic brusqueness in his *Commentary on St Paul's Epistle to the Romans* (1861). A series of critical studies of the Pentateuch confirmed and extended the alarm of orthodox churchmen. His intimate friend, Frederic Denison Maurice, was permanently alienated. Colenso became the storm centre of an embittered controversy. In South Africa he found himself confronted by a bold and bigoted Tractarian in the person of his Metropolitan, Gray, bishop of Cape Town. Gray would make no terms with "heresy", and acknowledge no subordination of the Church to the State in spiritual matters. Thus the doctrinal issue expanded into a controversy on the whole relation of Church and State. Gray had no doubt as to his competence to deal effectively with one of his own suffragans. Orthodox zeal was united in his mind with a desire to vindicate the spiritual independence of the South African Church. Thus colonial sentiment joined with theological conservatism and Tractarian clericalism in clothing the South African conflict with gravity. The notion of a Conference of the Anglican Communion for the settlement of a dispute which was assuming formidable proportions arose in Canada.

It arose, strange to say, from the interest awakened in North America by the Church affairs of South Africa.

At the Provincial synod of the Canadian Church, held on September 20th, 1865, it was unanimously agreed, upon the motion of the Bishop of Ontario, to urge upon the Archbishop of Canterbury and the Convocation of his Province that means should be adopted "by which the members of our Anglican Communion in all quarters of the world should have a share in the deliberations for her welfare, and be permitted to have a representation in one General Council of her members gathered from every land".[1]

It is, perhaps, worth noting the expression "General Council" employed by the Canadian Synod, for that expression carries a suggestion of that spiritual authority which the Lambeth Conferences have frequently disavowed, but which none the less is increasingly associated with them. Considerable apprehension was expressed in England when the project of a Conference was disclosed.

In the Upper House, Archbishop Longley took the utmost pains to "diminish the doubts and difficulties of some of his brethren". "It should be distinctly understood", he said, "that at this meeting no declaration of faith shall be made, and no decision come to which shall affect generally the interests of the Church, but that we shall meet together for Brotherly counsel and encouragement.... I should refuse to

[1] *The Five Lambeth Conferences*, compiled under the direction of Archbishop Davidson.

convene any assembly which pretended to enact any canons or affected to make any decisions binding on the Church.... I feel I undertake a great responsibility in assenting to this request, and certainly if I saw anything approaching to what (is apprehended) as likely to result from it, I should not be disposed to sanction it, but I can assure (my brethren) that I should enter on this meeting in the full confidence that nothing would pass but that which tended to brotherly love and union, and would bind the Colonial Church, which is certainly in a most unsatisfactory state, more closely to the Mother Church.[1]

The complaisant primate unquestionably meant what he said, but he did not allow for the natural progress of events, nor consider the inevitable effect upon the authority of an episcopal assembly of the more exalted theory of the episcopal office, which the Tractarians had proclaimed, and which has rapidly established itself in the Anglican mind. There is significance in the change of style with which the pronouncements of the Conferences are issued to the Church. Instead of the modest formula of 1867—"we, the undersigned Bishops, gathered under the good Providence of God for prayer and conference at Lambeth"—there is the imposing phrasing of 1930— "We Archbishops and Bishops of the Holy Catholic Church in full communion with the Church of England". Moreover, as the numbers attending the Conference increased, from 76 in 1867 to 308 in 1930, it could not but follow that the practical importance of the decisions at which the Conference arrived should become greater; and, as the nature of the questions dealt with was more closely bound up with the principles of religion and the credenda of the Church, it was unavoidable that the resolutions which dealt with them should tend to acquire the character of doctrinal definitions. General Councils are indeed no longer possible since the Catholic Church

[1] *Ibid.*

is so divided as to be incapable of united action: but Councils which are less than "General" are not therefore destitute of authority in faith and morals. Surely, it might fairly be thought, the Lambeth Conference could not be less authoritative than the older episcopal assemblies. It is certain that, in the view of those numerous clergy and laity of the Anglican Communion who hold the high episcopalian theory of the Oxford Movement, the resolutions of the Lambeth Conference are not destitute of spiritual authority, undefined indeed, but none the less binding *in foro conscientiae*. Dr Pusey, writing to Archbishop Tait a few weeks before the Lambeth Conference of 1878, assumed for the pronouncements of the bishops a far more authoritative character than Archbishop Longley would have allowed:

You are going to preside, my dearest Archbishop, over a band of men who have been called of God to an Apostolic burden of authority.... We can expect, and we do expect with confidence, that God the Holy Spirit will guide your deliberations, and—what you say will come to us with the Lord's own stamp upon it, and we, your children, will receive and obey the message you deliver to us.[1]

It is not to be forgotten that the purely episcopal composition of the Conference, the secrecy of the debates, and the almost invariable affectation of unanimity in the adoption of the published resolutions are all features of the Conferences at Lambeth which, while emphasizing its authoritative character, detract from the interest and importance of its decisions. It is only in a very general sense that the bishops can be described as representatives of their churches, for they attend officially, and not as specially chosen deputies. Apart from their episcopal consecration, it is difficult to discern in many, probably in most, of the bishops any special qualifications for pro-

[1] *V. Life*, II, 413.

nouncing judgment on the perplexing questions which may be submitted to them. Episcopal consecration conveys no "donum veritatis" which shall compensate for the absence of learning, experience, intellectual ability, and a sound judgment. Episcopal assemblies have no good record in the past: it is difficult to place much confidence in their fitness for the functions with which the enthusiasts for episcopacy would clothe them. It would always be valuable to know the reasons which determine the votes which the bishops give, especially when the resolutions submitted to them are such as arouse strong passions and prejudices. Unanimity destroys more confidence than it creates, while learning, sound argument, and proved saneness of judgment will always command the attention of reasonable men.

Probably the most useful work of the Lambeth Conferences is that which is done by the committees to which, at the start of the sessions, is entrusted the task of preparing reports on the principal subjects with which the bishops are to deal. These reports are debated by the entire Conference, and form the basis of the official resolutions which are finally issued to the public. As the members of the committees are generally selected with a view to their special qualifications, these reports are often of substantial and permanent value.

There can be little doubt that the effect of the Lambeth Conferences on the Established Church has been very great. They have tended to deepen the sense of Anglican fellowship, to strengthen denominational solidarity, to stamp Establishment with an invidiously "Erastian" character, to mitigate the intense parochialism of English churchmanship, to deepen interest in foreign missions, and to stir the imagination of the rank and file. The spectacular effectiveness of these great episcopal gatherings is arresting, and is made the most of by journalists and photographers. It does something to relieve the drabness of normal churchmanship, and, in an age devoted to "pageants", it is something that once in a decade the Anglican Communion can make so impressive a figure. To the bishops from overseas, especially those who labour in loneliness and extraordinary strain to mind and body, it may well be the case that the splendours of ecclesiastical pomp, as seen in the marvellous setting of Canterbury, Westminster and St Paul's, may help them to realize the greatness of their vocation. Readers of Archbishop Benson's life will recall the enthusiastic references in his Diary to the opening service of the Conference of 1888 in Canterbury Cathedral. The Archbishop's historical sense and temperamental fondness for ceremonial would enable him to enjoy to the full the almost patriarchal dignity which invested him as he addressed the lines of bishops from St Augustine's Chair. Probably Lord Northbourne ("a very sharp and experienced critic of such things") expressed the view of thousands of others who with him witnessed the spectacle, when he said, "It is simply the most impressive thing I have ever beheld."[1]

Yet a considering man, acquainted with the facts of our religious life, will chasten his enthusiasm by the reflection that no certificate of ecclesiastical strength and efficiency is less trustworthy than the number of bishops and the magnificence of sacred pageants. It is a sobering fact that while the number of the bishops in England has notably increased during the last century, the number of parochial clergy, both incumbents and stipendiary curates, has notably fallen. There seems but too good reason for thinking that what is true of England is not less true of the whole Anglican Communion.

V. Archbishop Benson's *Life*, II, 213.

IV. THE CHURCH ASSEMBLY

The end of the Great War released into activity a volume of reforming purpose, which the long conflict had held in check. On all hands the cry was for such a reconstruction of the national system as would, in the slogan of the hour, make Great Britain "a country fit for heroes to live in". The general sentiment was eagerly expressed within the Established Church, which was felt to be intolerably hindered in its spiritual work by irrational and largely obsolete restrictions. The experience of war is never favourable to the normal conservatisms of social and religious habit. The younger clergy, who had served as chaplains at the front, and had grown familiar with a freedom of pastoral experiment which could by no means be confined within the limits prescribed by the Act of Uniformity, were clamorous for ecclesiastical reform. For many years indeed dissatisfaction with the Establishment had been growing in Anglican minds. The evangelist, the Anglo-Catholic, and the democrat, differing widely in temper, outlook, and objective, yet agreed in finding the legal system intolerable. The general ferment offered an opportunity, which was eagerly embraced. A brisk agitation for "Life and Liberty for the Church of England" was set on foot, and made rapid progress. When it succeeded in securing the sympathy and approval of the Archbishop of Canterbury, its success was assured. In 1919 the Enabling Bill was passed into law, giving legislative force to the scheme of self-government which had been set out in the report of the Archbishops' Committee on Church and State issued in 1916. The ease with which the great innovation was effected reflected rather the indifference of the nation than the general opinion of the Church. Certainly it is the case that no Act of equal importance was so little demanded by the country, so little understood by the Church, and so little debated in

Parliament. The measure of the Church's decline in social and political importance, which had been taking place during the years preceding the Great War, and which had been long suspected by the more thoughtful students of the national life, was suddenly revealed when Parliament surrendered without reluctance its control of ecclesiastical legislation, and sanctioned without discussion a new constitution for the National Church.

If Parliament were no longer to be accepted as competent to legislate for the Church of England, it was necessary to create an alternative legislature sufficiently representative of English Christianity to justify the retention and rights of the National Church. That was the crux of the practical problem. So far as the clergy were concerned, they possessed their ancient Convocations, which only needed reform and letters of business to become again what they had been before 1717, effective organs of the clerical mind. But the laity of England had hitherto expressed their will, directly or indirectly, through Parliament, directly in legislation for the Church or indirectly in choosing the statesmen by whose advice the sovereign exercised his ecclesiastical prerogative. What alternative to Parliament as an organ of the lay mind should be provided? Had the Church of England been a non-established denomination like the Nonconformist and Roman Catholic Churches, or a disestablished denomination, like the Church of Ireland and the Churches of Wales, Canada, and Australia, there would have been little practical difficulty about defining its membership, but an Established Church has a character of its own, and both the theory and the tradition of the Church of England were inconsistent with a narrowly denominational definition of its membership. Given the necessity of a legal definition of Anglican membership, it is perhaps difficult to find fault with the actual definition provided by the Enabling Act. Every person of either sex who is baptized and above the age of eighteen years may, on signing a simple declaration, be enrolled as a parochial elector, and as such vote for the parochial church meeting, which, by an extremely indirect process elects the lay members of the Church Assembly. To this Church Assembly Parliament has delegated its legislative authority, retaining nothing more than a naked veto on the measures which the Assembly passes, and which have been submitted by the Ecclesiastical Committee of the Privy Council to the two Houses of the Legislature. How far, it must be asked, have the English people, baptized members of the Church, availed themselves of the new franchise? How far have they shown any disposition to use the powers bestowed on them? The success or failure of the Enabling Act is really determined by the answer to these questions. That the Church Assembly has done much useful work, and passed measures which have been long desired, proves nothing: for a merely nominated body could have done as much, and what was desired was a constitutional instrument through which the mind of the English laity could express itself. This will certainly not have been found if the English laity take no part, or only a trifling part, in working the new system. So long as the matters dealt with by the Church Assembly are non-controversial, or affect no considerable public interest, the non-representative character of the Assembly matters little, but so soon as its action extends to matters respecting which opinion within the Church is sharply divided, or affects interests of large general importance, the whole validity of its action, and certainly the success of its legislation must finally turn on the extent in which it is truly representative.

The agitators for ecclesiastical autonomy were divided in their objective. Some desired to strengthen the Establishment by facilitating ecclesiastical legislation and serving the interest of practical efficiency. Others desired to make an end of the Establishment in the interest of complete denominational autonomy. This dissidence of objective disclosed itself in connexion with the new franchise. Should baptism or confirmation be the necessary qualification of the parochial electors, who were to take over from the citizens their immemorial concern in ecclesiastical government? Since 70 per cent of the nation was known to have been baptized in the parish church, it was not unreasonable to regard the baptismal basis as securing an electorate large enough to justify a national claim. To insist on confirmation would be to exclude from potential membership the great majority of the nation. The scheme as originally drafted adopted the narrower basis, but the Representative Church Council after considerable debate changed its ground in order to facilitate the passage of the Enabling Bill. Baptism was to be sufficient. Bishop Gore was so distressed that he chose the moment for announcing his resignation of the See of Oxford. He stated his reason in a letter to the Archbishop of Canterbury:

I am convinced that in abandoning the present basis of franchise which includes confirmation we have sacrificed principle to the desire for larger numbers on our rolls, and that largely for the sake of maintaining the "national" position of the Church. I know this does not represent your point of view, or that of others of my friends who gave their vote for the baptismal franchise. But it represents, I think, the effect of the vote on the whole. And it leaves me in a very embarrassing position. I cannot fight against a movement towards autonomy for the Church to which for many years past I have largely devoted my life, but I cannot any longer co-operate cordially with the movement now that it has placed itself on what I think is so false a basis.[1]

The latest published *Official Year Book of the Church of England* (1938) states that the parochial rolls through-

---

[1] *V.* Bell's *Randall Davidson*, II, 971

out the country contained 3,559,926 names. The population at the last census (1931) was 37,510,817. The parliamentary electors numbered about 18,000,000. It must not be forgotten when parliamentary electors are compared with parochial electors that while the one must be above the age of 21, the other may be as young as 18. But this is not all. If it could be shown that the parochial electors displayed a keen interest in their ecclesiastical duty, the situation would be disturbing, but not actually scandalous. But when it is known that they care so little about their duty that no more than a petty fraction of their number attend the annual meetings at which the parochial church councils are elected, it is apparent that the new system has not succeeded in arousing interest or attachment. In 1924 the Bishop of Durham was at the pains of ascertaining the facts in his diocese. It appeared that out of nearly 160,000 parochial electors, only 8838 attended the annual meetings, where they elected 6828 councillors. There is no reason whatever for supposing that Durham was exceptional. If then, it may fairly be assumed that the parochial electors generally are as indifferent to their duty as those in Durham, we must conclude that the Lay House of the Church Assembly (which by the Enabling Act was charged with the legislative functions of Parliament so far as the Church of England is concerned) is chosen by no more than 200,000 persons of both sexes above the age of eighteen years.[1]

Though, however, the Church Assembly is so feebly rooted in popular support that it cannot reasonably claim to represent the national institution, it may fairly speak for the religious denomination. It includes the entire episcopate, the lower Houses of both Convocations, and a numerous body of laity drawn from all the dioceses. For most purposes it may be trusted to express

[1] V. Quo Tendimus? Primary Charge delivered at his visitation in November 1924, by Herbert Hensley Henson, Bishop of Durham.

the mind, not of the English nation, but of that part of it which values membership in the English Church. In the House of Lords, when introducing the Prayer Book Measure, the Archbishop of Canterbury was rightly careful to indicate the character and the limits of the Assembly's claim to attention. "The House of Laity in the Church Assembly", he said,

do not profess to represent the people of England, but they do profess to represent the Church of England, the people who care about these matters and go to church, who want to use their Prayer Book, who care about the form that Book should take, who understand the question, and who are the people really qualified to speak.[1]

In the course of twenty years the Church Assembly has achieved much, and learned something. The list of measures which it has passed, and which, under the provisions of the Enabling Act, have been legalized by Parliament, is long and impressive. Many salutary reforms have been effected, and some long-standing anomalies have been remedied. The reports of the Assembly's committees are often learned, sometimes interesting, and occasionally valuable. It may be questioned whether the procedure of the House of Commons is really well suited for the guidance of an Assembly so different in structure, in power, and in purpose. There is a growing opinion that the arrangement by which the Archbishop of Canterbury is *ex officio* chairman is unfortunate. The Archbishop is the head of the Hierarchy, and as such must necessarily exercise a dominating influence on ecclesiastical policy. His position in the Church Assembly is more properly regarded as analogous to that of the Prime Minister in the House of Commons, than to that of the Speaker. Indeed, there is an apparent incongruity between the two positions,

[1] *V. Life*, II, 1545.

which must make their union in the same hands very unsatisfactory. Yet something very like this union is involved in the Archbishop's chairmanship of the Assembly in which he is the inevitable leader. It is only the remarkable ability of their Graces which has made possible the working of an essentially irrational arrangement. In the hands of less competent persons it might work very badly. And there is this additional disadvantage involved in it. The Assembly does not always receive from the Archbishop the guidance which it needs, and is entitled to expect, for his Grace's position in the chair is rarely compatible with his intervention in debate, never really compatible when the subject of debate is one on which there is acute difference of opinion. The efficiency of the debates would probably be increased if the chair were occupied by a layman who could fulfil in the Assembly the function of the Speaker in the House of Commons, and the Archbishop of Canterbury were relieved of a laborious and incongruous duty. There can be no question as to the gain which the Church would derive from a franker and more frequent expression of the Primate's personal judgment on policies and projects.

CHAPTER 10

RELATIONS WITH
OTHER CHURCHES

The Christian Society was not permanently contained within a single ecclesiastical system. From the first its visible unity was endangered by the personal ambitions of hierarchs, and by the dissident teachings of heretics. Constantine's establishment of Christianity as the religion of the Empire bound Church and State so closely together, that the one perforce shared the fortunes of the other. When the single Empire was organized on a dual basis, having an Eastern capital in Constantinople, and a Western capital in Rome, the unity of the imperial Church was perilously strained, and long before the formal severance of the Churches in 1054 a breach destined to be permanent had been effected. The schism was stereotyped by isolation, by difference of language, race, and cultural type, by political interest, and by personal ambition. Yet it was never accepted without misgiving and reluctance. Serious Christians could not but perceive the magnitude of the scandal implicit in the fact that the Society of Christian Believers could not be included in a single system. From the time when the fellowship between the Church of the East and the Church of the West had been broken, the problem of reunion has pursued and perplexed devout Christians, and, from time to time, has forced itself on Christian politicians. The Crusades both attested the reality of the religious fellowship, and embittered the absence of ecclesiastical unity. The passion of spiritual fraternity, which had unquestionably driven the first Crusaders to their great venture, speedily gave place to less ideal motives. The policy of monarchs, the greedy enterprise of merchants, social discontent, and the spirit of adventure, lowered both the level of crusading intention and the methods of crusading warfare. The sack of Constantinople in 1204 was not only a political blunder of the first magnitude, but also a gross moral outrage and a grievous spiritual disaster. It destroyed the possibility of any reunion of the Churches. Under the waxing pressure of the Mohammedan aggression, the Eastern Empire turned again to the West, and again pleaded the case for common action of Christians as such.

On the eve of the final catastrophe a formal union of the Churches was achieved at the Council of Florence (1439); but the panic-stricken diplomacy of the Eastern representatives had underrated the strength of dissident feeling in Constantinople, and the union of the Churches, which had been proclaimed with great parade of thanksgiving in the West, perished as soon as it was announced to the East. The failure of Eugenius IV provides an impressive example of the futility of arranging religious agreement by diplomatic expedients. Where personal convictions, vested interests, and long-standing traditions are involved, the popular method of the "Round Table Conference" can never achieve any lasting agreement. Nemesis pursued the diplomatic achievement of Florence. The Eastern Church fell into its long servitude to Islam. The Western Church moved quickly to its final disruption. Less than a century elapsed before Western Christendom was shattered by the crisis of the Reformation.

The separated fragments, now organized as independent churches, local and confessional, had to face the old issue of reunion in an aggravated form. What should be their relations to the truncated Western Church, from which they had broken away? to the Eastern Church which, by reason of their schism, had become both more intelligible and more attractive? to one another? The complicated problem of reunion was, in the case of the Church of England, rendered both more urgent and more difficult not only by the character of its reformation, but also by the legal establishment, which involved so close an association with the State, that no ecclesiastical action could be regarded as lying outside the range of the State's interest and concern. We may consider the problem in its Anglican expression as it relates to the Church of Rome, to the Eastern Churches, and to the non-episcopal Churches throughout the world.

I. RELATIONS WITH THE CHURCH OF ROME

The hope of recovering England to the Roman obedience was not soon abandoned by the Popes. At first the prospect was not unfavourable, but it soon worsened. The dramatic victory of the Counter-Reformation under Mary Tudor was so mismanaged as finally to ruin the Papacy in England. The brief space of restored Papal jurisdiction under the unhappy queen and her Spanish husband was marked not only by a savage persecution of Protestants which created in English minds an un-quenchable hatred of the Roman Church, but also by a subordination of English interests to Spanish policy which gave mortal offence to the sensitive patriotism of the people. The union of moral repugnance and national feeling associated with the less respectable influence of the vested interests created by the secularization of the monastic property was quite irresistible. The accession of Elizabeth secured the complete and irreversible triumph of the Reformation in England. When, in 1570, Pius V excommunicated the great queen, he did but give formal expression to an accomplished fact. Elizabeth's successor was a conceited pedant with a foible for theological controversy, who imagined himself uniquely qualified for the rôle of ecclesiastical peacemaker. The futile negotiations which James I carried on seemed to imply that the reconciliation of his kingdom was not wholly impracticable, but they rather amused the foolish monarch than commanded any serious attention from the experienced diplomatists of Rome, and whatever prospect of success may have existed was finally extinguished by the murderous treason of Guy Fawkes and his associates. The far-resounding scandal of the Gunpowder Plot renewed in the public mind the fear and loathing of Papistry, which had been the bequest of "Bloody Mary". The matrimonial projects of the Stuart sovereigns kept alive in diplomatic circles the quite futile notion of the reconciliation of England, but those projects served only to damage the prestige of the monarchs, and to stimulate the Protestant feeling of their subjects. This alienation of Protestant confidence was not the least potent of the causes which brought about the overthrow of Charles I. In the Great Rebellion, when the original association of the monarchy with the English Reformation was obscured and jeopardized, the hopes of the Papists revived. Might they not fish in the troubled waters with good prospect of success? The conspicuous loyalty of the Roman Catholics in the Civil War, and the heavy sacrifices which they made in the Royal Martyr's cause, brought them considerable credit when at length the Restoration was effected, for the taint of disloyalty had passed from themselves to their Puritan adversaries. Their hopes were raised, and their influence increased by the Papalist sympathies of the restored monarch, and the loudly professed Papalist convictions of his brother, the heir apparent. But English Protestantism was inexorable. Accordingly, when Charles II attempted to mitigate the legal hardships of his Roman Catholic subjects, he found himself confronted by an unconquerable aversion. His attempts did but stimulate the suspicious Protestantism of his people. The outburst of popular feeling in the disgraceful episode of the Popish Plot stained the nation's honour, but it disclosed the magnitude of the breach between the court and the nation. Not even the fervid loyalty of the Cavaliers could mitigate their fear and hatred of Rome. Their experience of Roman intolerance in France during the interregnum had not tended to moderate their Protestant prejudices. The stars in their courses fought against the Popes. Louis XIV, whom they regarded with alarm and aversion, and whose policy they laboured to defeat, was, in English eyes, their most conspicuous champion, and the very embodiment of their persecuting fanaticism. The bigotry of Louis XIV in France told against Papal interests in England, for the revocation of the Edict of Nantes in 1685 confirmed the worst suspicions, and when it was followed by the arrival in England of swarms of Huguenot refugees, the Protestant feeling of the people was deeply stirred. The refugees were so many living proofs, not so much of French despotism, as of Papal intolerance. That the reigning Pontiff had regarded with something more than benevolence the expedition of William of Orange counted for nothing beside the fact that he was the head of the French king's persecuting religion. It must be admitted that James II was singularly unfortunate in the time and circumstances which conditioned his resolute effort to restore his kingdom to the Papal obedience. When, therefore, the stupid fanaticism of the king led him to strain his legal prerogative in order to advance his religious purpose, he alienated the people, and lost his throne. With the flight of the last Roman Catholic sovereign, the possibility of Romanizing England perished. The Revolution would run no risks. It bound the monarchy definitely to the Protestant religion, and thus made for ever impracticable any repetition of the attempt to recover the spiritual allegiance of the people by the "short cut" of winning the monarch. This favourite and fruitful procedure of the Counter-Reformation could not be applied to England.

It is certain that within recent years the decay of theological interest has favoured the growth of kindlier sentiments between the Churches of Christendom. Even in the case of the Church of Rome, though the exorbitant claims of the Papacy must ever continue to prohibit religious fellowship, yet it is the case that the old fierceness of antagonism has largely abated. The admission of Roman Catholics to the universities has brought Roman Catholic scholars into the republic of learning on equal terms, and created a consciousness of common purpose. In short, the "climate of opinion" has wonderfully changed. Roman Catholics no longer arouse the old fears and resentments. Not even the alliance with the Fascist State can galvanize into reality the temporal power of the Pope. It survives as an interesting archaism, but counts for nothing in the serious politics of the modern world. Diplomatic relations with the Vatican have been restored in spite of the protests of "die-hard" Protestants. Most English people look upon the renewal of direct negotiations with the Papacy as a reasonable consequence of the removal of Roman Catholic disabilities, and a judicious recognition of the fact that a large number of British citizens throughout the Empire profess the Roman form of Christianity. Moreover, the dangers which in former times were found to attach to a Roman Catholic sovereign are now securely guarded against not only by the Act of Settlement, but also by the constitutional limitation of the sovereign's powers. The declaration of Protestant belief, which the law requires every sovereign to make at the beginning of his reign, has, with general assent, been modified in deference to the reasonable objections of Roman Catholics, but it has not been abandoned. It may, perhaps, be said that so far as the State is concerned, a tolerable *modus vivendi* with the Church of Rome has been discovered.

The Roman Catholic community in Britain is now composed of three distinct sections—the descendants of those who never accepted the Reformation, the converts from the non-Roman churches, mainly, but not exclusively, from the Church of England, and the considerable number of Irish immigrants. The hereditary Papists may be left out of count. In Elizabeth's glorious reign patriotism carried most of them into the Establishment, and the penal laws had some effect in reducing the number of the rest. They had dwindled to a petty sect, too conservative to arouse political suspicion, and too few to justify ecclesiastical alarm, when the Tractarian Movement changed the situation. First Newman, and then Manning, carried into the Roman camp a considerable number of English Churchmen. The Tractarian version of Anglicanism survived the secession of the Tractarian "converts", and created a new attitude of mind towards Roman doctrines and usages within the Established Church. The stream of conversions has never wholly ceased, but it is negligible. Far more important is the transformation of faith and feeling among English churchmen, and especially among English clergymen, and, though it does not seem likely to multiply conversions, this transformation enfeebles the Church of England by loosening its hold on the public mind and conscience, and not less by providing Nonconformity with a new justification to replace that which the abolition of its legal disabilities had destroyed. The immigration of Irish Papists has been stimulated by the restrictions on the admission of indigent foreigners imposed by the Government of the United States. The destitute Papists from Celtic Ireland, who are turned back from America, are invading Liverpool and Glasgow, and creating social problems of considerable perplexity. A comparatively high birth rate increases their number and a sharply accentuated racial distinctiveness hinders their assimilation. The Roman Church exerts its immense authority to stimulate the birth rate, and to stereotype the social isolation. Thus the problems created by the Irish immigrants are less religious than social and economic. Their ecclesiastical distinctiveness is mainly important as adding difficulty to the solution of the secular problems. The Irish Papists are numerous in the districts where unskilled labour is required; but save for the effect of the mixed marriages which the Roman Church utilizes as a proselytizing instrument, they do not affect the religious distribution of the people.

Ever since the breach with Rome at the Reformation, there have been members of the Church of England who have indulged the hope, that some concordat between the Churches might be agreed upon. From time to time essays, more or less authoritative, have been made in this direction. When internal dissidence within the Roman Communion has seemed to permit the hope of actual disruption, there have never been lacking Anglicans who have made approaches to like-minded Papists. Gallicans, the victims of the French Revolution, Modernists—all have looked longingly to the one reformed Church which (save for the partial exception of the Church of Sweden) retained the broad essentials of the Catholic system. But negotiations with the Church of Rome are condemned to failure for two sufficient reasons. On the one hand, there is no agreed basis on which the differences between the Churches can be debated. Anglicans assume that the claims of the Papacy are capable of being so explained as not to conflict with their own principles, whereas those claims are matters of religious conviction with Papists, and could only be moderated by an act of spiritual treason. On the other hand, the negotiators are never adequately representative of the Churches which they profess to represent. It is very significant that the Encyclical Letter of the last Lambeth Conference (1930), while describing in highly optimistic language the relations of the Church of England with Eastern and Protestant Churches, omitted all mention of the Church of Rome; while the numerous committees of the Conference, which considered the Unity of the Church, reported both the failure of the Conversations at Malines, and the decisive action of the Roman Church:

Since the death of Cardinal Mercier, such Conversations have been forbidden, and Roman Catholics have in the Encyclical letter *Mortalium animos* (1928) been prohibited from taking part in any Conference on unity. The Committee desires to express its conviction of the value of such Conversations and Conferences carried out in a spirit of loyalty, and it much regrets that by the action of the Pope all such meetings have been forbidden, and Roman Catholics have been prohibited from taking part in conferences on Reunion. This regret, they have reason to believe, is shared by many members of the Church of Rome. They regret also that in the Encyclical the method of "complete absorption" has been proposed to the exclusion of that suggested in the Conversations, as, for example, in the paper read at Malines, "L'église Anglicane unie, non absorbée". There are difficulties greater than perhaps were realized in the scheme proposed, but it has the great merit of attempting to recognize to some extent at any rate the autonomy which might be possible in a united Church.[1]

The language of the committee, it may be conjectured, reflects rather a desire to "save the face" of the Archbishop and the Anglican negotiators, than any genuine belief in the wisdom or potential effectiveness of the

[1] *V. Report of the Lambeth Conference*, 1930, p. 131.

Malines Conversations. Probably the general view will incline to credit the Roman Catholic authorities with a clearer vision of possibilities. If the Vatican had been more complaisant, and some concordat between England and Rome had been formulated at Malines, does any one who knows the religious situation in England imagine that it would have been received with any other feelings than those of astonishment and indignation?

How far is it true to say that the Roman Catholic Church is making progress in Great Britain? Zealous Roman proselytizers and apprehensive Protestants agree in asserting that such is the case. While the Established Church is notoriously paralysed by its domestic dissensions, and the Dissenters are handicapped by the weakness of their systems, the crudity of their distinctive beliefs, and the repulsiveness of their "corybantic" methods, the Roman Catholic Church preserves an aspect of impressive stability, and pursues a consistently aggressive policy. Emphasis is placed on the prominence given to Roman Catholic activities in the newspapers, on the notable increase of priests and nuns, on the successful maintenance of Roman Catholic schools, on the numerous "conversions" of more or less prominent individuals, on the numerously signed statements of Anglo-Catholic clergymen who are prepared to accept the Pope's authority. Politicians and men of the world, accustomed to identify religious influence with ecclesiastical activity, are easily persuaded to adopt the opinion that, in the bewildering unsettlement of the public mind, which now menaces the very bases of social order and personal morality, the strongly organized Church of Rome is alone competent to hold its ground, and must finally monopolize the representation of Christianity in the civilized world. It may not, indeed, be denied, that the non-Roman Churches are in present circumstances at an apparent disadvantage. Protestantism addresses its appeal to the reason and conscience of the individual: Rome appeals to the hopes and fears of the multitude. Modern conditions tend to enfeeble the Churches which magnify the pulpit, but to leave unaffected the influence of the altar. The Protestant exaltation of the preacher's function was a source of strength so long as society was settled, but it has become a source of weakness since society has become, beyond all precedent, fluid. The development of society has robbed the pulpit of much of its importance, both by limiting its range, and by creating rivals in its sphere. The Press and the Platform, to which must now be added Broadcasting, have taken over much of its work. Preachers can never again wield the social or political authority which attached to them when "tuning the pulpits" was a part of State policy which not even the strongest statesman could afford to neglect. In any case, the preacher's influence is bound up with the habit of public worship, itself inseparable from Sunday observance. Both presuppose a society which is stable, resident from father to son in the same place, governed by tradition, coloured and led by personal example. If the Sunday be secularized, and the churches empty, if the close-knit fellowship of immemorial neighbourhood lose reality, and men live as strangers in the places where they rather pernoctate than reside, it needs no argument to show that the preacher's opportunity has vanished, and his function been destroyed. No learning, ability, or devotion in the pulpit can wake response from empty pews. The preacher's *raison d'être* is a congregation. If the last has disappeared, the first has no apparent reason for remaining. When, however, Christianity has once been practically identified with the priest's ministry at the altar and in the confessional, it is apparent that it has been largely released from local attachments. There is no insuperable difficulty about effecting a *modus vivendi* between the Church and modern society. One altar is as effective as another: and the confessional may be everywhere available. Both appeal to fundamental human needs which may be satisfied by any priest anywhere. The elasticity of sacerdotalism matches with comparative facility the bewildering mobility of modern society.

It it be objected that the amazing success of peripatetic preachers like Wesley and Whitfield in the eighteenth century, and Moody and Sankey in the nineteenth, disproves the impotence of modern preaching, it may suffice to reply that the mobility of modern society, which is now threatening the Protestant pulpit with practical futility, had no existence before the twentieth century. Whether the Protestant Churches will prove able to develop an elasticity of system which shall equal the elasticity of Rome is a question which will be variously answered. Those who believe that evangelical principles are essentially true will not doubt their ultimate triumph. History is full of surprises, and there are not wanting evidences, that the rapid and apparently irresistible advance of secularism is already waking reactions which may presently develop into a great revival of the Christian religion, albeit in forms widely different from those which have hitherto been its instruments.

II. EASTERN CHRISTIANITY

Eastern Christianity possesses for the considering Christian student a dignity and an interest which are unique. Its famous churches link the age of the Apostles with our own. The New Testament is written in its mother tongue. The creeds and liturgies of Christendom were its workmanship. In language, organization, liturgical habit, and religious outlook it perpetuates that distant age when the Christian society was still united, and could utter its corporate mind in doctrinal definitions. The solid

fabric of Catholic theology remains the supreme monu-
ment of constructive religious thinking, and it has not yet
been superseded. To these considerations must be added
the pathetic appeal which Eastern Christianity can base
on its calamitous history. In deepening measures it has
suffered oppression since the tide of Mohammedan conquest overwhelmed civilization in the Eastern Empire.
The Eastern Churches have borne the brunt of the battle
with Islam, and, at infinite cost to themselves, have been
the barricade for the West against disaster. Inevitably
they carry the disfiguring scars of their long martyrdom.
They have acquired the distinctive vices of the oppressed
—suspicion, servility, deceit. Isolated from the progressive influences which have created the civilization of the
West, and subjected to the harsh dominance of a culture
inferior morally and intellectually to their own, they have
sunk into an almost barbaric superstition. In fact, the
Eastern Churches carry into the modern world the temper
and outlook of that older time, when doctrinal controversy was the primary interest of Christians, and
Christ's religion was generally identified with a meticulous
theological orthodoxy. Thus the Churches of the East are
incorrigibly archaic. The justice of this description is not
really affected by the circumstance, in itself of considerable importance, that within recent years there have been
many Eastern ecclesiastics who have studied in Western
universities, and even attained distinction in critical and
theological learning. They carry large hopes for the future,
but for the present can do but little to affect the prevailing
low levels of their Churches. The Great War, and the
tremendous social and economic upheavals which have
followed it, have told with great, perhaps, decisive effect
on the Churches of Russia and the East, but whether
the final outcome will be favourable or not remains
doubtful. The time for forming a judgment has not yet
arrived.

Eastern Christianity has attracted the sympathetic regard of English churchmen, less by its venerable antiquity and pathetic history, than by its controversial significance. Whatever may be thought of its religious quality, there can be no question as to its ecclesiastical character. It is the last rather than the first which has most relevance to the issue at stake in the continuing conflict with the Papacy. Reunion with the Eastern Churches is facilitated by the very factor which obstructs reunion with the great Church of the West.

When from the Church of Rome we pass to the Churches of the East, we are conscious of entering into a different ecclesiastical atmosphere. Here most of the obstacles to mutual understanding are absent. There are no bitter memories of long-continued strife, no accumulations of controversy, no continuing exasperation of proselytizing activities on both sides, no strong tradition of patriotic suspicion, no evil legacies of polemical hatred. In the standing conflict with the Papacy the Eastern Churches might seem to be the natural allies of the Church of England. An episcopal church in the West which had repudiated the Pope's jurisdiction could not but have common ground with the Churches in the East which had never acknowledged it. In point of fact, English churchmen have realized the polemical value of Eastern Christianity. Their perception of the obligation of Christian fraternity has in their case not been unassisted by the motive of controversial advantage.

If controversy has coloured the attitude of English churchmen, it is probably true to say that the attitude of Eastern Christians has been affected by the inveterate Erastianism of their ecclesiastical tradition. They credit to the English Church much of the prestige of the English State, and interpret Establishment in England as carrying with it something of the political significance of Establishment in the East. Thus on both sides there is an element of potential misunderstanding in the negotiations between the Church of England and the Churches of the East. Moreover, in both cases "distance lends enchantment to the view". Neither Church knows very much about the other. Neither Church is well placed for learning the truth about the other. The discussions between them do not really get to the root of the questions which need answering before any spiritually effective fellowship can be created between them.

The internal dissidence of the Church of England both facilitates and disallows the negotiations with the Churches of the East. There is a section of the English clergy to whom the Reformation has the aspect of a great spiritual calamity, and who regard the fact that the Eastern Churches have never traversed any analogous crisis as rather a help than a hindrance to reunion. No less than 3715 of such clergy signed in May 1922 a "Declaration of Faith", which was addressed "To his holiness the Oecumenical Patriarch and the Holy Synod of the Great Church of Constantinople". This Declaration is stated to be designed

to set forth plainly that which we hold to be the genuine teaching of the English Church on certain matters of faith, touching which we gather from utterances of Eastern-Orthodox hierarchs and theologians that they would welcome some explicit statement from us.

The statement is set out in ten articles, and merits very careful study. It affirms a view of Christianity which would certainly be repudiated by the great majority of Anglican churchmen, which conflicts with the pronouncements of successive Lambeth Conferences, and which could only mislead the Eastern churchmen if they regarded it as anything more than an unauthorized private pronouncement. Its solitary allusion to the Reformation is indirect and belittling. It is implied in a reference to the

Thirty-nine Articles as "a document of secondary importance concerned with local controversies of the sixteenth century". When it is remembered that the Thirty-nine Articles, so far from being merely "concerned with local controversies of the sixteenth century", treat of the fundamentals of all Christian belief, of the rule of faith, of the canon of Scripture, of the creeds, of the Church and sacraments, and of the Church's traditions, it is apparent that the signatories of the Address are not candid or trustworthy representatives of the Church of England. The Thirty-nine Articles set out the "platform" of the Church of England, and constitute its principal doctrinal standard. As such the law requires the English clergy to subscribe to them. In any honest negotiation with other Churches they cannot but have a position of primary importance. It is an unfortunate by-product of negotiations with the unreformed Churches of the East that the Anglican negotiators tend to belittle the distinctive characteristics of the Church of England. Discipline within the English Church, already distressingly weak, is still further weakened. Experience suggests that it is easier to create fresh dissidence in England than to achieve unity abroad. Misconceptions are facilitated on both sides.

Eastern ecclesiastics, visiting England under the guidance of Anglicans who are more anxious to make a favourable impression on their visitors than to bring home to them the truth about English religion, are shown aspects of the Church of England which are little representative of its formal doctrine and actual procedure. Some great ceremonial at St Paul's or Westminster, where archbishops and bishops make a brave show in copes and mitres, reception by the monastic communities of Cowley and Mirfield, a visit to an Anglo-Catholic Congress, or attendance at "High Mass" in some "advanced" church can hardly fail to create in the minds of the foreign visitors a notion of Anglicanism which is curiously remote from the actualities of law, history, and current procedure.

The direct results of Anglican approaches to the Eastern Churches are not likely to be considerable. Those Churches are too far removed from the normal experience of English churchmen to make their attitude important. Whether they regard the Church of England with sympathy or with repugnance makes little practical difference. The indirect results, however, may not be so inconsiderable. The Eastern Churches may be the gainers by being brought into friendly contact with English ecclesiastics, the movements of reform within them may be strengthened and directed, and they may be assisted to withstand the unceasing and unscrupulous aggressions of the Roman Church. In England the effects are less apparently satisfactory. If it may fairly be maintained that negotiations with the Eastern Churches tend to correct the narrowing influence of Anglican insularity, it cannot be reasonably doubted that the inevitable concentration on the specific issues, doctrinal, liturgical, and constitutional, which form the staple of such negotiations, tends to widen the gulf between Anglicans and Non-conformists, and thus to drive into the background the nearer and far more urgent problem of Home Reunion. The eager effort to present Anglicanism to Oriental Christians in an attractive form involves those who make it in a certain lack of candour, a derangement of religious perspectives, a diplomatic concealment of the deeper divergences. Thereby the gulf which separates Anglicans from other Christians of English race and speech is widened, and the profound agreement which, under a bewildering multiplicity of denominational descriptions, does really bind them together, is calamitously obscured. It is notorious that the protagonists of union with the Eastern Churches look coldly on all efforts to effect union with Protestants. Even the recognition of the Church of

Sweden is only defended because the Swedish Lutherans retained the episcopal succession, a fact to which they themselves attach little, if any, religious importance. They do not suffer it to affect their fellowship with the Lutheran Churches of Scandinavia and Germany which are Presbyterian.

III. HOME REUNION

The theory of a National Church, which determined the ecclesiastical policy of the Tudor and Stuart sovereigns, which was expressed in the Prayer Book, in the Thirty-nine Articles, in the Canons of 1604, and in the Acts of Uniformity, and which was powerfully championed by Richard Hooker, was at no time successfully expressed in practice. But its radical unsoundness was only gradually perceived. Puritans generally clung to it not less tenaciously than Anglicans, though they differed as to its rightful application. They sought to shape the National Church on other lines than those which the State had laid down, but as to the rightfulness of the national organization of the Christian society they had no doubt. Neither Anglicans nor Puritans would tolerate dissidence from the national system. Sectaries were abhorrent to both. National churchism may be said to have expired in the violence and confusion of the Civil War. It did indeed reappear at the Restoration, but its course then was embarrassed. With the Revolution it was definitely abandoned. Richard Baxter was its latest Puritan advocate. Toleration, which conflicts with its essential principle, had long been legally secured when, late in the eighteenth century, "the Establishment" was championed by the paradoxical genius of Warburton, the noble eloquence of Burke, and the cold wisdom of Paley. But while on political grounds men had come to acquiesce in religious separations, they always resented them as spiritually enfeebling and apparently scandalous. They could not be harmonized with the interest of Christianity itself, the very interest which all Christians professed to regard as their own.

The final argument for toleration was the necessity of uniting "their Majesties' Protestant subjects in interest and affection". Protestantism could unite where Christianity must divide. Accordingly, while Roman Catholics were held to be properly incapacitated by their religious allegiance, Protestant Dissenters were regarded as loyal in spite of their denominational distinctiveness. The legal and generally unchallenged test of Protestantism was ready to hand in the Thirty-nine Articles. It was provided that the benefits of the Toleration Act should be restricted to those dissenting ministers who, with certain exceptions which did not touch doctrinal issues, subscribed to the Anglican formula. So long as this assumption of a common Protestantism could be made, agreement between Anglicans and Dissenters did not seem wholly impracticable. The breach between them tended to become less religious than social and legal. Relations were embittered by the steady opposition of the Established clergy to every proposal to remove the civic disabilities, which the Toleration Act had not affected, and which, though reduced by a curious legal procedure to the shadow of a shade, were resented as humiliating. With the final disappearance of these civic disabilities, there seemed little reason why the dissidence should not cease.

Three principal reasons may be perceived as explaining the persistence of this unfortunate division, and also the extreme difficulty of bringing it to an end.

1. The political decline of the Papacy has removed the main condition of religious unity in England. It is difficult now to realize the depth and reasonableness of the dread of Rome which haunted English minds before the

final defeat of the Stuarts had been effected. Everybody assumed that some religious establishment was indispensable in a rightly constituted State, and none could doubt that the English Establishment was probably better than any substitute which could be suggested. "A constitution of civil government without any religious establishment is a chimerical project, of which there is no example", wrote Bishop Butler in 1747. Dissenters had stood firm against the blandishments of James II, and their union with the Church in the Revolution had been recognized as the token and pledge of a common Protestantism. The Established Church was confessedly the principal barrier against (to use Bishop Butler's words) "that great corruption of Christianity, popery, which is ever at work to bring us again under its yoke". So long, then, as the Papacy was reasonably held to be a formidable danger to the civil and religious liberty of Great Britain, the spiritual fellowship of churchmen and Dissenters was generally admitted. Occasional conformity was practised by Dissenters, and approved by churchmen. As against the Roman adversary, the essential unity of Church and Dissent was apparent. With the secularization of politics the political power of the Popes has passed away. They use the old language, and still have their nuncios in the European capitals, but they no longer command any serious attention. Thus the old cementing dread of Rome has vanished, and with it has vanished also the consciousness of fundamental agreement. Dividing influences of class, habit, and vested interest, have gathered force, and created a new sharpness of denominational frontiers.

2. While the Church of England, established and endowed, has suffered from the loss of elasticity inseparable from legal establishment, and from the spiritual lethargy fostered by security of income, the Dissenters have been exempt from both disadvantages. They have been able without restraint to adventure and expand: they have

given free course to individual enterprise and enthusiasm. No doubt it is true that they have been exposed to the distinctive dangers of their situation. Individualism has sometimes run riot in the sectarian sphere, and the voluntary system has often stimulated the growth of pharisaism and plutocracy. The broad result of the religious development of English Christianity during the last three centuries is the indisputable fact that alike in the English-speaking communities outside Europe, and in non-Christian lands, the dominant type of non-Roman Christianity is not Anglican but Dissenting. Presbyterians, Independents or Congregationalists, Paptists, and the various descriptions of John Wesley's followers, to say nothing of less important bodies of Dissenters, took the lead both in organizing Christianity among the colonists and their descendants, and in evangelizing the non-Christian world.

These fruitful activities outside Great Britain have synchronized with a hardly less amazing expansion within the island itself. Before the rise of the Methodists, Dissent had shrivelled into a relatively petty force: but Methodism, which originated within the Established Church, soon moved outside its pale, and finally ranked itself as a powerful reinforcement of Dissent. It would not be excessive to say that, at the present time, the effective Christianity of England is almost equally divided between the Establishment and some description, Roman and Protestant, of dissent. Expansion abroad has enhanced the importance of the parent denominations at home.

It needs no argument to show that the problem of Home Reunion could no longer be regarded as possessing a merely domestic character. The intense localism of the Reformers, which was reflected in the legal Establishment, was perforce abandoned, and all questions of ecclesiastical politics had to be treated in universal connexions. The amazing development of obscure insular sects, tolerated but discountenanced by the State, into great Churches, whose members numbering many millions were spread throughout the world, and whose missionary efforts were founding new Churches among the heathen, could not but add greatly to the significance of Dissent.

3. Nor must it be forgotten that numerical expansion has coincided with a remarkable advance in social and intellectual importance. The abolition of the Anglican monopoly in the ancient universities opened a door of opportunity to non-Anglicans which they were quick to pass through. Dissent had always possessed an educational tradition of its own, which was precious and potent when Oxford and Cambridge were at the lowest ebb of academic quality. In Scotland and on the Continent Dissenting students had been able to pursue their studies and gain degrees. The association of dissent with illiteracy, which was created by the sectarian excesses of the Interregnum, and disproved by the eviction of the Nonconformists after the Restoration, was in some measure restored by the Methodists, who spread over the country the type of enthusiastic evangelism which, when grotesquely exhibited by the early Salvationists, was scornfully described as "corybantic Christianity". It cannot be reasonably questioned that at the present time the ordained ministries of the "Free Churches" are not inferior, socially or intellectually, to the Anglican clergy. The intellectual standard of the average Presbyterian minister is probably superior to that of the average Anglican parson. Free Churchmen hold with great distinction theological chairs in the English Universities, and contribute their full share to the national output of critical and theological literature. The religious press connected with the Free Churches is probably superior to that connected with the Established Church.

In these circumstances the problem of Home Reunion has to be considered in a new setting. It has acquired an oecumenical character. It is seen to require another method of handling. It affects no merely local interests, but the cause of religion in every part of the habitable earth. The change is already apparent. A new note of modesty is becoming audible in Anglican proposals; a new note of rightful self-assertion marks the Dissenting rejoinders. The current nomenclature of the religious world is reflecting the altered situation. The Puritans who had been persecuted as Nonconformists, and then tolerated as Dissenters, have now, since the triumph of democracy has secured them in the full enjoyment of civic rights, taken the more impressive name of "Free Churchmen". The sectarian character is repudiated, and the status of churches is claimed for the sects. It is perceived on both sides that negotiations for Home Reunion must proceed on the basis of confessed denominational equality. So far as the Anglican Church is concerned, the "Appeal to All Christian People" put forth by the Lambeth Conference of 1920 may fairly be taken as decisive.

That Appeal is expressed in the language of penitence, of fraternity, of an unaccustomed open-mindedness, of a brave spiritual versatility. But there is ambiguity in it, and, perhaps, a lack of perfect candour. It lies open to the suspicion that those who voted for it were by no means agreed as to its proper significance. These misgivings, which were certainly present in the minds of some of the bishops at the time, have been more than justified by the experience of the following years. Every attempt to translate the "Appeal to All Christian People" into appropriate action has been more effective in arousing suspicion than in facilitating agreement. The natural assumption, that forms of ecclesiastical polity were not henceforth to be included in the essentials of Christianity, which commended the Address to the acceptance of the Protestant denominations, was nowise accordant with that insistence on episcopacy as alone ultimately permissible, which conditioned the votes of many, perhaps most, of the bishops who voted for it at Lambeth. The discovery of the divergence of fundamental assumption has certainly not improved the prospect of Home Reunion. The outlook was more favourable in 1920 than it will be in 1940. The possibility of any reunion with non-Anglicans, whether on the right hand or on the left, which does not involve the disruption of the Anglican Communion remains as doubtful as ever. Yet a process of education is proceeding on both sides. Schisms which are so deeply rooted in history and entrenched in vested interests cannot be quickly healed. The conditions under which the Church of Christ now finds itself living are so novel and so alarming that even the barriers of tradition and bigotry cannot arrest the movement of salutary innovation. Christians of every denominational description are being forced to learn much and to unlearn much in the School of Experience. Facts seem to be disallowing the wearisome debates about the forms of ecclesiastical polity. Where the fruits of the Spirit are clearly seen, who can deny His Presence? The considering Anglican, confronted by the demonstration of redeeming grace in the Dissenting communions, says with St Peter in the House of Cornelius, when the unbaptized Gentiles began to speak with tongues and glorify God—"*Can any man forbid the water, that these should not be baptized, which have received the Holy Ghost as well as we?*" (Acts x. 47). The inference is irresistible: but it was not soon or easily drawn in the first century; it will not be soon or easily drawn in the twentieth. The most formidable obstacles to Home Reunion are not those which come under the consideration of ecclesiastical diplomatists. There is a dissidence of traditions which only time can remove. A fissiparous individualism, on the one hand, confronts an Erastian complaisance, on the other. Education and experience are silently destroying the first: the secularization of the State is plainly disallowing the last. Had it not been for the change effected by the Oxford Movement in the temper and outlook of the Church of England, it is not wholly unreasonable to think, that the historical breach would have been healed by the normal development of religious thought and life in England.

The Oxford Movement has been the subject of a voluminous literature. Its apologists and its critics have been equally decisive in their estimates of its character and value. To the one it has meant for the English Church little less than spiritual resurrection. To the other, it has seemed hardly distinguishable from spiritual apostasy. The truth certainly lies with neither. As in all human works, it was mingled of good and evil. A right judgment is hard to come by, yet some of its consequences are neither obscure, nor inconsiderable, nor disputed. Here it suffices to indicate its effect on the prospect of Home Reunion. The Tractarians repudiated the Protestant character of the English Church, and thereby destroyed the foundation on which Anglicans and Dissenters had hitherto been able to unite. Not agreement in the essentials of Protestant Christianity was henceforth to be emphasized as the indispensable condition of ecclesiastical unity, but identity of polity. This implied a profound alteration in the whole theory and attitude of the Established Church. Episcopacy which, under Elizabeth, had been justified as a political necessity, was, under Victoria, exalted as a religious principle. National establishment which, under the one queen, had been urged as religiously indispensable, declined, under the other queen, into a temporary expedient. The Tractarian logic was simple, ruthless, and exact. Given the premises, the conclusion was inevitable. For a Church to be without bishops, holding office by title of unbroken succession from the

Apostles, was to lack the hall-mark of ecclesiastical legitimacy. A non-episcopal church was, in the propriety of language, no church at all. Variously stated, crudely and offensively, or with learning and a disarming courtesy, that was, and is, the Anglican position as formulated by the authors and disciples of the Oxford Movement. Many circumstances have compelled a salutary change of temper, but, in spite of the new moderation of tone and more generous appreciation of non-episcopalian churches, to which reference has already been made, the official attitude of the Church of England still involves an exclusive claim for the episcopal ministry which has hitherto wrecked every serious attempt to effect Home Reunion. It is certainly true, that many Anglicans deceive themselves into imagining that the fatal character of their own theory can be avoided. An attempt to combine insistence on episcopacy with a frank recognition of non-episcopalian Christianity has recently been made, and secured wide acceptance. A distinction is drawn between the fact, and the theory, of episcopacy. All must agree to accept bishops, but none need believe in their necessity. The polity is indispensable but the only principle which can make it so may, or may not, be held! This position assumes that episcopacy can be justified on the ground of its practical efficiency. But to base an exclusive claim on the ground of practical efficiency is really to accept the verdict of experience. That verdict in the case of specific polities, whether secular or spiritual, is not doubtful. Neither the Papacy, nor Episcopacy, nor Presbyterianism, nor any other polity bequeathed by the past to the present can make good at the bar of history an *exclusive* claim to efficiency. All have served, in varying measures of success, the essential objects of ecclesiastical government. None has been immune from failure. All stand in the same condemnation. No specific form of polity can be an *essential* constituent of ecclesiastical legitimacy.

Meanwhile the development of Dissenting Christianity has not been wholly favourable to Home Reunion, for if it may not be denied, that its spiritual achievements at home and abroad have disallowed the old attitude of contempt, and compelled a measure of respectful recognition, yet its incorrigible individualism has multiplied fresh causes of distrust and dislike. What Rome has done on the one side, America has done on the other. In both cases foreign-born extravagances have widened the breach in England, and rendered the peacemaker's task indefinitely more difficult. Nevertheless, the deeper tendencies of the age, intellectual and religious, are in the direction of ecclesiastical union. The articulated and stereotyped denominationalism, which still humiliates and enfeebles English Christianity, has no future. It draws its strength now from vested interests and obstinate habits, less and less from intelligible principles, and strongly rooted convictions. The set of the spiritual tide throughout Christendom, and most apparently throughout the English-speaking part of it, is towards Christian fellowship and co-operation, and the final result cannot really be doubtful. There is a note of prophetic certitude in the glowing language of the Lambeth Appeal, and the Appeal itself outlines an ecclesiastical ideal which is cherished far beyond the limits of Anglican Christianity:

The vision which rises before us is that of a Church, genuinely Catholic, loyal to all truth, and gathering into its fellowship all "who profess and call themselves Christians", within whose visible unity all the treasures of faith and order, bequeathed as a heritage by the past to the present, shall be possessed in common, and made serviceable to the whole Body of Christ. Within this unity Christian communions now separated from one another would retain much that has long been distinctive in their methods of worship and service. It is through a rich diversity of life and devotion that the unity of the whole fellowship will be fulfilled.

EPILOGUE

The day of Nationalism is over. On every plane it is becoming apparent that civilized mankind has outgrown the garments of its nationalist past. As Nurse Cavell said when she went to her martyrdom, "Patriotism is not enough." In religion, in ethics, in politics, as well ecclesiastical as civil, nationalism is exhausted. It follows that the epoch of national churches is closed. Of all national churches the Church of England has been the most magnificent and the most efficient, but it too is passing. Disestablishment would but give formal recognition to an accomplished fact. The Spiritual Society is bursting the bands of nationalism, and can only be confined within them at heavy cost to its true life.

The day of nationalism is over. What will take its place? Imperialism has a wider range and weaker roots. It can be no more than a transitory phase. Moreover, it conflicts with fundamental Christian principles, being indeed pre-Christian in origin, and in essence pagan. Earth-born and earth-bound, it has no promise of permanence. It has survived in the Papal Church, which expresses and perverts the genuinely Christian ideal of Catholicity. It too will pass. Such success as it obtains is garnered from the hopes and fears of men who in their deep disillusionment are groping after that Christian ideal.

"*The difficulty about the Church of England is to*

believe that the Supernatural is in her : the difficulty about the Church of Rome is to believe in the Supernatural at all" observed a devout Anglican layman in the course of a discussion on the possibility of a union of the Churches. This observation enshrines a true judgment. Both Churches are profoundly disappointing. If the record of the one is mean and limited, that of the other is paradoxical and arrogant. But the Church of Rome moves the deeper scepticism in the considering Christian's mind because the discrepancy between spiritual claim and moral quality is more extreme. In a remarkable volume, *The Vatican as a World Power* (Longmans Green and Co. 1939), a learned Roman Catholic apologist has advanced a paradoxical argument. After reviewing with knowledge and candour the scandalous history of the Papacy, and showing how, in spite of great Popes and noble achievements, it has failed to fulfil the presumed purpose of its original institution, he draws the surprising inference that since, in spite of all, the Papacy has survived, it must be what it claims to be, viz. the infallible Guardian and Interpreter of the Christian Revelation, the Divinely ordained Witness and Warder of Christian Morality in the world. This is indeed to "put the cart before the horse". It ignores the only Divinely authenticated test of spiritual quality—"*By their fruits ye shall know them*"—and fastens on a mere accident of history, the survival of the Papacy, as alone sufficient to sustain the fabric of the Roman theory. The Papal System is totalitarian, and, as such, conflicts with the human spirit itself.

Within the non-Roman sphere denominationalism has developed, but denominationalism is only individualism "writ large", and has no deeper root. Neither nationalism, nor totalitarian institutionalism, nor denominationalism can finally satisfy the human hunger for spiritual fellowship, or provide a tolerable embodiment of the Christian ideal of Catholicity.

But the end is not yet. Mankind, God-inspired, God-guided, pursues its spiritual quest through passion, disillusionment, and defeat. It cannot be that its faith shall finally fail. The words which Browning places in the mouth of the dying Paracelsus, may utter its deepest thought—

> If I stoop
> Into a dark tremendous sea of cloud,
> It is but for a time: I press God's lamp
> Close to my breast: its splendour soon or late,
> Will pierce the gloom: I shall emerge one day.

INDEX

CAMBRIDGE: PRINTED BY WALTER LEWIS, M.A., AT THE UNIVERSITY PRESS

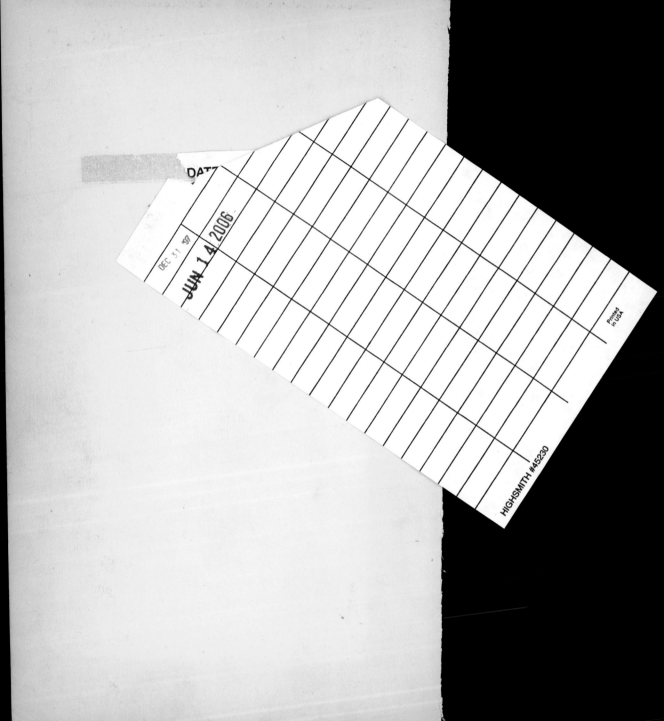